Lesbian and Gay Visions of Irel

*The Cassell Lesbian and Gay Studies list
offers a broad-based platform to lesbian, gay
and bisexual writers for the discussion of
contemporary issues and for the promotion
of new ideas and research.*

COMMISSIONING:
**Steve Cook
Roz Hopkins**

CONSULTANTS:
**Liz Gibbs
Keith Howes
Christina Ruse
Peter Tatchell**

Lesbian and Gay Visions of Ireland

Towards the Twenty-first Century
Edited by Íde O'Carroll
and Eoin Collins

CASSELL

Cassell
Wellington House   215 Park Avenue South
125 Strand   New York, NY 10003
London WC2R 0BB

First published 1995

British Library Cataloguing-in-Publication Data
A catalogue record for this book is available from the British Library

ISBN 0-304-33227-5 (hardback)
      0-304-33229-1 (paperback)

Typeset by York House Typographic Ltd, London

Printed and bound in Great Britain by Biddles Ltd,
Guildford and King's Lynn

Contents

Acknowledgements vii
'The Glen': Mary Branley ix
Editors xi
Contributors xiii
Editors' Introduction 1

Part I: Background

Criminal Law (Sexual Offences) Bill 1993, Second Stage Speech,
 Tuesday 29 June 1993
Senator David Norris, Seanad Eireann 13
Interview
Mary Dorcey 25

Part II: Socio-political

Anatomy of a Campaign
Chris Robson 47

Lesbians: The Lavender Women of Ireland
Joni Crone 60

The Tenderness of the Peoples
Kieran Rose 71

Living Visions
Ger Moane 86

Identity, Existence and Passionate Politics
Joan McCarthy 99

I Used To Be an Activist, But I'm Alright Now'
Izzy Kamikaze 110

Letter from a Gay Republican: H-Block 5
Brendí McClenaghan   122

Ghetto-blasting
Marie Mulholland   131

Glimpses
Suzy Byrne   138

Part III: Arts and Culture

Oscar's Mirror
Eibhear Walshe   147

Noises from Woodsheds: Tales of Irish lesbians, 1886–1989
Emma Donoghue   158

Artist–Activist
Louise Walsh   171

Part IV: AIDS

*Prelude to a Vision: The Impact of AIDS on the Political
Legitimacy and Political Mobilization of Gay Men in Ireland*
William O'Connor   183

Part V: Emigrants

The Accidental Immigrant
Anne Maguire   199

A Land Beyond Tears
Fr Bernard J. Lynch   212

Keeping it Close: Experiencing Emigration in England
Cherry Smyth   221

'Geasa' by Cathal Ó'Searcaigh   234

'The Bond' by Frankie Sewell (a translation of 'Geasa')   235

Acknowledgements

We extend our deepest appreciation to our contributors who worked so hard to realize this project. We would like to acknowledge Nexus Research Co-operative's sponsorship and the assistance of Margaret Kelleher and Angela Rickard. Some of the papers in this collection were presented at the Public Lecture Series in Lesbian and Gay Studies, Trinity College, a series organized under the auspices of the Centre for Women's Studies. We would like to acknowledge the support of our friends who haven't seen that much of us in the last year. Also, we would like to thank Steve Cook and Roz Hopkins of Cassell for their patience and help. Finally, Íde would like to say a special word of thanks to Annie G. Rogers whose love is a constant reminder of the joy of being lesbian.

Dedication

We acknowledge the wonderful energy and enthusiasm that exists in the lesbian and gay communities in Ireland and abroad, the energy that has brought us thus far, and to these individuals and groups we dedicate this book.

Go néirí linn!

The Glen

At the entrance of the Glen
seven silver birch stand guard,
at ease, resting one foot on a soft leaf rug.
They have grown complacent in this time.
I slip between their lines of vision,
each rustling step betrays me.
My education years are useless to absorb
this valley, precisely cut,
when ice-age mountain thawed and slid
and ripped a vein of solid rock right out.
In the melt, alpine plant seeds fell
and orchids juxtapose their tiny brilliance.

I swear I'm being watched
by Maeb, the warrior queen
her woman's army know my name
and waits behind the ivy wall –
the air is humming with a swirl of cries.
I embrace the ivy strands
soft as a lover's flowing hair
and I remember now my warrior queen
the battle and my death.
Her glorious face before me breathes,
her green eyes call,
her arms invite me to her breast,
where her red hair falls.

'How can I serve my Queen?' I ask.
With her finger tip she lightly traces
a circle round my sinister eye.
'This eye, pierced in battle
looks inward to the heart of things.
Let it be your guide,' she says,
and taking hold of my two hands
she turns the palms to heaven.
'Love all you touch, touch all with love.'
Her lips kissed mine, her last words were:
'Tell of our love and speak my name.'

Mary Branley

Editors

Íde O'Carroll

Íde O'Carroll is a Research Associate at the Centre for Women's Studies, Trinity College and Nexus (Europe) Research Co-operative. She has conducted research on Irish women at home and abroad, most notably *Models for Movers: Irish Women's Emigration to America* (Dublin: Attic Press, 1990), and numerous articles in publications such as *The Irish World Wide* (vol. 4): *Irish Women and Emigration* (Leicester University Press, 1995). With Nexus, she has worked on many Irish and European social research projects including the GLEN/Combat Poverty study of poverty in the lesbian and gay communities. She teaches Women's Studies at the National College of Industrial Relations, organizes the public lecture series in Lesbian and Gay Studies at Trinity College, is a member of LOT's Publishing Group, and contributes regularly to *Gay Community News*. Her Irish language poem, Mná I mBoston/Women in Boston, will be published in the forthcoming fourth volume of *The Field Day Anthology of Irish Literature*.

Eoin Collins

Eoin Collins is a member of GLEN and Nexus (Europe) Research Co-operative. He has been involved in the GLEN research on poverty in the lesbian and gay community and has worked extensively on other social research projects in Ireland and the European Union. These projects cover a range of issues including the Dublin Transport Initiative and information technology in less favoured regions. He is currently part of a joint Nexus/GLEN research team undertaking work on HIV and AIDS in Ireland.

Contributors

Mary Branley

Mary Branley is a poet who works as a teacher in London. She was born and brought up in Sligo and has lived for many years in the USA. Her work appears in several publications: *The Field Day Anthology of Irish Literature* (forthcoming volume on Irish women's writing); *Working Papers in Irish Studies* (Northeastern, 1989). Her first play, *Silk Kimonos* was staged in Sligo during the Yeats Summer School in 1995.

Suzy Byrne

Suzy Byrne is co-chair of GLEN (the Gay and Lesbian Equality Network), is the co-author of *Coming Out* (Martello Press, 1994) and has written extensively for *Gay Community News*. She is also involved in a number of youth organizations and is treasurer of the International Lesbian and Gay Youth Organization.

Joni Crone

Joni Crone is a founder member of Dublin Lesbian Line, Liberation for Irish Lesbians and the Lesbian Disco, where she was DJ for thirteen years (1977–90). Elected to the steering committee of the Irish Gay Rights Movement and the National Gay Federation in the 1970s and 1980s, she was interviewed on national TV in 1980 and again in 1993. A community arts worker and writer of fiction, plays and TV drama, she has been actively involved in promoting the rights of lesbians in Ireland for many years.

Emma Donoghue

Born in 1969, Emma Donoghue grew up in Dublin and now lives in Cambridge. Her history documenting the diversity of lesbian culture, *Passions Between Women: British Lesbian Culture, 1668–1801*, was published by Scarlet Press in 1993, and productions of her play, *I Know My Own Heart*, have been staged in Cambridge and Dublin. She has written two novels: *Stir-Fry* (Hamish Hamilton, 1994) and *Hood* (Hamish Hamilton, 1995).

Mary Dorcey

Born in County Dublin, Mary Dorcey's works include two collections of poetry, *Kindling* (Onlywomen, 1982) and *Moving into the Space Cleared by Our Mothers* (Salmon, 1991), and a book of short stories, *A Noise from the Woodshed*, (Onlywomen, 1989), which won the Rooney Prize for Literature in 1990. The most recent collection, *The River That Carries Me*, will be published in September 1995 (Poolbeg/Salmon), and her first novel, *A Biography of Desire* will be published in the spring of 1996. She is currently working on a new collection of short stories.

Izzy Kamikaze

Izzy Kamikaze has been active in the Women's and Gay Rights movements for many years. She has worked full time with AIDS organizations, was heavily involved in the resurrection of Dublin Pride, and more recently has concentrated her efforts on writing articles on lesbian and gay issues.

Fr Bernard Lynch

Bernard Lynch, an SMA Father, studied at the African Missions College, twenty-six miles from Belfast, during the inception of the present 'Troubles' in Northern Ireland. He worked with the Benda people in north central Zambia for two years before going to the USA. He has an inter-disciplinary doctorate in counselling psychology and theology from Fordham University and New York

Theological Seminary. For ten years he has been theological consultant to the board of directors of Dignity New York, an organization for lesbian and gay Catholics and their friends. He founded the AIDS Ministry of Dignity New York in 1983.

Presently he works with people living with and affected by HIV/AIDS throughout the UK; he also has a private practice in psychotherapy. His book, *A Priest on Trial* was published in 1993 by Bloomsbury, London.

Joan McCarthy

Joan McCarthy was a member of Cork and Dublin Lesbian and Gay Collectives and Cork Women's Place in the 1980s. She contributed to *Out for Ourselves* and sang in a lesbian band, Eile. Today, she is a development worker in childcare and teaches philosophy on community and women's studies education courses.

Brendí McClenaghan

Brendí McClenaghan is thirty-seven, and is currently in the process of being released after seventeen and a half years' imprisonment in the H-Blocks of Long Kesh. A Republican activist, he was arrested and sentenced to five terms of 'life' at the age of twenty. He was in the H-Blocks during the blanket and hunger strike periods. It was his imprisonment which encouraged and inspired him to come to terms with his own personal struggle and come out as a gay man in prison and the Republican movement. To date he has written articles about his sexuality and Republicanism, and has effected a change in Sinn Féin policy on gay and lesbian issues.

Anne Maguire

Born in Dublin, Anne Maguire is a lesbian feminist, who was involved in many political campaigns in Ireland before emigrating to the USA in 1987. A founder member of the Irish Lesbian and Gay Organization (ILGO) and the Lesbian Avengers NYC, she has been at the forefront of the campaign to establish the right of Irish lesbians and gays to march in the St Patrick's Day parade in New York City, a battle which continues to this day.

Ger Moane

Ger Moane has been active in the women's movement since 1976, particularly in the areas of violence against women, education, reproductive rights, and lesbian issues. She was involved in Dublin Lesbian Line from 1989–1994 and is currently active in LOT, LEN and the Irish Women's Land Project. She is a lecturer in Psychology and Women's Studies in University College Dublin, and has published in the areas of health care, women's psychological development and gender and colonialism. She spends as much time as possible having fun in Lesbiana, indulging esoteric interests.

Marie Mulholland

Marie Mulholland is a Republican, a trade union and community activist from Belfast, presently living in Derry. In 1987, she was the first recipient of the Constance Markiewicz Award presented by the Irish-American Labour Coalition for services to the community by a trade unionist. She has edited and contributed to several publications: *Unfinished Revolution* (Meadbh Publishing, 1988); *Green Peas and Barley-O* (Meadbh Publishing, 1989) and *Women's Voices: An Oral History of Women's Health* (Attic Press, 1992). She has been out as a dyke and a Republican for seventeen years. These two influences ensure that she never becomes complacent. She keeps grounded with the love and support of some very special and strategically placed friends.

David Norris

David Norris is one of Ireland's best-known gay activists and its first openly gay senator. From the late 1970s he was centrally involved in legal action to change the laws in Ireland which criminalized sexual relations between gay men. After many disappointments, he finally won his case in the European Court of Human Rights in 1988. The Court held that Ireland's laws contravened the European Convention on Human Rights. He teaches

English literature at Trinity College, Dublin, and is an internationally recognized Joycean scholar.

William O'Connor

William O'Connor was born, grew up and came out in Cork. Over the past seven years he has been active in numerous lesbian and gay community groups and HIV/AIDS organizations. In 1994, he graduated from University College Cork with a Masters degree in social science. He currently lives in London where, among other things, he is experimenting with a career in social research.

Cathal Ó'Searcaigh

Cathal Ó'Searcaigh is a poet who writes in the Irish language/ *as Gaeilge*. He lives and works in Gort a Choirce. Co. Donegal. His collections include: *An Bealach'na Bhaile* (Cló lar Chonnachta, Galway, 1991), *Suile Shuibhne* (Cóiscóim, Dublin, 1987) and *Shuibhne* (Cóiscóim, Dublin, 1983).

Christopher Robson

Christopher Robson is an architect working in Dublin. As co-chair of GLEN he was continuously involved, through campaigning and negotiation, with the series of legal reforms of the last few years. He has also worked on AIDS issues at national and international level as a founder member of both Gay Health Action (Ireland) and EuroCASO. He is a co-author of *Equality Now*, published by the Irish Council of Civil Liberties.

Kieran Rose

Kieran Rose is the author of *Diverse Communities: The Evolution of Lesbian and Gay Politics in Ireland* (Cork University Press, 1994) and co-chair of GLEN (the Gay and Lesbian Equality Network).

Cherry Smyth

Cherry Smyth is a journalist and poet living in London. Her non-fiction book, *Queer Notions*, was published by Scarlet Press in 1992, and her fiction appears in several anthologies. Her poetry is published in *Frankenstein's Daughter* (Stride Publications, 1993) and *Virago New Poets* (Virago Press, 1993). An essay on lesbian pornography, 'The pleasure threshold' is published in *Feminist Review*, no. 34, spring 1990 and on 'The transgressive sexual subject' in *Queer Romance* (Routledge, 1995).

Louise Walsh

Louise Walsh is an artist who works in diverse media. She was born in Cork, lived in Belfast and Limerick and now lives in Dublin. She is actively involved in the lesbian community in Ireland and teaches at Limerick School of Art and Design.

Eibhear Walshe

Eibhear Walshe is a lecturer in modern English at University College Cork. He has edited *Ordinary People Dancing: Essays on Kate O'Brien* (Cork University Press, 1993) and *Sex, Nation and Dissent* (forthcoming). He is Academic Director of the Shaw School.

Editors' Introduction

ONE of my earliest memories is of my father telling stories *as Gaeilge* (in Irish), based on encounters he had with *sióga* (fairies). One story he told was of an experience he had had as he cycled home on a particularly cold winter's night. Hearing fiddle music coming from a field, he witnessed *sióga* emerging from their homes beneath the soil, and watched them dancing merrily, playing music and having fun. When he realized they had spotted him, he broke out in a cold sweat and fled from the place, terrified of what they might do to him. At the end of the story he revealed that actually it was all a dream, and that the vision he had witnessed was only in his imagination. To this day I am not sure.

As I shift this story through to my present, it provides powerful elements for understanding myself and my identity as an Irish woman and a lesbian. On the one hand it reminds me of a tradition – the *Aisling*/Vision, deeply immersed in Irish poetry, in which an image of a being, usually a woman, symbolic of Ireland, appears to declare something about the nation's future. In my father's story he is fearful of what he does not know – spirits of another world, the *áit eile*. His reaction mirrors the reaction of many individuals who witness lesbian and gay life from afar, who dismiss it as high jinks, or flee with fear, refusing to engage with a different way of being. *Lesbian and Gay Visions of Ireland: Towards the Twenty-first Century* is an effort to engage many people with stories of individual lesbians and gays (some of whom live outside the country) who have been part of the changes that have occurred for lesbians and gays in Ireland. It also offers a set of dreams, visions of the future for Irish lesbians and gays as we come to the end of one century and move towards the next.

In this, the 95th anniversary of the death of Oscar Wilde, and the 150th anniversary of the Great Hunger, we mark in our collective memory a significant period of Irish lesbian and gay history, for the last 25 years have been a time of enormous struggle and success. Hopefully, by the twenty-first century the visions contained in this book will be realised, and the changes documented and presented in collections such as this, celebrating further achievements for Irish lesbians and gays.

Background to the project

To understand the roots of this project I must tell a story of my own, one that has elements that are reflected in many other pieces in this collection – the search for identity, the reality of discrimination, the safety net of emigration.

I returned to Ireland in the autumn of 1991 fired by the election of Mary Robinson as President, to conduct my doctoral research, after five years of being a graduate student in Boston. In the USA I had grown up as a lesbian, even though I'd first come out within a wonderful lesbian community in Cork in the 1980s while working as a teacher. Back in Ireland, I quickly learned that the situation for lesbians and gays hadn't changed all that much. On a personal level, it was extremely difficult for me to get work to support myself while I did my research, even though I had plenty of qualifications and experience, including a newly acquired Harvard degree. It wasn't just the unemployment situation – averaging almost 20 per cent – but rather the fact that I made no point of hiding my sexuality. However, I had support from friends and family, and from the Centre for Women's Studies at Trinity College, which offered me a base as a research associate.

For almost two years I worked alone, gathering the voices of Irish women for my research topic, allowing myself to document in a feminist way the reality of women's lives in Ireland. By 1993, however, I was despondent. Though LOT (Lesbians Organizing Together) had been established in 1991, and was blossoming as the main umbrella body for lesbian organizations, in Dublin, I was still without paid work. So I decided to move to London for the summer, en route back to the USA. My spirit was low and my bank account registered a zero sum.

In London, working as a temp by day and writing up my research by night, I experienced racism personally for the first time. In the USA, being Irish had always been a plus factor; in Britain I was exposed to people who stereotyped the Irish as either 'stupid' or 'terrorists'. It was a terrible time, softened only by the love and support of a handful of Irish lesbians and gay friends. When GLEN (Gay and Lesbian Equality Network) won their long battle for the decriminalization of male homosexuality that summer, we toasted the efforts of David Norris, Kieran Rose, Chris Robson and many others. We took heart: perhaps things would change and some of us could return 'home' to build a life without fear of discrimination in the place we most wanted to be.

And in September that's just what I did, after receiving an offer to conduct a piece of research for Nexus Research Co-operative. It was there that I met Eoin Collins, who at that time was working on a study of poverty in the lesbian and gay community, commissioned by GLEN and funded by Combat Poverty (a statutory agency). For many, many months Eoin and I worked side by side on this project. We forged a bond that goes beyond work, one that reinforces my belief in the ability of lesbians and gays to unite in common cause. His kindness and insights were then and now the root of our friendship.

While working on this project I was invited by the National Forum for Equality of Opportunity in Third Level Institutions to give a paper on the position of lesbians and gays in academic institutions in Ireland. The result, 'Queers in the Quad' was delivered at University College Cork, where I met Steve Cook of Cassell, who was there to present a background paper on OutRage! He asked if I had any book projects in mind. I *had* been thinking of a particular book, one that would gather together the voices of those who had been central to the changes that have occurred for lesbians and gays in Ireland. However, such a project could only come about if it were based on a good working relationship between a lesbian and a gay man, two people who could act as gatherers of stories. Eoin and I knew many of these individuals, some were friends, all were people we admired. We discussed the idea and decided to submit a proposal.

Changes in Irish society

Ireland is at a critical stage in its socio-political history, not least because of the possibility of an end to the war in the North, but also in relation to the position of lesbians and gays: the Republic's Law Reform Act of 1993, the result of a hugely successful campaign to establish equal age of consent with heterosexuals, and by default a recognition by the state of a lesbian presence in Ireland. More importantly the inclusion of sexual orientation in the Unfair Dismissals Act provides guaranteed rights for lesbian and gay workers. Lesbian and gay issues are included in Equal Status legislation now being prepared (1995) by the Department of Equality and Law Reform; and a statutory agency has commissioned a study of lesbian and gay poverty. There is now a lively public discussion of lesbian and gay issues. In just a few years Ireland has witnessed changes in the Republic's public policy that some of us could only dream of in the past.

At the grass-roots level, lesbian energy is high: writers such as Emma Donoghue and Mary Dorcey have received awards; the Cork Women's Weekend is in its twelfth year; annual Women's Camps have been established; Lesbian Lines exist, both in the North and South. LOT is entering its fifth year and has just received a grant of £50,000 from the Department of Social Welfare. Gay men's groups have focused primarily on law reform, Gay Switchboards and massive efforts to respond to the horror of AIDS. Abroad ILGO's (Irish Lesbian and Gay Organization) fight to be included in the St Patrick's Day parade in New York has forced worldwide attention on a re-definition of Irishness, while ironically, at home, President Robinson welcomed lesbians and gays into the Árus (the presidential residence) for the first time.

Those who view such changes from afar must attempt to reconcile this shift with the impression they may have of Ireland as a Catholic-run, backward little nation. The reality, in my view, is that as a small nation we have been subject to a particular history of colonization (and are still partially colonized). In pre-Christian Gaelic Ireland, for example, homosexuality was recognized and could be cited as a reason for divorce under the Gaelic Brehon Law system. This particular history of colonization by the Christian and then the British empires heightens our ability to connect with issues of inequality and injustice. Senator Norris's legal battles and GLEN's campaign built on this ability, always presenting the case for decriminalization in terms of equality. It is an argument which must be deployed again and again, especially in light of the findings from the lesbian/gay poverty study. Side by side with such campaigns is the groundwork that has been carried out to establish coalitions with other community groups, for example LOT's Outreach Group and GLEN's Campaign for Equality.

A key element in this shift in attitude is the number of lesbians and gays who have used the media to great effect. I contend that we are a nation of great newspaper readers. One of the remarkable differences between Ireland and the USA, for instance, is that here there are three national newspapers, and a national TV and radio network. Whatever the news, it is discussed from Bundoran to Ballydehob: whether people agree or disagree, there is at least a national debate. The other significant factor in our favor as lesbians and gays is that we are all someone's daughter or son, sister or brother, aunt or uncle, and in Ireland, a small country by any standards, people know people's people. It is a tool that we have to use to greater effect in the future – to come out over and over again, despite the possible negative consequences, in order to build allegiances with family, friends and, indeed, the other organizations working for a more socially just Ireland.

What I write of here is best exemplified by incidents which took place around our 'national' holiday. While certain American-Irish continue to refuse to admit Irish-born lesbians and gays to the St Patrick's Day parade in New York City, lesbians and gays received an award as the 'Best new entry' in the Cork parade in 1992. So, for me there is hope for further change, but we must be vigilant too. AIDS continues to claim lives; harassment and violence are a reality; constructive dismissal is used to weed out lesbians and gays who come out at work; custody of children is an issue that remains unresolved. We still don't have one lesbian-owned pub or club in Ireland. We need properly resourced community development programmes, and we need to ensure proper representation of lesbians and gays in our national parliament. These are just some of the future campaigns for Irish lesbians and gays as we move towards the twenty-first century.

The book

This has been much more than a book project. It has been an enormous learning experience and a co-operative process. We decided early on that we would view ourselves as gatherers of stories, and asked individuals to use a personal narrative style when reflecting on social change and imagining the future for lesbians and gays in Ireland. We believe that this collection is important, not least because it brings together a number of key individuals, but more importantly, because it builds on our Irish tradition of storytelling and makes personal and immediate the political experience of Irish lesbians and gays at home and abroad.

Issues emerging

One theme that emerges from our collection is identity: the need of Irish lesbians and gays to combine their sense of Irishness with their sexuality. This is poignantly evident in the chapters by those who by choice or circumstance are emigrants, and those who live in Northern Ireland. But identity is, in truth, an issue for us all. It is often difficult to articulate what Irishness means – for me it was there before I grew breasts and realized I was becoming a woman, before I loved and desired women. It is there in a knowing before words and beyond words. It happened to a nation viewing Riverdance – a collective 'Yes'.

Another theme is the desire to reconcile being lesbian or gay with being part of a heterosexual family and a society dominated by heterosexuals, while still remaining true to what we know is our way of being in the world. The difficulties encountered by many contributors in the coming-out process warn us of the need to continue to educate, so that the next generation of lesbians and gays do not suffer loss and exclusion. What is also clear is the desire of all the contributors to work towards change, within lesbian and gay organizations or alone, to unashamedly declare our right to be equal players in the society of which we are a part, and more importantly, to celebrate the joy of being lesbian or gay.

Íde O'Carroll

When I was growing up my first positive sense of what it might mean to be gay came from studying economics in school, when one of our more progressive teachers told us that John Maynard Keynes had had a relationship with a man. I almost hit the floor with excitement, and with assistance from the teacher, who was probably surprised by my sudden interest, began to read about Keynes and his association with The Bloomsbury Group. From this point on, my reference points for 'gayness' were to be British and American: Bloomsbury, Berlin decadence and, eventually, Stonewall and Gay Liberation. To be gay was to be urban, intellectual and sophisticated.

With all these notions in mind, I went to London in 1987 to recreate myself in the image of those I had read so much about. However, the GLC had recently been abolished, Clause 28 was about to be introduced and most of the people I worked with talked of the escalating price of property and the profits to be made in buying shares in the recently privatized British Gas. It was a depressing time to be in Britain: the Welfare State, the trade unions and local democracy were all under attack. In this environment, and faced with the attitudes of some gay men who felt moved to commiserate with me on the backwardness of Ireland, I reacted with anger: I even found myself defending the Catholic Church on the basis that it, unlike Margaret Thatcher, believed in 'society' and the concept of the common good. I took great offence at the notion that we were 'priest ridden' or almost psychically reactionary and conservative. In argument, I pointed out that in the town I come from people identified strongly with the Catholic Church, but many remembered the times when Catholics could not obtain loans from the local bank, and worked for low pay in the local mill without any possibility of advancement. That such people could simply be dismissed as unreconstructed bigots seemed inaccurate and unfair.

Some time after returning to Ireland I attended a debate at University College Dublin. My memory of the motion is impressionistic and went something like 'Lesbians and gay men deserve equal rights in the new Ireland'. The first speaker was a rather crude and silly homophobe who presented a particularly nauseating case against the motion. I was sitting in the audience, aching to express my anger and hurt. Then Kieran Rose moved to the podium and calmly dismissed the motion, refusing to debate about rights which he believed were inalienable and self-evident. Instead, he talked about what the lesbian and gay community was doing in Ireland, the years of activism, the progress made in redressing prejudice, the strength of the community and its contribution to Irish society. His only concession to what the first speaker had said was that the views she had expressed would find little favour among the people of Ireland who, with a renewed confidence, were rediscovering and embracing more progressive parts of their political and cultural heritage.

I relate these experiences because they explain why I have found working on *Lesbian and Gay Visions of Ireland* so exciting. Many of the contributors, whether they know it or not, have had a profound impact on my life and have enabled me to reconcile my identity as Irish and Gay in a way which makes me proud of both. It is my belief that the tremendous fondness for our country which comes through in all the contributions has been the key to the changes that have taken place for our community in Ireland. Long may the change continue!

We open the collection with pieces by two prominent Irish activists. Senator David Norris's speech, delivered in June 1993 on the occasion of the introduction of a bill to repeal the laws which criminalized sexual activities between men, to replace them with new legislation based on a common age of consent with heterosexuals and no privacy restrictions, a law firmly based on equality. He presents a broad historical view. He outlines the roots of the anti-sodomy laws and the impact these laws had on the lives of gay men up to the mid 1970s when the emerging gay movement began to mobilize against them. He also describes his own groundbreaking challenges to these laws.

This is followed by an interview with Mary Dorcey, one of the early feminist activists of the 1970s movements, and a founder member of the Irish Sexuality Liberation Movement. She chronicles life in Ireland in the 1950s and her emergence as a feminist, a lesbian and an activist. Mary Dorcey speaks of what it is like to be a writer and lesbian.

In Part 2, Chris Robson provides a detailed analysis of the role of GLEN in changing anti-gay laws in Ireland. It sets law reform in the context of earlier battles for justice. Joni Crone has the distinction of being the first Irish lesbian to appear on our national TV. She provides a testament to the energy of the lesbian liberation movement in Ireland, and describes her involvement in campaigns for women's rights throughout the past two decades. To complement Joni's article, Ger Moane, a psychologist, looks at the roots of homophobia within an Irish context and focuses our attention on the vibrancy of the lesbian community, in particular the work being undertaken by LOT in Dublin and by Lesbian Lines throughout the whole of Ireland.

Kieran Rose's chapter juxtaposes the rights of Irish lesbians and gays against a backdrop of international human rights, arguing that we must be aware of the socio-political environment in which some lesbians and gays find themselves by birth.

Joan McCarthy, in a philosophical vein, examines lesbian identity and existence, forcing us to consider the personal base our selves, to examine what it means to be lesbian, and to acknowledge our need to remain firmly aware of our roots, while respecting difference in others. Building on this discussion, Izzy Kamikaze describes her own radical roots and her belief in the need to challenge complacency in the lesbian and gay communities. She examines in particular the issue of exclusion, which she believes operates in established lesbian and gay organizations.

Brendi McClenaghan wrote his chapter in his prison cell in pre-ceasefire Northern Ireland. He gives a poignant account of his experience of being a gay man and a Republican prisoner. Another Northerner, Marie Mulholland, warns of the dangers of the ghetto, where the unity of a particular group can in itself become exclusionary, ignoring diversity within the group and the inequalities and struggles faced by others.

Suzy Byrne, a young lesbian closely involved in the law reform campaign, describes her background in Catholic youth groups and her role as a very public spokesperson for GLEN.

In Part 3, Arts and Culture, academic Eibhear Walshe writes of what he calls his 'Epiphany' – the discovery of lesbian and gay writers in the Irish literary tradition. Emma Donoghue, herself a prolific writer, tells another tale of discovering the lesbian voice in Irish literature. Louise Walsh, a visual artist and teacher, describes her emergence into a lively lesbian community and her commitment to events such as the Cork Women's Fun Weekend, Women's Camps, Lesbian Lines – all vital events in bonding Irish lesbians. Much of this activism has informed her own works of art, which celebrate the strength of Irish women in the face of adversity.

In our only chapter to deal specifically with AIDS, William O'Connor explores how its emergence, both internationally and in Ireland, has increased the urgency to organize and dismantle laws which discriminate against gay men.

In our final section, Emigrants, Anne Maguire, one of Ireland's best-known emigrants, paints a harrowing picture of the Hibernian homophobia of the American–Irish, and describes the role of ILGO in attempts to participate in the New York City St Patrick's Day parade.

Another equally well known emigrant, Fr Bernard Lynch, looks at his own struggle against homophobia within the Catholic Church and describes a spirituality that embraces lesbian and gay sexuality as divine love. Finally Cherry Smyth, a London-based lesbian, presents the voices of Irish lesbian immigrants in Britain, and shows how racism is an extra burden in lives lived 'across the water'.

Eoin Collins
Dublin, 1995

Part I
Background

Criminal Law (Sexual Offences) Bill 1993

Second Stage Speech, Tuesday 29 June 1993

Senator David Norris, Seanad Eireann[1]

THIS speech was given by Senator David Norris to the Irish Senate in June 1993 on the occasion of the passage of a bill into law abolishing all previous laws criminalizing homosexual acts between men, and replacing them with a new gender-neutral law with a common age of consent with heterosexuals and no special privacy restrictions. We reproduce the speech in its entirety because of its historic significance and because we believe that Senator Norris, a long-standing activist for gay rights in Ireland, displayed his usual ability to be forceful and witty in presenting his case.

This is for me a happy day, for my fellow legislators have chosen as the law makers of a free and independent Republic to liberate the gay community from an oppressive, corrupt and deeply damaging law whose origins are shrouded in the mists of ancient religious prejudice. Although I regret that this bill did not originate in the Upper House as had been at first intended, I cannot do other than commend today the courage and clarity of the Minister's handling of the passage of the bill through the Lower House and the humanity she demonstrated not just in her opening words in introducing the legislation but most particularly in her final reply just before midnight on that historic day, when she dealt effectively and with dignity with a number of contentious speeches from the back benches. Such reform had been made part of a programme for government by the PD's [Progressive Democrats] some years ago but this was never acted upon, and I would also like to thank the Labour Party and in particular the Minister for Equality, Deputy Mervyn Taylor, for ensuring that on this occasion the government's nerve did not falter.

I have already stated in public my disappointment at the fact that at a late stage the Fine Gael Party acting against the advice of its front bench sought, through a series of mean-minded and unfortunately motivated amendments, to introduce some marginal measure of discrimination. However, I would like also now to place on the record my gratitude to those humane and civilised members of that party who by the technique of filibuster managed to prevent these regrettable amendments from their own party being reached and voted upon. It took courage, tenacity and humour to achieve this.

By effectively wiping the lingering shame of British imperial statute from the record of Irish law our colleagues in the Dáil have done a good days work. I confidently anticipate that we in this House will complete that work honourably. I have always said in defiance of comments from abroad that the Irish people were a generous, tolerant, compassionate and decent people and that this would one day be reflected even in that sensitive area of the law governing human sexuality. By enacting such a law in what is admittedly a delicate area we are extending the human freedoms of all citizens in this state. As the great apostle of Catholic emancipation Daniel O'Connell said in pleading his case at the bar of British public opinion, human dignity and freedom are not finite resources. By extending these freedoms to others one's own freedom is itself enhanced and not diminished. This is the kind of Irish solution to an Irish problem of which we as Irish men and women can feel justly proud.

But surely it would have been odd had it been otherwise. In granting equality under the criminal law to gay citizens the Minister, in the legislation she is recommending to this House, is not bowing to the ridiculous demands of some eccentric pressure group. She is on the contrary following the clear dispassionate advice of our own expert Law Reform Commission in their reports on Vagrancy, on Rape, on Sexual Offences Against the Mentally Handicapped and on the Problem of Child Sex Abuse. Moreover, full decriminalisation with an equal age of consent has been urgently called for by the World Health Organisation as a health measure against the spread of venereal infection. In addition, just such proposals have either been welcomed or called for by the Irish Congress of Trade Unions, by the Church of Ireland, by the Council for the Status of Women, by the National Youth Council of Ireland as well as by the political parties represented in the House here today.

We already in fact have in place certain articles which clearly indicate that the feeling of the Irish Parliament and people is set against the discriminatory practices of previous ages. For example, since the late 1970s when I succeeded in persuading my union, the Irish Federation of University Teachers, to send forward resolutions on the matter to the annual conference of the ICTU [Irish Congress of Trade Unions] the trade union movement in this country had solidly backed the struggles for equal treatment. In 1988, in a highly significant move the then Minister for Finance, Ray McSharry, introduced a binding code throughout the Civil Service outlawing discrimination on the basis of HIV status, full blown AIDS (as long as the capacity to work remained) and sexual orientation. This very House saw the first successful battle to introduce sexual orientation clauses into Irish legislation in both the Video Bill and the Incitement to Hatred Bill. So this is not a revolution, rather the culmination of a growing awareness of injustice and discrimination in our society.

It would be tedious and wrong of me to inflict an academic lecture upon this House on this occasion. Nevertheless some glance at the source of this legislation is I think relevant. Those who believe that there is an innate horror of homosexuality occurring generally throughout mankind in history are quite wrong. Some kind but anonymous correspondent sent me yesterday morning an article from a Jewish newspaper entitled 'Judaism and gays: a faith divided'. In this the American lecturer Denis Prager examines from a hostile point of view the whole question of homosexuality. Although I do not agree with his opinions they are founded upon an accurate historical assessment, and I quote from the article:

> Prager begins by noting that Judaism alone among religions of the ancient world opposed homosexuality. In Greece and

Rome, among the Phoenicians and the Canaanites, a man's preference for other men was of no more consequence than another's choice of beef over mutton.

This is indeed a fact, although one might well have included other civilisations such as the Egyptians who also celebrated homosexuality officially, to such an extent that not only ordinary mortals but even their gods engaged joyfully in homosexual activities. It was for this very practical reason that the Old Testament Children of Israel sought to define themselves against the stronger surrounding culture by outlawing and condemning as blasphemy something that was widely regarded in the ancient world as an integral part of the culture of the main civilisations.

The proscription on sexual activity of a non-reproductive kind also had the incidental advantage of increasing a small and vulnerable population group. And this naturally enough is reflected in the commands of Yahweh to the ancient people recorded in Genesis 'Go forth and multiply'. Whatever relevance this command may have had to a threatened tribe four or five thousand years ago attempting to survive in the desert in hostile circumstances, that relevance must surely be questioned today with the world population set to double in the next twenty-five years. I cannot but admire the gusto and lack of restraint with which my heterosexual colleagues have carried out the commands of God in this instance, although not in many others.

For amateur theologians it is worth noting that the principal attack upon homosexual practice is contained in the Book of Leviticus in a section which deals mainly with dietary codes. It is remarkable that the same harsh penalties as for homosexual behaviour are held also to exist for the eating of shellfish and for the wearing of worsted cloth. I have yet to hear of a campaign by a Board *lascaigh Mhara* [Irish Fish Board] or the Textile Board for full implementation of the code of Leviticus in Irish law. In other words, we have very sensibly understood the concept of historicity. The fact that even sacred texts must be seen in their social, cultural and historical context and not uprooted and transplanted, unexamined, into modern life.

It is clear from what I have said that the source of the taboo for homosexual behaviour can be found in ancient religious pages. It is reflected even in the language of the legislation which we are setting about to dismantle this afternoon. Even the terms 'sodomy' and 'buggery' have roots in the religious power struggle. Sodomy comes from the tales of the cities of the plains, Sodom and Gomorrah, a tale in the Old Testament, whose development is complex and difficult to interpret. Anyone indeed who seeks enlightenment upon this point could do no better than to consult *The Church and the Homosexual* by the distinguished Jesuit biblical scholar Fr John McNeale SJ. Buggery comes from the middle French, *boulgre* (meaning Bulgarian), because of the attempts by the Vatican to smear the adherents of the Albigensian heresy, seen as Cathars or Bulgars with a reputation for unorthodox sexual practices.

It is also worthwhile noting that the behaviour which is this afternoon in the process of being decriminalised was, until the sixteenth century, a matter for the ecclesiastical rather than the civil courts, a question of sin rather than crime. It was only when King Henry VIII seized the monasteries, and incidentally took control of the ecclesiastical courts, that this behaviour made the transition from sin to crime for the first time in an Act of Henry VIII of 1533. Under this law the possible penalties included death and forfeiture of property. The first recorded conviction was that of a clergyman, Reverend Nicholas Udall, headmaster of Eton and author of the first English comedy, *Ralph Roister Doister*. It is perhaps instructive to note also that the first Irish victim of this law, whose conviction and execution came a century later, was also a clergyman, Bishop John Atherton. There is a grisly appropriateness about his end, since he was the very cleric who, having noticed the failure of this law to extend to Ireland, mounted a 'Save Ireland from sodomy campaign' that was so successful that he paid for its introduction with his own life, hoist one might say with his own ecclesiastical petard – let bishops beware!

This law survived with its provision for capital punishment until 1861 when in the Offences Against the Person Act of that year, which now seems to us a harsh and unsustainable enactment, the penalty was reduced from death by hanging to a possible term of life imprisonment. The last execution took place in Scotland in 1830. I need hardly say that to the modern imagination the judicial murder by the state of two of its citizens for consensual erotic activity is morally repugnant. The other law which mercifully will vanish from our statute book as a result of our deliberations is the so-called La Bouchere Amendment of 1885. This was introduced late at night in the British Parliament as an adjunct to a bill to which it had no connection, and criminalizes what it describes as 'acts of gross indecency between males'. Because there is no definition of precisely what constitutes gross indecency this remained to be determined by case law, and it will I am sure surprise and horrify the House to learn that in the 1950s two airmen in Britain were sentenced under this act for the crime of having looked lasciviously at each other. This gross invasion of human relationships would threaten all of us if it were allowed to remain in force. On the whole, however, the Irish police and Irish courts have shown a great deal more common sense than their British counterparts. The 1885 Act has been aptly described as a blackmailer's charter.

The modern gay liberation movement effectively started in the late 1960s in the United States of America by analogy with the struggle for black and women's civil rights. By the early 1970s these ideas had spread to Ireland. I was involved in those early movements, and among the tasks which confronted us was that of dealing with a considerable number of men who were arrested in what appeared to be compromising circumstances by the police. I know that it has been said that there have not been prosecutions for over forty years, but this is not the case at all. In fact in the 1970s when gay people were arrested by the police, we defended them so successfully that within a few years the number of arrests by young police officers anxious to accumulate high score convictions had dropped to virtually none. But I do remember very clearly the humiliation caused to those accused even when we secured their acquittal. In particular, I recall one occasion on which a young man was forced in the Dublin District Court to describe in detail and repeatedly an act of fellatio or oral intercourse in which he had engaged with another man in the Phoenix Park. The judge amused himself by making comic remarks about this particular form of practice, to the huge enjoyment of those in the body of the court and to the understandable human distress of the accused. I should also point out that within the last couple of years the 1861 Act has been invoked by a judge in a case involving the accusation of a rape by a man upon his wife which was successfully defended through plea of consent, whereupon the judge relied upon the provisions of the 1861 Act which held that, regardless of consent, an act of buggery even between husband and wife was a criminal matter, and sentenced the man involved to a term of imprisonment. This was a spectacularly unsavoury case, but it does highlight the fact that one can never presume the total intertia of the law.

By 1974, partly as a result of our experiences in the courts and partly because many of us with our new-found dignity as members of the gay community found the whole notion of being labelled criminal offensive, we decided to go on the offensive and to sue the State of Ireland in the High Court in order to seek to demonstrate that the existing provisions of the law conflicted with the notion of civil and human rights in Ireland and were therefore unconstitutional. We mounted a powerful case involving international expert witnesses. Our intention was to end the conspiracy of silence that has for so long surrounded this whole subject of homosexuality from the days in which it was described as a *peccatum, illud, horribile, inter christiani non nomindaum*, that crime which is so horrible that it must not be mentioned among Christians.

In his judgment Mr Justice McWilliam found that he was persuaded by our evidence that there was a very large minority of people in the state who were homosexual. That they were not mentally retarded. That they were not emotionally sick. That they were not child molesters. And so the list went on until we were convinced that we had won. But at the very last minute there was a swerve in the judgment, and the learned judge found that he could not determine in our favour because of the Christian and democratic nature of the state.

The case had been built around my own experience as a gay man, because although the ideal would have been to get one of our clients as a victim of the law to challenge its constitutionality, understandably no one was prepared to do so. One of the principal elements of my case was the fact that in the late 1960s I had collapsed in a Dublin restaurant and had been rushed to Baggot

Street Hospital with a suspected heart attack. After examination it emerged that what had occurred was in fact an anxiety or panic attack, rather than a genuine heart attack, and having been referred for counselling the sources of this anxiety emerged as the recent death of my mother, the emigration of a close friend and the fact that subconsciously I had apparently felt deeply threatened by the existence of the criminal law. I was referred to a psychiatrist whose advice to me was to leave this country for ever and find refuge in a jurisdiction where a more tolerant attitude towards homosexual men prevailed, specifically the South of France. This well-meant advice I found deeply offensive. I would ask this House to consider how any member of the House would feel if they were professionally advised to leave their own country merely on account of something over which they had as little control as the colour of their hair. This outraged me and propelled me into the moves that led to the foundation of the Irish Gay Rights Movement. It also proved useful in putting together a legal case.

When we appealed to the Supreme Court we got another moral and intellectual victory but a divided judgement. On the one hand the Chief Justice argued that the criminal provisions of the law were necessary in order to induce homosexual men into marriage. This struck me as a rather peculiar view of that sacred institution. I was not however surprised when within a couple of years one of those judges who had collaborated in this opinion unburdened himself, in a case involving nullity, of the view that if a gay man contracted a marriage it was not by virtue of his orientation a valid marriage in any case. This was what one might reasonably describe as a no-win situation. Gay men were to be terrorized into marriage by the full vigour of the criminal law, but once inside that institution it turned out to be a mirage as a result of their sexual orientation. It defeats me how the family can be thought to be supported as a institution by these irrational views. Moreover, anyone who thinks that the criminal law has remained a dead letter would do well to read the transcript of my case in the European Court of Human Rights, which was ultimately successful thanks to the brilliant legal work of my then counsel, now President, Mary Robinson. She unearthed a series of cases in the matrimonial court in which the learned judge had stopped evidence being given by one of the spouses in a marriage to the effect that he was and continued to live as a homosexual after marriage. This stopping of the evidence was done on the basis that if it continued the judge would feel required to refer the book of evidence to the Director of Public Prosecutions and a criminal prosecution might well have followed.

In other words, what I am saying this afternoon is that despite appearances to the contrary the provisions of the criminal law continued and will continue, until they are extinguished by our acts, to exert a malign social and legal influence upon the population of Ireland.

It has been argued, however, on abstract grounds that this change in the law is a retrograde step because homosexuality is an unnatural practice. It may be useful to enquire the way in which this word 'natural' is used. The American researchers and sociologists Margaret Meade, and Forde and Beech, found in their surveys of primitive societies that in 67 per cent of these societies (i.e. man in his and her natural environment) homosexuality was accepted and to some extent institutionalised. Turning to the animal kingdom, the distinguished scientist Wainright Churchill has established that homosexual behaviour occurs throughout the mammalian order in nature, increasing in frequency and complexity when one ascends the phylogenetic scale, and that most wonderful, intelligent and endearing of marine mammals, the dolphin, is among those non-human creatures that have been known to establish lifelong monogamous homosexual relationships. One must therefore question the sense in which the word 'natural' is employed. It is clearly a theological derivative of the Roman Catholic notion of natural law. But even here one can raise a question mark. For the great theologian St Thomas Aquinas actually instanced the existence of homosexuality as an example of his proposition that what is natural for the individual may be natural for the species and vice versa. In other words, to force a homosexual man to behave heterosexually is just as much a violation of his nature as it would be to force a heterosexual man to behave homosexually.

This leaves us with the problem of what God intended if one is a religious person, and I am. I have heard repeated again the hoary old joke, God made Adam and Eve not Adam and Steve. This is an unnecessarily narrow view of God's intellectual horizons. I have no reason to doubt that God created both Adam and Eve and Sam and Steve. If God did not create Adam and Steve then who did? It is also simplistically argued that the same God designed the various organs of the human body for specific purposes. This is an argument persistently engaged in by those right-wing pressure groups whose minds are firmly stuck in the human plumbing. I do not intend to venture too far into this distasteful area of controversy, but I may point out that when the late member of this House, and Nobel Prize-winning poet, William Butler Yeats wrote in 'Crazy Jane and the Bishop' that

> love has pitched his tent
> in the house of excrement

he was speaking of heterosexual and not homosexual love. I wonder if my friends of the misnamed organisation Family Solidarity would seriously suggest that because the penis is used for the purposes of bodily elimination it should be restricted to this function and not employed in sexual relations.

I only make this point because members of both Houses have been inundated by these groups with squalid pamphlets purporting to describe in lurid detail the grosser aspects of what they imagine to be common sexual practices in the gay community. The apparent source of this material is something described as the Canadian Intelligence Service, which seems to me to be a contradiction in terms.

Disease has also disreputably been invoked as an argument by these same groups. They have used the tragic situation with regards to AIDS as a stick with which to beat the gay community. This is to my mind an unspeakably sad and disreputable thing to do. May I place on the record of this House the fact that according to the World Health Organisation statistics the mechanism of transmission of the AIDS virus in 70 per cent of the cases reported on a global basis is straightforward heterosexual intercourse. The remaining 30 per cent is divided between intravenous drug users sharing needles, mother-to-infant transmission, use of untreated blood products for haemophiliacs, and homosexual relations. It would be grotesque if I were to call for the banning of heterosexual relationships as a result of this information. Moreover, even were this disease confined entirely to the gay community this would scarcely be an argument for legal repression. There are certain diseases that are apparently confined to specific groups. If I may give one instance, sickle cell anaemia occurs only in the black population. It would rightly be regarded as abhorrent if these medical facts be used as a basis for a theory of racial inferiority. This is the direction in which, if one takes up this kind of argument, one will inevitably travel. Let us remember it is but fifty years ago that gay people were systematically victimised with the complicity of church and state in Germany under the Nazi tyranny when they were made to wear a pink triangle in the concentration camps as a badge of infamy. They were the first group to be incarcerated in the concentration camps, to be tortured, to be medically experimented upon and finally to be exterminated. The gay movement of which I am proud to be a member has adopted this pink triangle as its international symbol and turned a badge of infamy into a badge of pride and humanity.

There is one other argument that I would like to address. I heard in the Lower House one member say that if this law were passed it would be the thin end of the wedge and he might have to witness the horrible spectre of two men holding hands at a bus queue. May I say that if his mind were to be genuinely disturbed by such a prospect then his mental balance is precarious indeed. From the cradle I have been brainwashed with heterosexuality, I have frequently witnessed the spectacle of young heterosexual couples holding hands and enthusiastically kissing at those very same bus stops, and I merely wished them well and passed on my way. May I reassure the House that should two young men or two young women hold hands at a bus stop in Dublin the island will not be overwhelmed by earthquakes and turbulence, nor will the world come to an unexpected end.

It is therefore with pride that I welcome this bill to the House in its provisions dealing with homosexuality. Young people will no longer have to grow up in the shadow of the taint of criminality which had blighted the vulnerable youth of so many of our citizens with terror and shame. The talent that has been destroyed and repressed in so many people will now be freely and generously available to the wider community, and much of what has been unnecessarily squandered in the past will be added to the richness of Irish life. This therefore is in that sense a happy day. Nevertheless, I cannot in conscience vote for this bill in its present form. This is because of the provisions regarding the matter of prostitution. It would go hard with me to accept my liberation without a murmur at the expense of the victimisation of another vulnerable group. It is for this reason that I have put down a series of amendments opposing Sections 6 to 13 of the bill which seek to criminalise prostitution. I believe that this is both unwise and ungenerous, although I perhaps understand the tactical reasons for which it was done. I shall argue the case against such provisions and in favour of the unlinking of the two issues of prostitution and homosexuality so that the matter of prostitution may be calmly and rationally considered at another date. I shall speak further on these issues when we come to deal with the particular sections of the bill.

Note

1.　　Seanad Éireann is the Upper House of the Irish Parliament, the Lower being Dáil Eireann. All members of the Dáil are elected by the general population. Some senators are nominated directly to the Seanad by the Taoiseach/Prime Minister, while others are elected to represent five particular panels of candidates, for example an agricultural panel, a social and cultural panel. A small number of senators are elected by graduates of the NUI universities and Trinity College. Senator Norris represents the Trinity College constituency. Bills are passed from the Lower to the Upper House for discussion and ratification. However, the Seanad can only discuss and on occasion delay the passage of bills; it cannot veto legislation coming from the Dáil.

Interview with
Mary Dorcey

Can you first tell us something about the Ireland you grew up in? Have you seen great changes in the last twenty years?

The Ireland I live in now is so far removed from the Ireland of twenty years ago it might be another country. And the Ireland of my childhood remembered from this perspective seems like another planet.

So you grew up in the 1950s and 60s? Could you summarize the most striking characteristics of that period for you?

Silence. Repression. Censorship. Long dark winters. Poor food. Nuns and priests everywhere. Drab clothes. Censorship of books and films. Fear and suspicion surrounding anything to do with the body or the personal life. The near total repression of ideas and information. A Catholic state for a Catholic people. It is hardly possible to imagine the extent of this censorship, because the cultural climate has changed so radically by comparison. Needless to say modern Ireland is still a profoundly conservative society, a Catholic theocracy, but the boundary walls have been demolished and the power of mass communications has transformed our lives. It is still easy to be right wing, bigoted, sectarian and sexist, but it is now impossible not to know that there is an alternative viewpoint.

In the 1950s all was silence. An almost perfectly homogenous society brooking no divergence from the norm. I remember the taboos, the concealments. All the things that couldn't be said. Divorce was a bad word. I knew *one* woman who was divorced when I was growing up. She came from England to live on our road.

She wore bright lipstick and dyed her hair red. She played cards. She drove her own car. She was a scandalous woman, exciting and shocking, outside the lives of our mothers.

Contraception was not known or spoken of. The Pill was mentioned only as a medical means to regulate a woman's cycle (so many irregular periods). Condoms (rubbers as they were known then) was a dirty word, a word only whispered. You went to Belfast to buy them, a couple of packets at a time. Abortion was unheard of except in English films, where from time to time a woman suffered an indescribable horror at the hands of a corrupt doctor. One knew without it being said that this was the blackest sin of all – a back-street abortion. Sex. Never written or spoken of except in Catholic church pamphlets for the education of the young, where it was described as 'marital relations' – intimacy takes place between husband and wife for the purposes of procreation. Homosexual. The worst of all forbidden words, never spoken or published until 1973.

Can we talk a little of your own childhood? Did you feel different when you were growing up?

In spite of what I've said about the general climate of repression and bigotry, at the time I had a life of great freedom and variety. I was athletic, extrovert and gregarious. I had wonderful friends and grew up in a beautiful place. I had three older brothers and a sister, so our house was always full of people. I seem to have spent most of my life out on the sea in boats, or swimming, cycling, going to the cinema, talking, reading and in adolescence, dancing and partying.

My father died when I was seven, leaving my mother to care for five children. This meant there wasn't a lot of money, so although we were middle class we didn't have middle-class security. It also meant that being the daughter of a widow I had more freedom perhaps than a child of two parents.

But I did feel conscious of difference. It seemed to me that girls and women spent their lives in a game of concealment; forced to conceal their intelligence, their strength, their instinctive life, their need for action and self-definition. Girls learned very early to hide their ability and their desires – to defer pleasure, to efface them-selves, to disclaim achievement. I found it hard to fit into the confines of the world offered to girls. I had the freedom and opportunity of a boy until I reached adolescence. It felt as if I had to deny my own essential self, my integrity and sense of identity, to become a young woman. I learned to play the game well and to enjoy it, but I had to conceal more than I expressed. Talking to feminists and lesbians, this is something we all seem to have in common – rebellion or escape from the confines of femininity in childhood that made us impatient with this constraint in adulthood.

Did you know that you were lesbian when you were growing up?

No. I knew nothing about it. I did not hear the word, I think, until I was thirteen. My best friend at school asked me if I knew anything about the subject. We were sitting on our bicycles, leaning against the convent wall, talking before going our separate ways home to six o'clock tea. She had stolen a copy of *Lady Chatterley's Lover* from the back of her father's wardrobe, and we were reading it together. Neither Lady Chatterley nor her gardener mentioned the word 'lesbian', but my friend wanted to know all about it, as with any other taboo subject. I had to admit I knew nothing except that it must be the female equivalent of male homosexuals, a word which conjured up images of distorted bodies, sad lonely people, dark streets and foreign cities.

I first heard the word homosexual when I was ten. My sister was rehearsing *The Ballad of Reading Gaol* by Oscar Wilde, to recite at the Fr Matthew *Feis* in Milltown. My brother said. 'You know he was a homosexual?' (My brother was at university and knew about things!) My mother said it couldn't be true and she didn't believe it. It was a British plot to disgrace him, like Parnell and Kitty O'Shea. And how could it be true? How could a man with another man? No one answered the half-phrased question. But I remembered the word and after dinner went to look it up in the dictionary. 'Pertaining to one's own sex.' That was not a lot of help. It clearly applied only to men (but then so could most things looked up in the dictionary in those days). I forgot about it for the time being. It was many years before this awkward, unattractive word came to have anything to do with my life, but Oscar Wilde quickly became a favourite author. I read all his plays aloud on winter evenings after that, act by act, to my best friend, while we sat on our bicycles leaning against the convent wall. When we discovered that he had been prosecuted and imprisoned for the practice of homosexuality, betrayed by his best friend, separated from his wife and children and had died in exile soon after his release, it left an impression of great sadness and foreboding. But it made us admire his wit and iconoclasm all the more.

Shortly after that I discovered the French writer Colette and the *Claudine* novels, and the first door on the road to enlightenment opened before me.

Can you explain why the subject seemed to catch your interest at such an early age?

Now this is one of the strangest things. Many gay people report the same phenomenon – sensing that they are different before they have anything definite to go on. Having a need to discover what certain words mean even before they hear them.

As I have said the word 'lesbian' was never spoken. The word 'homosexual' was not spoken or written in Ireland before the 1970s. The word 'gay' didn't exist. I had never heard of a bisexual. I had never seen one or spoken to one. So how did I manage to become one? But isn't this one of the great mysteries of social development? How truth and desire triumph over ignorance and deception? The wonder is how so many people, so many thousands manage this discovery for themselves, given the immense effort society puts into making it hidden and making it seem unattractive. Lifelong brainwashing from the cradle to the grave to remain faithful to heterosexuality is still not sufficient to keep everyone suppressed. The entire force of Church and State, the entire weight of international culture, is not enough to suppress the strength of nature. The instinct to joy and love and intimacy is irrepressible. Centuries of repression have not worked and can't work. Here we are, all of us, in every country, in every culture, in every epoch, finding ourselves, finding one another, even in countries where no one has ever spoken the word, in countries where you can be sent to prison for it.

Somehow we know and find others who know and tell them and they tell someone else and so we reproduce ourselves in every generation.

Before we get into the large questions of sexual identity and creative impulse, could you first tell us a little about yourself? Could you tell us for instance when you first came out?

That depends on what you mean by the expression. It is a strange phrase, isn't it? Coming out – from where to where? Do we mean discovering our sexuality? Do we mean discovering our lesbian sexuality? Do we mean acknowledging it to ourselves? To a lover? To our friends and relations? To the public at large? To the nation?

I think in this case we mean your first lesbian experience

Ah well, in that case I can say I came out when I fell in love with a woman at seventeen. This is a very common way for lesbians to come out – by falling in love – and it is one of the very odd things about this expression because 'coming out' usually means that you stay in bed for weeks, months, even years, unable to part from the joy of one another's flesh for more than five minutes. So it is a strangely inappropriate term to describe this process of self-discovery. However, be that as it may, I came out, I found out, when I fell in love with a woman in 1969.

Did you define yourselves as lesbians at this time?

No, not until we got involved with feminism. Until then we saw ourselves as two unusual individuals with a special passion, a capacity for friendship and affection that was greater than the average. I think that young women still experience lesbianism in this way, even in contemporary Ireland.

Would you have come out as a lesbian if you had not become a feminist?

For me it is impossible to separate life as a lesbian from my life as a feminist. While it is possible, of course, to express physical attraction to one's own sex without adopting a radical political philosophy, it is impossible to make this a reality for anything more than a few if we do not create a feminist revolution.

Women's position in society as a subservient class, existing to service the needs of men and children, means that the mass of women cannot hope to establish a self-determined sexuality within the existing patriarchal power system. Realizing this at twenty-one made me a feminist. And becoming a feminist gave me a tremendously strong self-image and a cultural context in which to be a lesbian.

Before we get into all those deeper questions, perhaps you could first tell us what the word 'lesbian' means to you?

It seems to me, to put it at its most simple (which is not always easy), that I am a lesbian because I have loved women more than men. That is, I have loved women more deeply, more completely. It is not a matter only or even primarily of sexual desire, but rather of erotic love. That is, attraction and engagement with another individual at the deepest levels of emotional, psychic and physical discovery. I think erotic love is not so much a matter of lust as of who and what inspires the imagination, awakens psychic passion. With women I can be most fully myself. The relationship between two women lovers is immensely more empathetic, passionate, creative than is possible in present-day heterosexuality. A lesbian is a pioneer, a woman who has escaped from the controlling grasp of masculine heterosexuality, a visionary, a free spirit, an adventurer, a self-creator.

There is a profound and personal liberation made possible by the discovery of the erotic in its purest sense, and by the erotic I mean self-empowerment through integration of the emotional, spiritual and sexual.

Are lesbians made or born? Do women choose to be lesbian?

I think I was born bisexual and chose to become a lesbian when I fell in love with a lesbian feminist, because feminism changed a private sexual encounter into a cultural happening, a psychic happening, a way of seeing, a way of being in the world, a life of personal and political exploration, self-realization at a level that was so much more exciting, fulfilling than collusion with heterosexism or what seemed then to be apolitical bisexuality.

Can you explain why lesbianism is such a closely guarded secret?

Why indeed? This is a question many women ask themselves when they have their first sexual experience with a lesbian. And the answer is that homosexuals don't tell us because they don't know themselves, but they suspect and fear it is something so exciting, so passionate, so time-consuming, so addictive, that once started there will be no getting people away from it. And of course they are right. It is engrossing, time-consuming, passionate, romantic. If gay men are often considered to live a life of rampant sexuality, lesbians could well be said to live lives of rampant romance and erotic passion. It's a wonder anything else gets done, but it does because lesbians are a powerhouse everywhere, within the feminist movement and throughout the world. Anywhere women are organizing together, breaking silence, breaking new ground, there you will find a lesbian or two or three (and that's where the trouble comes in, but it does get worked out) and the work does get done all the more powerfully for being fuelled by such passion.

What kind of women become lesbians?

All kinds, every physical type, every personality type, every class, every culture, all age groups. Schoolgirls falling in love with each other. Mothers of young children falling in love with other mothers. Childless women falling in love with mothers of teenage children. Nuns falling in love with their sisters. It can happen at any age, at any stage. It happens to straight women and to bisexual women and mothers and to celibates. It is encouraged by contact with others of the breed, it is highly dangerous when exposed, it is spread by education and personal contact, it changes lives, it distracts from the nuclear family, it takes up a lot of time that could be gainfully employed with housework or knitting. It is highly contagious. It is rife among feminists. The contraceptive/divorce mentality does often lead to the lesbian mentality, feminism encourages it. Lesbians *are* self-indulgent, joyful, self-sufficient. Lesbians are not good wives: lesbians are not obedient, dutiful, ignorant or asexual.

People like to discuss lesbianism as though it were a social problem. It reassures heterosexuals to consider it only in terms of their own reaction, that is to say, their own homophobia, their own fear and hostility. They talk about what we need, what we have fought for, what we've gained. Oppression, suppression, action and reaction. A social sort of problem like any other disadvantaged group. But the difference between us and many other marginalized groups is that a lesbian loves to be a lesbian, a lesbian wants to be a lesbian, a lesbian wants lesbians, a lesbian wants to love women, a lesbian is in love with women, a lesbian loves it this way, a lesbian wouldn't go back.

If you had to choose one thing above all that you like about being a lesbian, what would you say?

I like kissing. This is a very good reason for being a lesbian. Women are so good at kissing. Then I like being able to lie in bed for hours, and we might kiss or we might not because literally you get distracted talking about the revolution, talking about books and movies and parties and lovers and food, movies, and talking about the revolution. Of course, not all lesbians are consciously involved in the revolution; some of them work in the bank, but all of us are part of it whether we know it or not, whether the bank knows it or not (all those phone calls – all that photocopying and faxing!).

I like being a lesbian because women are fabulous lovers, especially with other women (they don't get much of a chance with men). I have a theory that heterosexuality was invented to keep a check on sexual desire, lust, Eros, all those things. Because men and women together aren't very good at it, they have to spend so much time learning and trying hard not to do the first thing they think of – the thing they would really most like to do – and remembering instead to do something else first in the hope that if they do their partner will get into the mood to do the thing they first thought of, the thing they most want to do. There is an awful lot of incompatibility to get over: the bodies aren't the right size, the geography is wrong, the tastes are different, the messages get fouled up, and then there's all the cultural stuff. All the hard work of being heterosexual means that attention is only left over for making money and babies. Of course, lesbians make money and make babies too, but maybe not so many of them? (Is my theory falling down here?) Anyway, back to sex, because homosexuality is about sex isn't it? Or why would they call it that?

How are lesbians different from heterosexuals?

Making women the 'centre of our lives' – the early 1970s phrase, 'women - identified - woman' probably expresses it better than most others. Lesbians are too deeply self-realized and self-assertive for the willing suppression of their own instincts and personalities. They want to love as equals and in a patriarchal world this is condemned as neurotic. The heterosexual establishment is afraid of the power of lesbianism, because it is a radical threat to the system as we know it. It demands the empowerment of women, the autonomy of women, the freedom of women to define themselve, to choose their own sexual partners, to determine their manner of life without reference to male needs.

As far as sexuality is concerned the greatest constraint on women is the denial of agency, of spontaneous emotion, of freedom and equality. Heterosexuality, as we know it, romanticizes and eroticizes the domination of women by men. In order to truly desire a man, a woman (to a greater or lesser extent) has to surrender her own agency and collude with her own oppression. When a woman is unable to picture her own suppression and self-denial as romantic or sexy she finds it impossible to be romantic about men. This makes her either cynically divided against herself (through living a split personality, she agrees to abandon herself from time to time in order to relate romantically/sexually with men) or frustrated and lonely. Most women feel this sense of alienation from their true selves in sex with men: the sense of playing a part, the sense of playing the eternal feminine and of being desired as a representative of the species rather than for their individual self. Probably men feel this too, but I think it would take a gay man to tell us about it.

But is it not a very painful way of life? This makes it all sound fun and good times? There must have been hard times, surely?

There are. Don't worry. There are always hard times. Everyone has them – even gay people. Your lover leaves you. You leave your lover. (Why is it no one ever writes about how painful it is to leave a lover – to be the one who leaves?). There are angry parents, hurt parents, there are bewildered friends who wonder if this means that they might be too, there are people staring at you when you hold hands in the street, and people putting you out of pubs when you kiss on the mouth. People ring up radio stations and denounce you. You might lose your job if your boss finds out. Break your mother's heart. Disappoint your mentors. These are all hard things. If you go to visit your lover in hospital it is difficult to kiss her without causing shock waves. Property rights are uncertain. Who gets the house if you split up?

Straight people write angry letters to the paper denouncing you as the detritus of the polluted river that will overwhelm the country when the floodgates open. One is always being accused of 'living on the slippery slope' and 'opening the floodgates'. Now these are very erotic images, and gay people certainly do their best to express the adventure suggested by them, but why they should be considered the only ones to do so is hard to understand. Heterosexuals lack self-confidence, I'm afraid.

Heterosexuals worry so much about other heterosexuals catching homosexuality. They say it is unnatural, neurotic, disturbed, deviant, sick, and yet it must be kept secret at all times in case anyone would want to try it. Very strange. They don't worry about any other so called 'disordered state' being infectious, only homosexuality, which must be kept in the closet because it's too exciting to be let out.

Will you tell us about the early days of the Gay Rights and Women's Rights[4] movements?

I was living in Paris with a male lover and going to university. At university I met a group of older women who I thought might be lesbian, though they did not say so. For the first time in my life I sensed the possibility that adult women could live as lesbians, that they could have an independent financial existence, live without the support of men, choose not to have children, have their own self-sufficient (with gay men) social world. That it need not necessarily mean social extinction and penury.

I came back to Ireland. I went to the Women's Movement (then in its second year). I met wonderful women. I was enchanted by the exhilaration, the self-confidence, energy, wit, anger, vision but, to my surprise, no one declaring themselves lesbians or speaking about it. Then one dark wet November night my girlfriend and I were walking past Trinity College and we saw a poster which amazed and excited us: 'The Sexual Liberation Movement Meets Tonight at Eight O'clock'. Bewildering and ludicrous as it seems from this vantage point, that night twenty-two years ago was the first time I think the word 'sexual' was written anywhere in public. The Women's Movement had been in action for one year, the Pill train had taken place and I had seen some of the group on the *Late Late Show*, but while they demanded the right to legal contraception, I don't remember that anyone talked about sex.

We went upstairs to the meeting in Trinity (a place that intimidated us both and we would never have entered if it weren't for the hope of meeting gay people). We sat round in a circle and introduced ourselves. There were five gay men, two bisexual women and one lesbian. My girlfriend and I, for reasons of solidarity, decided to define ourselves as lesbian. So now there were three lesbians in Ireland!

I started to talk about lesbianism at the Women's Movement meetings and discovered that there were five other lesbians closeted in the group. But very quickly the numbers grew. The Sexual Liberation Movement (SLM) had its first public meeting, a symposium on Gay Rights in 1973. Noel Browne, an Irish psychiatrist, and Babs Todd, an English activist attended it. Hundreds turned up, turned on and came out. Gay Byrne invited the guest speakers onto the *Late Late*. She was the first ever lesbian to be seen on Irish television, but fortunately Babs Todd was British and going back in the morning, so that was all right.

It is almost impossible to believe the euphoria and manic fun of this period when we thought the world could be changed utterly by twenty lesbian feminists and some gay men wreaking havoc on Dublin. The world seemed transformed overnight. We gave parties. We went to bed. We fell in love. We went out in the streets and clamoured for our rights. We discovered ourselves to be new, extraordinary, exhilarated beings. We shouted in the streets. We had a lot of wild parties and a lot of wild protests and workshops and conferences. We were intoxicated with the joy of change and discovery. They were times of great sexual extravagance. Everyone slept with everyone. Possessiveness and monogamy were the work of the patriarchy and so we had to learn to do things differently. We kept in close touch with events in the USA. We felt part of an international movement. Alix Dobkin sang what became a theme song: 'Every woman can be a lesbian', and we knew she was right. All around us women were coming out and joining in.

I began to be invited to universities and other venues to give talks on Gay Rights. Everywhere I went I was met with horror and amazement. I spoke at Women's Week in University College Dublin on sexuality. I spoke as an open lesbian describing heterosexuality as sado-masochism. And declared: if feminism is the theory lesbianism is the practice. It was like a Roman arena. I was the Gladiator. I just about escaped with my life. It was reported in the papers the next morning. The *Irish Times* ran a front-page headline: 'Self-Confessed Lesbian Denounces Heterosexuality'.

On the following night I attended a debate on contraception. When I spoke from the audience a young man interrupted: 'What would a pervert like you know about contraception?' And I was booed and prevented from speaking. This was my first experience of the censorship and restriction that would be forced on me.

As the country got to hear about us we were subjected to intense vilification – we were declared freaks and lunatics. Outcasts. We frightened our friends and families. Made strangers angry. We were no longer trusted with young children. Happier than ever before. But freaks.

Then the Irish Gay Rights Movement (IGRM) was formed and David Norris came into prominence. Eventually the lesbians split and, after much debate, formed their own group, 'Women for Radical Change', which lasted two years. The original Women's

Liberation group broke up and many of us joined a new coalition, Irish Women United, which was an umbrella organization for lesbians, radical feminists, socialists, communists, trade unionists, liberal feminists, workers, students, the unemployed and house-wives. About 40 per cent of the group were lesbian. A shifting population with new women coming out all the time and many lesbians emigrating.

After a time my mother found out. She read about my speech at Belfield, as did all her friends and neighbours and relations. A great silence descended. People stopped talking to me. I was dropped from the circle I had grown up in. I had become an embarrassment. An unmentionable name except to a small circle of radicals. I didn't really notice. I was so busy being in love and changing the world.

I went to Japan. My mother heaved a sigh of relief. When I came back I joined up with the women's army again. (We used to sing a song called 'The Women's Army is Marching, Oh! Sisters Don't You Weep'!) By then we had added Rita Mae Brown and Kate Millet to the list of heroines. There were now three public lesbians in the world. *The Well of Loneliness* by Radclyffe Hall was reprinted. Wow! And we thought we had it bad! Huge changes were taking place. The movement had won a catalogue of social and legislative reforms. Structures and attitudes were beginning to give way. But the movement that spearheaded this remarkable progress was begin-ning to flounder. So many factions, so many issues. Socialists and republicans, liberals and radicals and an awful lot of lesbians. The lesbians as always crossed all the divisions and wreaked chaos in tightly knit socialist cells. I went to North America.

In the USA I found that 'feminist' was a word no one wanted to hear. The dykes were all into good living. They wanted to make out on the beaches, in the fields, at the women's festivals. Feminists? They wanted to know would you sleep with them. And what did you do – that meant a career, making money. (Americans are always very uneasy until they know what you do.) It wasn't easy for me to answer that, but something I had always done a lot of, without thinking anything about it, was writing, so I said 'I write', and they said 'Great!', and gave me a typewriter and a room to write in.

And so to writing. When did you decide to become a writer?

I don't know if I was born a lesbian but I know I was born a writer.
The desire to write certainly predates any of my sexual identity. I
would have become a writer no matter what kind of life I led or what
political viewpoint I held. My need to write springs from some deep
psychic level more akin to a religious sensibility, I think, rather than
a political one. It is a need to make sense of existence in order to
experience, to find in language a way to reflect the rhythm and
cadence of the natural world. Most definitely I would be a writer
even if I were not also a feminist and a lesbian. My pleasure and
fascination with words existed long before any political awareness.
I can't remember a time when I wasn't full of curiosity and delight in
language. As a small child I was forever making up stories and songs
and poems, and exasperating anyone who would listen by reciting
them. I loved to be read to, and to be told stories. I wrote from as
early as I can remember and I took it for granted that I always
would. But this did not mean that I saw myself becoming a writer!
That was a dream too outlandish to be spoken, one which seemed to
me, as a teenager, impossible to make real.

Women writers so far as I knew, if Irish, were rich, Protestant, upperclass and living in exile. It was considered that Irish
Catholic women were incapable of any vocation other than the care
of men and children (and real Irish women were always Catholic).
An Irish woman who wrote? Somerville and Ross – rich, idle
Protestants. (How long before I discovered that they were lovers?)
There was a poet, Kathleen Tynan, who wrote a poem about Jesus
that we learned at school. Elizabeth Bowen? Oh, yes, a fine writer
within limits, but another rich 'Prod', of course living in England.
Kate O'Brien? Well, she was rich too – lived all her adult life in
England, and her books were out of print anyhow. Mary Lavin? Oh,
yes, some nice little short stories but wasn't she born in America?
And contemporary Irish Catholics? No such thing. Not one. Until
Edna O'Brien burst on the scene. Scandalous, flagrant and a Catholic country girl. At last, a proletariat Irish woman. An inspiration.

39: *Interview with Mary Dorcey*

What writers influenced you in your formative years?

When I was a child and a teenager I read everything in sight, everything that came my way. All the nineteenth-century classics and as much of the modern American and English literature as I could find. I was fifteen before I noticed if the books I read were by men or women. I began to identify with the authors and to be conscious of their position in society. What class they were, what nationality, what kind of education they had, and finally, what gender. And it was then that I stumbled on the extraordinary fact that 80 per cent of the books I read were by men. The nineteenth century gave us the Brontës. Austen and Eliot and the early twentieth century, Colette, Woolf, Mansfield. But the postwar period seemed to have returned women to the kitchen.

So what spurred you on? What was your particular aim in becoming a writer?

My principle desire as a writer (not formulated until I discovered feminism and lesbianism) was to find a voice that could express in literature the multifaceted reality of women's lives – the fusion of emotional, sensual and intellectual experience that women take for granted but that is foreign to men. I wanted to find a way of writing that would not only express this way of life but embody it. It's a truism to say that men and women experience the world differently, and one of the most striking features of this is women's reluctance to compartmentalize reality. Men seem to find it difficult to feel and think at the same time, and consequently adopt a suspicious and critical attitude to any combination of emotion and logic. Women, on the other hand, live in every sense in a mixed world. Pluralism is a daily necessity for us, a gift and an imperative.

This pluralism is especially true of lesbian existence. We live in what might be called an intensified female atmosphere. We combine in our way of living more fusion/confusion of heart, mind and the senses than most people would feel comfortable with or have time for.

So it seems to me the essential quest for a woman writer is to forge a language that creates this reality on the page. That makes an actual fusion of these elements in the very sentence structure so that the reader is drawn into that reality and experiences it from within. The struggle to find a language which reflects this is for me an artistic quest, but also an act of political resistance and creation. Creating the language, the way of saying, is also to form the fabric of our lives, to build the superstructure of a woman-centred culture.

Literature can do what theoretical writing cannot – involve and transform. The element of magic in poetry and fiction functions as a lure to draw the reader into the individual experience. In this way it's possible to bypass reason and contact the individual at the deeper levels of the psyche.

Have you written anything which typifies this process?

I don't know if I ever succeed, but in as much as I had a conscious intention in writing the title story of my collection, *A Noise from the Woodshed*, it was to write a quintessential lesbian story – expressing something special to our culture, a kind of gleeful energy which is seldom talked about and certainly doesn't find its way into literature. I wanted to capture the quality of fertile chaos and the common experience of women who have to balance the practical, the emotional, the political and the sensual all in one day.

Women are not allowed to organize and compartmentalize their lives in the way men do. We are not allowed a separate space for our work (the office), our sex lives (the club, the brothel), our social lives (the sports' ground) as men are. If we want something we have to make room for it. I think this juggling act that women spend their lives in is something essential to the way we experience the world, and is one of our greatest gifts. I think it's especially true of lesbian lives, where women not only have to balance these incredibly intense and romantic relationships with the ordinary life of minding children, working, tending to others and political action. Very often we are forced to express our love lives in secret, in a manner which will not upset the heterosexuals around us. So, for instance, we not only have to fit in sex somewhere between doing the laundry and fighting for abortion rights and putting the children to bed, but we have to do it without disturbing the neighbours. There is a great fund of pleasurable farce and hilarity in lesbian life which I haven't written about elsewhere, but I very much want to be able to express. The complexities and subtleties of my own life at any given time would seem quite incredible if set down in fiction. More than in any group, when talking to lesbians I hear the phrase 'Nobody would believe it if you wrote it'. There is a gleeful sense of the absurd in our own predicament as invisible people that is special to us.

What are the particular challenges of being a lesbian writer? Is it possible to be a lesbian writer without it becoming one's whole identity? Without setting up the expectations that one always writes about sex? That one's writing is sexy?

Yes, it is difficult anywhere for a lesbian or gay writer to be open about the subject without being shoved into a literary cul-de-sac. Homosexual people are not allowed a private life. We either have a secret one or a notorious one. If you keep quiet about your sexuality you can be taken seriously as a writer, but the internal pressure of concealment may damage the writing (enervating it, depriving it of depth and urgency) as much as it damages the life.

On the other hand, if one declares one's sexuality openly one becomes at once a 'lesbian writer'. A strange and peculiar animal unlike any other living creature. Scandalous or closeted. This is a false choice we are faced with and so the discrepancy/dichotomy between the personal life, the self-perception and the public stereotype. We live with this dual reality, caught between the rich diverse inner life and the distorted mirror image. It is like Wilde's wonderful metaphor, *The Picture of Dorian Gray*. The inner self may grow by leaps and bounds but the public image often seems incapable of growth. Stalled in some freak infancy. A stunted, amorphous creature. Is there any way to break the mirror? To have it reflect the inner reality? Is one condemned to a lifetime spent wandering in a hall of mirrors? This attempt to make the outer image reflect in some true measure the inner reality of lesbian life in all its complexity and diversity is one of the great spurs to my writing.

You must be very brave to live as you do.

I'm not so sure. I don't know if I would have the courage again to live as a heterosexual. Although I was brought up in a heterosexual household, raised by heterosexual parents and completely surrounded by a heterosexual culture, and lived as an active heterosexual myself for perhaps ten years, I'm not sure I would any longer have the courage for it. Heterosexuality is such a dangerous proclivity for women and children. When you consider the incidence of rape, battery, molestation, assault, child abuse, incest, paedophilia among heterosexuals, not to mention the legal and social problems caused by marriage and divorce and the great difficulties they experience with meeting and communicating, it would make any thinking person extremely cautious of becoming one. I am not sure I would have the courage. I think life in the lesbian community has spoilt me. I am not as young as I used to be. Or as foolhardy.

Is it a deliberate choice of yours to stay and work in Ireland?

Yes. As we all know most Irish people get pushed out of Ireland not only because they can't find work, but because of social pressure to conform to a narrow norm, since everyone knows you and talks about you. There are forty million people of Irish extraction living in the USA and eight million in Britain. In the whole island of Ireland there are only four and a half million.

I spent most of my early adulthood abroad. I have lived in the USA, England, France, Spain and Japan. When I was out of Ireland I came across so many people who had been forced into exile, who would have liked to return, but who find with each year that passes that it becomes more difficult. They are strangers at home and away. So I made a conscious decision ten years ago to come home and try to make my life and work in Ireland. I moved to the West because I wanted a cheap place to write in and because I wanted to confront what is in effect the forcing ground of Irish society. By returning to the West of Ireland I was entering the belly of the beast, as it were, the most westerly point in Europe. As far as I could travel from my starting point and still be in my own country. It was a special compromise between coming home and emigrating. In a sense I did it in one move.

43: *Interview with Mary Dorcey*

Is there any political significance to your living and working in Ireland?

There is a sense of wanting to assert a refusal to be banished, to be exiled. I want to be one of the first generation to say 'We are different. We dissent from the consensus. But we are staying here.' To be the first generation in Ireland to force the consensus to change from the inside. To be a queer who stays in Ireland and writes about it is to fly in the face of all our cultural expectations (which will accept any behaviour in the foreign streets so long as it doesn't frighten Irish horses). We like to export our troublemakers, our dissidents, our critics. I have a dream of Ireland in which all the troublemakers have come home to roost. But for that to happen some of us have to refuse to leave. To make a roost for others to return to. I think this is now happening. While at the institutional level the country is profoundly conservative, it is gradually becoming a pluralist culture. Ideas and debate are far in advance of the public position on just about every issue of national concern.

There is a growing secular and liberal constituency in Ireland, especially amongst those under forty. The public face of Ireland is defined by the over fifties. The reality of life for the young, whether it is the drug culture, permissive sexuality, the breakdown of the nuclear family, the effects of unemployment, are not reflected in the institutional life, but are just beginning to be found in the artistic world. There is a real hunger for artistic work. Music, film, television, literature. Work which expresses and comes out of this new Ireland, this concealed Ireland, which up to now has been stifled by emigration. When I was growing up the attitude was always 'If you want to live differently go and do it somewhere else!' This is changing and very fast. The causes of this are many. The international communications explosion, our entry into Europe, the great increase in emigration, the war in the North and the feminist movement. To my mind, the single greatest force for education in this country in the last twenty years has been the Women's Movement, in all its varied expressions. And a great part of this force has been the flowering of writing by women that has taken place in the last fifteen years.

44: Lesbian and Gay Visions of Ireland

How do you picture the future for lesbians living in Ireland

It's hard for me to imagine the future. So much has changed. So much has stayed the same. The struggle to survive as an open lesbian, a committed feminist, a political writer, has dominated my life in the last twenty years and it is difficult to see how that will become easier. The financial struggle is the hardest part. But when have radical artists ever had a comfortable life? If I can survive physically and spiritually I will count myself very fortunate.

As for the community, I can only hope that the gains we have made will be established and built upon. That we go from strength to strength. I hope the immense changes I have witnessed in my adult lifetime will continue and create a way of life immeasurably more diverse and open than we can now imagine.

When I first discovered lesbian society I made a vow that no young Irish woman would grow up as I had, totally ignorant of the existence of earlier generations of lesbians. But if that is to be made possible, then others like me have to create a body of work that can survive the vagaries of heterosexual fashion. Write books that can speak to our grandchildren. I want to contribute to the re-imagining of the relation between private life and public affairs. If we can truly re-invent/re-envision our own sexual identity all else is possible.

Part II
Socio-political

Anatomy of a Campaign

Chris Robson

AT the beginning of 1988 Ireland had a constitutional ban on any form of divorce, there was restricted access to non-medical contraceptives, and a new constitutional provision apparently prohibited entirely any form of abortion. It also boasted what was, on paper at least, the worst legal regime in Western Europe for lesbians and gay men. There was no recognition or protection of any sort, and gay men faced a total ban on any type of sexual activity. If these laws were almost never enforced (largely because of effective action by David Norris and others in the 1970s) they still insulted and marginalized tens of thousands of gay men and, by association, lesbians as well. There is a general perception that these criminal laws simply derived from British law, so it is perhaps important to emphasize that they were not merely similar to the old British laws, but identical. In 1922 the new Irish state had incorporated all British common and statute law into its legal system, and the 1967 Wolfenden-inspired 'reform' in Britain did not apply to us.

Seven years on from 1988, the legal regime for gays and lesbians now mandates:

- The abolition of all previous laws criminalizing gay activity, and their replacement by a new gender-neutral law with a common age of consent of seventeen, and no special privacy conditions. [June 1993]
- No exceptions from this law for the armed forces or for the merchant marine. [June 1993]

- A Prohibition of Incitement to Hatred Act, which includes in its title the category 'sexual orientation'. [November 1989]
- Specific protection for every category of worker from 'unfair dismissal' because of sexual orientation. [April 1993]
- Work codes in all government and local government employment statutes which include the sentence 'Discrimination on the basis of sexual orientation will not be tolerated.' The same codes also specifically protect those with HIV/AIDS. [First code implemented July 1988]

There are also two new laws which have received outline Cabinet approval (October 1994) and which are currently being drafted:

- An expanded Employment Equality Act, which will cover all forms of workplace discrimination and which will now protect under several new categories including 'sexual orientation' and a definition of 'disability' which includes HIV/AIDS status.
- A radical new Equal Status Act to prohibit discrimination in non-work areas including housing, education and social services, together with an Equality Agency to monitor the Act.

Meanwhile, there is still no form of divorce, and, despite horrendous confusion in the law, abortion is still prohibited. Condoms, however, are now widely available.

It can hardly be denied that, by any comparative standards, this is a remarkable outcome. As recently as 1992 at the Paris conference of the International Lesbian and Gay Association (ILGA), Kees Waaldijk put forward a comparative model of legal advances, commenting as he presented each element that 'the exception to this pattern, of course, is Ireland'. But by 1994, Waaldijk had to concede that even he could not quite credit that the Irish reforms occurred both so rapidly and so out of 'sequence'. This article attempts to explain how these surprising reforms were fought for and enacted. It is important to stress that I shall not attempt to cover the origins of this campaign: that long courageous struggle (begun in 1974, by David Norris and others) which eventually resulted in the October 1988 judgement of the European Court of Human Rights in Strasbourg. Nor can I document the many community organizations that did, and continue to do, so much essential work.

The Strasbourg judgement stated that the total ban on gay sex was too severe, and that some reform must be introduced. However, previous judgements had also indicated that if this reform were based on the 1967 British 'reform', then that would almost certainly be accepted. The real question therefore was 'What sort of law?' A series of meetings was held, under the title 'Unite for Change', to which every lesbian and gay group in Ireland was invited. Almost all did attend, and the result was the foundation of a new organization, the Gay and Lesbian Equality Network (GLEN). It was given a specific mandate: to campaign for an equal criminal law and for new equality-based labour and civil laws. No-one would expect, or even desire, that our diverse communities would agree on everything, but on this specific issue we did. To confirm and renew its mandate GLEN held annual national meetings to present its work and agree its priorities, and throughout each year it attempted, with reasonable success, to maintain a continuous liaison with its sponsoring groups. It might seem frivolous to attribute some of our eventual success to so simple a thing as a name, but GLEN sounds both friendly and Irish, and is easily remembered. It also carries in four words the essence of our entire programme. We were never asked who we were, or what our aims were. More crucially, we were never asked to compromise: to accept, for instance, a differential age of consent. The word 'equality' carries great power. You either have it in total, or you remain unequal.

The mandate we'd been given would have been daunting at any time but in 1988 it seemed almost impossible. It was not long since a referendum had decided, by 66 per cent of the vote, to reject divorce. The previous referendum on abortion had bitterly split the country and, by a similar percentage vote, abortion was (supposedly) rendered entirely illegal. Right-wing groups were successfully prosecuting women's clinics and student health centres for the heinous crime of providing the phone numbers of abortion information services in England. The same right-wing groups were gazing in admiration at Britain's 'Clause 28'. We nonetheless felt confident that there was no inherent majority for oppression. Irish people have for too long been on the receiving end of discrimination to be comfortable with the charge that they are discriminating against others. On the principle of equality the argument could be won.

Allies

It seemed (and does still) to be an elementary tactic that lesbian and gay groups should form coalitions with other disadvantaged groups as well as with more powerful allies. It is a matter of continuing surprise to people in GLEN that, year after year at international conferences, we hear a 'new' radical call for creative liaison with both marginalized and sympathetic sections of society. When we mention (again) that this approach has been at the core of our work for eight years, they listen politely and then change the subject.

People who were to become GLEN activists had already begun to work with the first and perhaps the most influential of our allies, the trade unions. Unions are not only comparatively well funded but strongly in need of some effective visible action on civil rights. Following initiatives within their own unions by lesbian and gay members, the annual conference of the Irish Congress of Trade Unions (ICTU) agreed to sponsor a conference on lesbian and gay workplace issues. An ICTU working group, with several lesbian and gay members, was duly set up to prepare 'negotiating guidelines' on lesbian and gay workplace rights. The result was an unapologetic and radical charter of rights, printed in thousands, and sent to every union in Ireland (June 1987). It also gave a mandate to the ICTU to intervene on our behalf in negotiations with government. They have done so ever since, to powerful effect.

A second union-based initiative had a more dramatic initial effect. The AIDS committee of one of the civil service unions (which included a future GLEN member) was mandated by a number of other unions to negotiate an 'AIDS policy for the Civil Service'. The combined union position was accepted almost in its entirety, and resulted not only in effective protection for those with HIV/AIDS but also in a statement that 'discrimination on the basis of sexual orientation will not be tolerated'. The real significance was that it was issued in July 1988, four months before the Strasbourg decision and at a time when the government was publicly stating that the criminal laws must be maintained. If the government considered such protection necessary for its own workers, then the argument for its extension to everyone else became unanswerable.

Approach

The above manoeuvres demonstrate that GLEN had agreed on its strategy at an early stage. Lesbian and gay activists have tended (in crude summary) to veer between two well-known stances: 'Please, please, be nice to us', and 'Give us our goddamned rights, and give them now'. The first tends to provoke contempt, the second to elicit the perfectly reasonable response, 'What's so bloody special about you?' There is, however, a third approach: 'You will agree that equality before the law is a basic principle. On the particular equality issue in question, your responsibility is to abolish Statute X, and to add "sexual orientation" to Clause Y, Statute Z. Please sign here. Thank you.'

The summary may be crude but it's not invalid. Politicians neither like to be grovelled to nor shouted at. And however well intentioned they may be, they are rarely well informed. (Ask any of them what the common age of consent is in Italy, or Belgium, or Spain.) Our programmes had to be clear, well argued, highly specific and, above all, be seen to demand no special privileges.

'Equality now'

An effective way to present demands is to get others to argue them on your behalf. At the suggestion of its GLEN members, the Irish Council of Civil Liberties (ICCL) set up a working party (which included those same members) to produce a report on legal and civil rights issues for our communities. It eventually became a book, *Equality Now for Lesbians and Gay Men*, which was significant in so far as it was probably the only such book ever published by a non-gay group, and also because it incorporated a model Bill on Equal Status legislation for all minorities. Despite the fact that the ICCL had almost as little money as we had, they still sent a copy to every TD (Member of the Dáil) and senator in order to initiate the discussion.

Law Reform Commission

Faced with the Strasbourg Judgement, the government, perhaps inevitably, delayed. But, for once, this proved to be to our benefit. The government asked the Law Reform Commission to examine various models of legislations, to invite submissions, and to make a report. Submissions arrived from all quarters, including, of course, a range of gay and lesbian groups. After an admirable process of research, seminars and consultations, the final report included the following key sentence: 'The same legal regime should obtain for consensual homosexual activity as for heterosexual and that, in particular, no case has been established that the age of consent (seventeen years) should be any different' (September 1990).

They were right of course, but it was formidably important to be able to quote a government commission as having said so. It became, and stayed, a pivotal argument, and the entire report was added to our list of resources. A second lesson had become clear: if a document is sufficiently well prepared its usefulness does not just continue, it increases. The ICTU guidelines helped with the civil service policy: both were incorporated into *Equality Now*, which in turn was presented in its entirety to the Law Reform Commission. Right up to the end of the campaign all these documents, and many more, have worked as interconnecting elements in a comprehensive platform. (The metaphor is deliberate: GLEN's membership includes people in planning, architecture, journalism and social research, and our approach has been duly influenced by these disciplines.)

Another lesson was learned during the inter-party negotiations leading to the renegotiated programme for the Fianna Fáil–Progressive Democrat government. We made a phone call to one of the negotiators to establish whether gay law reform was to be included in the programme. Informed that it was not, we asked why, to which the reply came, 'Good question'. Next morning it became part of the programme. One phone call.

Campaign for equality

Promises are one thing, action another. Law reform was obviously still distant, and our other concerns were pressing. Under the title 'Campaign for Equality' we asked for, and received, written commitments of support from political parties, national organizations, and from individual political leaders for anti-discrimination legislation and a Human Rights Commission. At the press conference launch, GLEN's co-presenters included the Forum of People with Disabilities, the Dublin AIDS Alliance, the Women's Coalition and the Travellers' Development Group, all of whom stayed on as core members of the campaign. Eventually, some forty organizations, including four of the main political parties, became supporters. Precisely because of our commitment to rights in the context only of equality, we now had a range of allies working to a common goal under a common slogan, 'Welcoming Diversity'. (The campaign continues: the day after the new criminal law was decided, a Technical Workshop on Equal Status Law was held under its banner.)

Friends in the media were another welcome addition. Some of Ireland's most powerful political journalists spoke as invited guests at our public meetings: their insights into strategies and tactics, and their opinions on our own proved invaluable. They were happy to be associated with our campaign, as we were so clearly aligned to the direction in which they hoped Ireland would move. The press also published long articles by GLEN itself, where the most radical possible programme was set out in quiet argument with which no reasonable person could possibly have disagreed. (That is the point, after all: everything we ask for is entirely reasonable, though we seem at times to forget this.)

Workplace protection lies at the heart of any lesbian and gay programme. Under a national employment agreement, the Unfair Dismissals Act was due for renewal. Getting it amended to include just two new words, 'sexual orientation', required long, grinding work involving hundreds of letters and calls to unions, employers' groups, national and even religious organizations, requesting that they articulate to the government our demands on their own behalf. (No file, we've been told, was ever bigger in the Department of Labour.) It worked. Travellers, lesbians, gays and (by understanding) those with HIV/AIDS are now fully protected from arbitrary dismissal in all categories of employment. We'd always said that if we'd had to choose, we'd have taken that rather than a reformed criminal law. Now, with both, we think it is still the more important. There is also, of course, the issue of those denied access to work. A proposal by GLEN to the Combat Poverty Agency was accepted, and we were commissioned to carry out a research project (now almost completed) on the mechanisms whereby discrimination leads to disadvantage and poverty.

A year earlier, however, all this had seemed impossibly distant. The new Taoiseach, after receiving complaints from the Council of Europe, simply stated that reform was 'at the bottom of his list of priorities'. A sardonic fourth birthday party for the Strasbourg Judgement, which we held outside the Dáil, didn't seem to shame him. At a bleak time, an international letter campaign, channelled through ILGA, kept up some real pressure.

In November 1992 the government fell, and while negotiations were proceeding after the election, we gained our most powerful ally yet. At an earlier suggestion of the Limerick Forum, representatives of gay and lesbian groups throughout Ireland were invited to a special reception at the official residence of President Mary Robinson. She had previously been a civil rights activist and had acted as David Norris's barrister in Strasbourg, and is easily one of the most admired public figures Ireland has ever had. The reception symbolized a national reconciliation with our community.

During the election, and after it, we continued to implement these lessons. After the Campaign for Equality's press conference, its policy statement was faxed to every party leader and director of elections. The Campaign, the ICCL and GLEN all subsequently made detailed submissions to the negotiators for the new Fianna Fáil–Labour Party government, submissions which reappeared, sometimes very exactly, in that government's programme. The new government created a Department of Equality and Law Reform with a Cabinet post and a brief that could have been written by the three groups. The new Minister for Justice, Maire Geoghegan-Quinn, also startled us by announcing that her early priority was gay law reform. Though the record of her party, Fianna Fáil, had recently been socially very conservative, she said it was a task she was delighted to have been given.

The first member of the new government to meet us was Mervyn Taylor, Minister for Equality and Law Reform. He told us that, despite his title, he had no direct interest in specific criminal law. In what proved a crucial discussion, we strongly disagreed: if the first act of the new government was to legislate for *inequality*, where would that leave either his or his department's credibility for the next five years? He became, and has stayed, a most powerful advocate of across-the-board equality.

In all our meetings on the criminal law we have had both lesbian and gay delegates. In the pivotal meeting with the Justice Minister, however, we also brought as a delegate Ms Phil Moore of Parents' Enquiry. The Minister was very well informed and took on all of our arguments and briefing papers, but with Phil Moore she achieved a remarkable rapport. Two Irish mothers decided the issue between them: 'You simply can't make criminals of young gay men. An unequal age of consent would be a huge injustice on our sons.' In all her subsequent statements, the Minister remained steadfastly unapologetic on the issue of equality. Which was just as well, as the next step of her department officials was to issue a 'Memorandum for Government' which was leaked to the press, with consequent furore. In retrospect, it helped greatly to clear the air, but it was unnerving to see robust arguments for various options including 'British-style' reform which spelt out more clearly than anything we'd ever written ourselves why the 1967 Act is no reform at all: 'It retains the principle in law that the sexual conduct in question is unacceptable.' In discussing the other option of complete equality, they suggested that this might mark homosexuality as 'an acceptable or parallel lifestyle', and might even encourage 'the most bizarre manifestations such as homosexual marriage'. Robust indeed.

We had already sent out position papers and briefing documents to every member of Cabinet and to the opposition leaders. The structured options of the memorandum greatly clarified our arguments. It also prompted us to use one very high-risk strategy. We contacted a member of the Cabinet and said that the only acceptable reform was one that abolished both the common law offences and the Victorian statutes. If these were retained, even with an equal age of consent, we would mount a campaign for the law's defeat and thus risk in one throw all the credibility we had gained. We subsequently learned that the Labour Party ministers, nearly half of the Cabinet, had agreed a common strategy: repeal of existing law, and a common age of consent.

Opposition

Where in all of this were our opponents? Some were in the Dáil and Senate, in government as well as opposition. Some remained quietly unhappy at what their parties were agreeing to, while others ventured the occasional speech saying so. The fight was left instead to the ideological right-wing groups, whose hugely successful manipulation of Irish politics in the 1980s had given them an aura of invincibility.

One such group, Family Solidarity, took on the 'Homosexual Challenge' and published a book with that title. Much of their resources and all of their statistics came from the ideological right in the US and Australia. TV and radio audiences became acquainted with the syphilis statistics in Oklahoma, as well as the forty-five sexual partners that all gay men were supposed to enjoy in a weekend. Politicians' offices were flooded with such stuff. In a country where most view gays and lesbians as peculiar or simply different, the objective was to make us appear loathsome and riddled with disease.

They received little help from the press. We don't have anti-gay tabloids in Ireland, and elsewhere our articles and letters more than answered theirs. However, they got a more sympathetic response from TV and radio. News programmes tended to be fair, but the political and discussion programmes were dreadful. Not once was there a serious analysis of any issue: right to the end they maintained a 'bear-pit mentality'. Happily television as a medium doesn't favour bigots. Our opponents made a further surprising contribution to the resulting laws. Because their own logic made any decriminalization simply intolerable, they were unable to comment on the various options open to the government. It was left instead to GLEN, and of course Senator Norris with whom we worked closely, to argue the detailed points of the emerging law.

And the role of the churches? Certainly not in alliance with ideological right, whom the churches mostly view with distaste. Every church leader and religious organization received letters from GLEN asking, not for support, but suggesting instead neutrality: 'Even if actions are considered sinful, why demand that they be defined as criminal?' Surprisingly often, instead of neutrality, we received statements of support. The (Anglican) Church of Ireland and other 'minority' churches backed law reform and anti-discrimination codes. The Catholic Church also took our point, and indeed quoted it. Their publicly expressed concerns were formal, and arrived late. The National Conference of Priests of Ireland even chided us for our pessimism, and suggested that identified lesbians and gays might have a positive role in the life of the church. Perhaps.

The parliamentary debate

If the mark of success of a good campaign is to have the crucial points set down in the printed bill, then we had reason to be happy. The section of the bill that referred to gay sexual acts contained virtually everything we had fought for. (Unfortunately, the second section contained unexpected and ill-drafted measures against prostitution, which affected women prostitutes particularly badly. The new gay laws derived from a painstaking five-year campaign, the other laws from no discussion at all. Yet another lesson.)

The most encouraging note in an encouraging Dáil debate on decriminalization was set by Maire Geoghegan–Quinn.

What we are concerned with fundamentally in this bill is a necessary development of human rights. We are seeking to end that form of discrimination which says that those whose nature it is to express themselves sexually in their personal relationships, ... in a way that others disapprove of, must suffer the sanctions of the criminal law.

The command from Strasbourg seemed forgotten: this was an Irish parliament extending Irish freedoms, and both the Dáil and Senate debates are worth reading in full. Listening in the gallery, we felt justified in our optimism that discrimination is not ingrained in Ireland, that diversity can be welcomed.

Perhaps the most astonishing moment came when the main opposition party, Fine Gael, proposed the raising of the gay age of consent to eighteen rather than seventeen. The proposal was treated with such general derision that the proposers filibustered their own amendment to ensure that there would be no Dáil vote.

By the most perfect of coincidences, the reforms were passed two days before the Dublin Lesbian and Gay Pride march, which turned into the happiest of street parties. ('What *did* we want? Equality!' 'When *did* we get it? *Yesterday*.') Saturday shoppers cheered us. They even thanked us. In a country used to the snail's pace of change in matters of social reform, this issue had been successful at the first attempt. To politicians and campaigners who had fought for divorce, and for the rights to contraception (let alone abortion), it marked a new era of possibility.

This article may appear to make large claims. I can only agree, and indeed I'd go further. It is, I would suggest, a sustainable claim that this campaign for legal and civil rights stands alongside the most successful campaigns undertaken in Ireland since our Independence, and is possibly even *the* most successful. The much-vaunted successes of the ideological right in the 1980s were largely negative holding operations and are in the (slow) process of being overturned. Of the positive reforming campaigns, it is very hard to think of one that has had virtually its full programme implemented at the first attempt and in a relatively brief period. I make the point because, even in our own communities, there is a vaguely articulated feeling that 'If it happened so easily, maybe it's not that important. Maybe Ireland was simply joining the rest of the world.' But it didn't happen that easily, and in the rest of the world there are only a tiny handful of countries with an equivalent spread of legislation. The entire Irish lesbian and gay community, acting in genuine accord and with a coherent programme, achieved a remarkable result. We deserved our celebration.

'What will you do next?' 'Relax. A little.' From the start GLEN had tried to learn from previous experience. Our working meetings were always open to anyone who was interested. The only question ever asked was 'What work will you take on?' Perhaps the question intimidated, as we never had more than seven or eight members, often fewer. We worked collectively with no defined roles (if you were prepared to put the case to government or before the cameras, you were appointed co-chair). In six years we've not had one fight or even one unfriendly meeting (the blood was still too vivid on the walls from earlier struggles). We also did without a constitution, premises, paid workers, accountants and, to a large extent, funds. (The National Lesbian and Gay Federation and Nexus Research both helped with office facilities; a few good friends helped cover the costs of occasional public meetings and mail shots.)

Most of us had at one time been members of collectives working towards liberation. In our work now for equality in law, that target had seemed further off though still an objective. The paradox was that by finding our voice, and by stressing the simplicity of equality, we moved a surprising distance towards changing national attitudes, towards a welcome for diversity, towards liberation itself.

Lesbians: The Lavender Women of Ireland

Joni Crone

Many songs have been sung
of the Irish Revolution
of the men who have fought
and have died
But you seldom will hear
of the women's contribution
though they all struggled there
side by side
Now the time has come
to set this wrong to right
the story of our fight for liberty
In the forefront of the fight
despite history's oversight
Strong and true were the Women of Ireland
Strong and true were the Women of Ireland

Mary O'Sullivan, 'Women of Ireland'
from the album *Mam Ceoil*, 1992

LESBIAN women have played a part in every liberation movement in Ireland over the past twenty years, but we have seldom been sung about, written about or given any kind of prominence. Our contributions have gone unrecognized because we have been content to work behind the scenes. As a native Irish lesbian who has lived through two decades of lesbian activism, I would like to bring our achievements out of the closet, to show why I can still say in the 1990s: 'I am Lesbian and I am proud.'

The lesbian movement in Ireland has suffered because our energies have been divided between the Women's Liberation Movement, the anti-nuclear Greenpeace movement and the gay movement. Gay men in Ireland have mostly been active on their own behalf in relation to law reform. They have succeeded thanks largely to the efforts of a few gay men, notably David Norris, Kieran Rose and Chris Robson, who have been consistently and doggedly active in the political arena. The story of liberation for lesbian women in Ireland, however, is very different. It is a story which has, remained of necessity, hidden from the public eye. A story of an underground minority, a subculture whose members have been unwilling or unable to court publicity, because to do so may have invited violence, rape, or even death. These are the hard facts of lesbian life in Ireland. They are not easy to live with but I believe it's time they were stated and acknowledged.

I have no wish to underplay the difficulties gay men encounter in 'coming out', or the suffering they have endured publicly and privately. What I want to emphasize is that the experience of coming out in Ireland is very different for a lesbian and for a gay man. There are times when our territories overlap, when we appear to have common ground – on law reform, for instance, or health issues or gay community centres – but the vast majority of lesbians and gay men in Ireland experience life very differently. This is not due to any lack of solidarity but to our gender differences.

'Coming out' to ourselves as lesbians, to our friends and family is a complex process. Lesbians are not strange, extraordinary or exotic women. We are ordinary women, and as ordinary women, reared in heterosexual families, we have been socialized into a mothering role as helpers, assistants and carers. 'Coming out' as an Irish lesbian involves undoing much of our conditioning. It means recognizing the external and internal barriers which prevent us taking charge of our lives, and resolving to become autonomous human beings, independent persons with a right to life, a right to love, a right to control our own bodies, a right to live free from harassment in our work and our homes, a right to choose who we love, how we love, and if or when we want to become parents.

These rights for men have been recognized for centuries. Heterosexual and gay men have created democratic institutions and interminable legal and political systems to protect their basic human rights. But women have had no part in framing the laws that oppress us or protect us because for centuries we were considered, in law, to be men's property. As wives and daughters we have been valued primarily for our capacity to be 'the vessels which carried the seed', as Aristotle taught. We have been valued solely for our bodies, the means to ensure the reproduction of males.

The abortion debate is very much a 'live' issue in Ireland, after twenty years and more of political campaigning. But it is not about the protection of female children or female foetuses. There is ample historical evidence of the murder of female infants who were considered worthless or unnecessary burdens, and far from equal to male children. And in Ireland, tragically, we have witnessed female infanticide far too often in recent decades. The furore around granting women – heterosexual and lesbian women – the right to say no to pregnancy is so intense because it goes to the heart of the power relations of men over women.

Historically, men have decided what is best for the human race. Men have declared themselves to be made in the image of God. Men have assumed the right to decide the fate of other men and *all* women and children. Men have considered themselves superior in body, mind and spirit. Men have produced endless tomes to justify this false claim. Women's legal status up to the early years of the twentieth century was equivalent to that of 'criminals and mental deviants'.

This is the backdrop we have to bear in mind in any consideration of the struggle for lesbian liberation in Ireland. The traditional roles of women – chattel, wife, mother, servant – have been reinforced by an educational system which, for most of this century, has been managed by religious orders. It is an amazing, indeed an Amazonian achievement, that despite the constant grinding down by church and state, lesbian women, walking arm in arm with our straight sisters, have managed to take a number of important steps in the defence of our basic human rights. In fact, we have been involved in political and social change since the 1970s.

A detailed chronology of events, including groups, campaigns, and social, political and cultural activities could fill a book. So, I would like to focus on certain key issues. These centre on the years 1978, 1980, 1983 and 1991. Another point to be borne in mind is that Cork, Limerick, Galway, Derry and Belfast have had their own lesbian history which has yet to be written. In this article, I concentrate on Dublin, and on the events which have had particular significance for the majority of lesbians in Ireland.

1978

1978 was a memorable year for feminists and lesbian feminists in Ireland. In January, a women's conference at Trinity College attracted over three hundred women. It was organized by an *ad hoc* group concerned with the issues of violence against women and free, legal and safe contraception. Sexuality was discussed only in the broadest sense. It was difficult to hold in-depth discussions among lesbians, because so few of us were out. A small number sported badges and T-shirts with slogans such as 'Sisterhood is Powerful', 'Women Unite in Armed Snuggle', 'Lesbian Nation', and 'Anarcha Feminism Unrules OK'. But most lesbian women at the conference were torn between their desire to be out, and supposedly free from constraints, and the perceived necessity for discretion.

It was only at the social events and women-only fundraising discos that the large lesbian presence became obvious. The preponderance of lavender T-shirts was a discreet but recognizable symbol. (Lavender had been adopted as an international lesbian colour after Betty Friedan had dubbed lesbians the 'lavender menace' in the early 1970s.) A small group of 'lavender women' got together a few days later, full of enthusiasm for a lesbian conference. We wanted a place where *we* could set the agenda. We were tired of attending and even organizing women's events where lesbian concerns were always last on the list.

We met in each others' homes once a week for four months. After the practical considerations had been attended to (such as venue, childcare, transport, food and accommodation) we began to deal with the topics that might be discussed and the other events that could be included, such as lesbian poetry readings or a music night with lesbian songs. (Alix Dobkin's album, *Lavender Jane Loves Women*, was very popular at the time.)

It was only quite late in the proceedings that we realized that if we called the event a 'lesbian conference' most of the organizing collective would be unable to attend because 'walking through the door would be a public statement'. Just when we believed that we were taking a giant step towards our own liberation, it was sobering to discover that most of the lesbian women we knew were leading double lives. At home, at work and even within the Women's Movement they were open about their feminism, but they disguised their sexual identity. Our compromise solution was to call the weekend a Women's Conference on Lesbianism. This meant that women of every sexual persuasion were free to attend.

After months of spreading the word through the grapevine, and distributing posters in the few locations which would accept them, we arrived at the Resource Centre on Rathgar Road hoping to meet the about fifty lesbian women who had attended the January conference. Several had promised to bring a lesbian or bisexual friend. By ten o'clock, sixty-five women had registered, and we began to worry about how we would accommodate them all. By the end of the night eveyone had found a bed or a floor to sleep on. No one complained about the overcrowding; in fact, several romances started as a consequence of these arrangements.

By Saturday lunch-time, we had eighty-one women on the books. The Junior Common Room in Trinity could no longer function as kitchen, eating area and workshop space. We prayed for a feminist miracle. It arrived in the form of hot sunshine, which meant that about half the workshops could be held in the open air.

The organizers relaxed and we began to enjoy ourselves. Monica Sjoo, a Swedish artist who had studied matriarchal cultures gave a workshop and slide show on 'Goddess Spirituality' which was spellbinding. Then an American woman arrived with a speculum and a mirror, and offered to help us all find our cervix. A small number of shy but determined lesbians offered their bodies to science, and a slightly larger number trooped off to another room, urging each other on with jokes and nervous laughter. The same women emerged at the end of this impromptu 'Find Your Cervix' workshop, beaming with pride and laughing wildly at their own daring, aware that below each navel was an interior undiscovered country they had just begun to explore. A music group named OVA gave several innovative workshops, using instruments made from plastic hosing. The sunshine beckoned us on to the grass, and several circles of women sat drumming and chanting into the evening.

The 1978 conference was significant for the boost it gave to lesbian pride, and had a lasting effect on the community. Lesbian feminists now recognized the contribution we had already made to the Women's Movement since 1970. It enabled us to form strong bonds of friendship across class barriers and to decide that the time had come to put energy into our own cause. The first Lesbian Line Collective was formed in September 1978, and a delegation from the lesbian conference joined with delegates from a conference on Family Violence (which had taken place during the same weekend) to plan a campaign for a women's centre. This broad-based alliance began a fundraising campaign for a women's building.

The lesbian conference had concluded with the tabling of a number of formal and informal proposals including: 'that this conference supports the establishment of an Irish Republican Amazonian Nation' and 'that marriage and motherhood should be illegal until the age of twenty-five, so that all women can make real choices about their sexual lives'. Questions that had triggered emotional exchanges related to a number of issues: whether lesbians should work with gay men on law reform, or put all their energies into women's concerns and live a separatist lifestyle; whether women who became 'political lesbians' were really lesbians at all; whether monogamy was an imitation marriage which enshrined the unequal power relation of men over women, and as such should be rejected in favour of open relationships and non-possessiveness; whether national liberation and the Republican question should take precedence over sexual liberation; whether all lesbians should be vegetarian as a matter of principle in striving for an alternative society where violence against women, animals and the planet generally was seen as the legacy of two thousand years of patriarchal rule; whether lesbians should join the Women's Right to Choose campaign as a group rather than as individuals; and why couldn't we all agree on all these issues and speak with one voice? The one formal proposal that everyone endorsed wholeheartedly was the need for a women's centre. This became a reality about four years later.

The debates which continued in the wider feminist community throughout the next decade received their first airing at the Women's Conference on Lesbianism in 1978, and the ripples are still being felt in the lesbian community in the 1990s.

1980

1980 proved to be a significant year because of the decision by a national television programme, with an audience of over a million, to feature a lesbian interview. I'm focusing on this, because so many lesbians have told me over the years how important it was in their lives that I had appeared on the *Late Late Show* and proclaimed: 'I am Lesbian and I am proud.'

Since my appearance on the show, I have answered questions from many lesbians, particularly from those who want to come out publicly. Did you suffer personally or professionally as a result of going on the programme? What motivated you and how did it come about in the first place? To answer the first question: I did suffer personally, but not professionally. The newsroom at RTE contacted me on the Monday following the interview to find out if I had lost my job. I was able to tell them that the managing director of the small computer firm where I worked had called me into his office and assured me that my job was secure and that as far as he was concerned my sexuality was irrelevant in relation to my work. However, the fact that I hadn't lost my job, was not considered news.

On a personal level, I suffered rejection from my family, received threats of violence and experienced ostracism. My parents had feared that their house would be set on fire or that they would be shunned by the neighbours. When these fears did not materialize, family relations began to improve, and I have since achieved a measure of understanding and acceptance. But it has taken more than ten years for the wounds to heal. In the 1990s I expect it is relatively easier for lesbian women to come out publicly, but there are still very few native-born lesbians, living in Ireland, who feel safe enough to do so.

I agreed to appear on the programme to dispel the ignorance and fear about lesbian sexuality. At the time, lesbianism was considered a taboo subject, suitable only for secret, scandalous and private conversation. It was my belief that if only one lesbian woman felt less shame and more pride as a result of the programme it would be worth doing. There was also a sense of urgency, because an opportunity to appear on the *Late Late Show* might never come again. This proved to be true. It was fourteen years later before Emma Donoghue appeared as a lesbian writer on the same programme. The 1980 interview came about as a result of various researchers passing on information to each other about previous coverage in the media of lesbian and gay issues. I had been interviewed by radio and newspaper journalists in 1976 and 1979, so I presume my name was on file. I am convinced now that it was due to rivalry between certain media personalities, rather than any desire on the part of the programme-makers to give lesbians a public voice, that the decision was taken to go ahead with the interview.

1983

1983 was a landmark year, because of two major public events which had lasting consequences for lesbians and gay men in Ireland. The first was the Fairview Park murder, when a gang of queerbashers assaulted and killed Declan Flynn. The gang held a victory march at the murder scene after they were given their suspended sentences. In his summing-up, the judge declared: 'This could never be called murder'.

In response, the Dublin Lesbian and Gay Collective organized a protest march, which proved to be the largest event in support of gay rights that Ireland had seen. It was significant, not just because of the large turnout, but because it was supported by feminist groups, parents of gays, some sections of the trades union movement and heterosexuals. All of them wanted to voice their outrage at such inhuman treatment of gay people.

1983 was also the year of the Abortion Amendment, which inserted a clause in the Constitution giving an equal right to life to both the foetus and the adult woman. This created huge controversy. The Anti-Amendment Campaign was unsuccessful at the polls largely due to an underhand tactic adopted by the Catholic Church, who registered members of religious orders who had never voted previously. However, a large number of people chose not to vote, apparently in protest against the acrimony and slander on both sides of the campaign.

The campaign also led to a split in the gay community, when the national lesbian organization, Liberation for Irish Lesbians (LIL), urged the National Gay Federation (NGF) to affiliate with the Women's Right to Choose campaign. A series of educational workshops was held, to illustrate how the 1861 Offences Against the Person Act had been used against gay men and all women in preventing them from making adult choices about their sexual lives. A vote was held within the NGF and a majority voted in favour of affiliation. This would have shown public solidarity among gay men and lesbians on the right to choose issue. But a minority of influential and vocal gay men cited a subclause in the original document detailing the aims and objectives of NGF which gave the steering committee the right to overturn decisions of the members in exceptional circumstances, 'in the best interests of the organization'. This betrayal of lesbian and heterosexual women who had campaigned previously for gay male law reform resulted in lesbians leaving the NGF. And it was the last time that many of us chose to work in any official capacity in solidarity with gay men.

1991

1991 marked the establishment of the first Irish national network of lesbian organizations. LOT (Lesbians Organizing Together) brought together the Lesbian Line collectives, the First Out groups, and other political, social and cultural groups. Resources were allocated to staff an office, establish a lesbian archive, form a publishing group and organize a whole range of new and exciting events, including the first lesbian and gay film festivals. The organization is young and vibrant and expanding year by year.

In the 1970s and 1980s lesbian energies were divided between feminist politics, the gay male reform movement and the immediate needs of lesbian women. Those two decades saw an ongoing struggle on all three fronts. The current lesbian community is gathering strength: fun Weekends, Women's Camps, film festivals and Lesbian Line conferences now take place on an annual basis. The future will surely bring more connections with international and global networks of lesbian groups (a Lesbian Studies Conference has already been planned for 1995). The lessons of the last two decades, often painfully learned, can now bear fruit.

My vision for the twenty-first century begins with the next five years, to the millennium and beyond. I believe that if we concentrate more of our energies on our concerns as lesbians we will connect directly to global movements for social change. 'What is most personal is most universal.' Our diversity, our activism across a wide spectrum of political, social and cultural activities will no longer be handicaps. Rather, it will assist us in our efforts to create greater understanding around our sexuality and our identity. The networks of women of all sexual persuasions will grow and expand within and beyond Ireland and Europe to North America, Africa, India, Australia, Asia, Central and South America, where we already have informal links. Our lesbian support networks at home, which are beginning tentatively to interweave across the barriers of class, race and religion, will grow stronger.

The historical fight for a united Ireland may give way to a unity in a larger whole, a federal arrangement perhaps, or a WISE (Western Island States Economic) community comprising five republics: Ireland South, Ireland North, Scotland, Wales and England. England without the monarchy could present a very different prospect in terms of political alliances in Ireland, North and South. We need to imagine these possibilities, and more, before we can begin to make radical changes.

The radical activism of the 1970s was followed by an extreme anti-women backlash in the 1980s. The new upsurge of activism among young lesbian women in Ireland augurs well for the future, but we need to remember the lessons of past decades. If we ignore our history we are doomed to repeat it.

One major event in gay history, the Stonewall Riots, needs revision. The anniversary celebrations which fuelled the Gay Pride movement internationally have concentrated too much on gay males. It is as if the riot happened in isolation, as if a few drag queens suddenly decided they had had enough and were going to start a revolution. The Stonewall riots undoubtedly did have a major effect on the lives of the gay men involved, but they also concerned straight men, lesbian and straight women, latinos and those of mixed race. A whole range of social minorities had suffered harassment and decided to fight back. We need to appreciate the significance of this if we are to place our concerns in a broader political context. We need to keep these connections and build on them, so that lesbian women and straight women, gay men and straight men, can build a future together where:

> there is only one religion, the religion of love,
> there is only one caste, the caste of humanity,
> there is only one language the language of the heart.

The Tenderness of the Peoples[1]

Kieran Rose

Hey Ronnie Reagan, I'm Black and I'm pagan,
I'm gay and I'm Left and I'm free.
I'm an unfundamentalist environmentalist,
Hey Ronnie don't bother me.

John Maguire[2]

OUR community, and indeed this country, is now at a critical moment. Nineteen ninety-five is the twenty-first anniversary of the founding of the Irish Gay Rights Movement (IGRM). The law reforms of 1993 and the forthcoming equality legislation mark the end of an era. Most, if not all, of the legal programme we set out to achieve many years ago is, or soon will be, in place.

These fundamental and radical reforms which established our equal citizenship in turn create many challenges and opportunities. We cannot now claim that progress is not possible in this country or that our movement is without any power to effect change. We could, of course, squander these opportunities in self-doubt, complacency or factionalism, but there is now a great challenge for us to bring together an optimistic, feasible and principled programme of community development for the next twenty years. There is an international dimension to such a programme.

We can now develop a set of policies and priorities which will provide a radical improvement in the daily and practical lives of lesbians and gay men and also contribute significantly to the betterment of the wider society. In particular, as equal citizens, we now have the responsibility to make our contribution to the peace process. Peace within and between these islands is too important a matter to be left to a few political leaders.

It has often been said that there can be no peace without justice. The fact that the killings have stopped is a wonderful achievement. But we know that a society whose structures produce intolerable levels of poverty, unemployment and oppression, whose structures destroy the lives of thousands of people (including lesbians and gay men) cannot be at peace with itself. As Gerry Adams, President of Sinn Féin, put it on the eve of the cease-fire, 'There must be equality of treatment, equality of opportunity and parity of esteem across the entire political, economic, cultural, social, legal and security spectrum'. Whether he intended to or not, Gerry Adams has presented us with a programme for the rights of lesbians and gay men as well as other disadvantaged groups. The demands of the lesbian and gay community, Travellers, people with disabilities, and others, for equality of treatment, equality of opportunity and parity of esteem must be incorporated into any peace settlement.

The immediate contribution we could make to the peace process is to involve ourselves in the Forum for Peace and Reconciliation, perhaps along with groups from Northern Ireland and Britain. (GLEN has recently made a submission to the Forum.) The war has blighted both islands and, besides the deaths and injuries, it has resulted in a pressure on democratic rights and a significant increase in oppressive legislation, which is directly and indirectly inimical to the interests of lesbians and gay men.

There are few models for a lesbian and gay contribution to a peace process. This reminds us again that while the lesbian and gay movement is quintessentially an international movement it tends, because of the unequal world we live in, to be dominated by the politics, culture and priorities of advanced capitalist countries and, in particular, of their metropolitan centres such as New York and London.

In examining the complexities and contradictions resulting from this domination we need to look at some issues relating to colonialism and neo-colonialism, and also to look at the current effects of imperialism – military, economic and cultural. Words such as 'colonialism' and 'imperialism' have become unfashionable and clichéd. But these concepts are necessary in any analysis of the reality of the world in which we live. At this point I would like to make clear that I am presenting a point of view for discussion and that I do not intend to be dogmatic or dismissive of other viewpoints. I am mindful of Edward Said's reminder in his illuminating study, *Culture and Imperialism* (1993) that

> In our wish to make ourselves heard, we tend very often to forget that the world is a crowded place, and that if everyone were to insist on the radical purity or priority of one's own voice, all we would have would be the awful din of unending strife. (Said, 1993, p. xxiii)

Clearly much of the impetus for, and the ideology of, the modern lesbian and gay movement has come from metropolitan centres. The Gay Liberation Front (GLF) was set up in New York in 1969 shortly after the Stonewall Riots. This radical activism soon spread to London, where a GLF was set up in 1970. There were reverberations in Ireland, and in 1974 the IGRM was established in Dublin.

However, in relation to many basic issues – historical, economic, social and cultural – Ireland is, arguably, almost the polar opposite to those situations in which the modern lesbian and gay movement was formed. Even if we are to understand our psyche and sexuality, let alone devise a feasible political project, we need to understand the historical forces shaping us. Joe Lee (1989) has written of the 'traumatic shocks' of nineteenth-century Ireland, not only colonization but famine, depopulation, language loss and religious revival. John Waters (1994) reminds us that the Great Famine is but three generations away and that its effects are to be seen in 'the cravenness of our dependencies, in our fear of self-belief, in the culture of amnesia in which we live our lives, in our willingness to imitate anything rather than think for ourselves'.

Traumatic shocks continued in the twentieth century: the War of Independence, the Civil War, Partition and the 'carnival of reaction'[3] which followed. The economic and social failure of the new state, according to Sean Lemass, a government minister at the time, 'created a situation in which the very disappearance of the race was a possibility that could not be ignored'. The crisis continued so that by the 1950s there was a sense of 'ignominious defeat'. Meanwhile the Western capitalist world was booming and engaging in significant domestic social reform. According to some commentators, the disillusionment of the 1980s in Ireland harkened back to the open despair of the 1950s (Breen *et al.*, 1990).

So, if the political projects developed in other countries in such radically different circumstances were transferred to Ireland, unthinking and undigested, without regard to the particular problems and opportunities that existed here, they would have been almost bound to have failed. In fact, I would say that perhaps the greatest achievement of the Irish lesbian and gay movement over the past twenty years is the development of an indigenous, organic political analysis and practice appropriate to the particular Irish circumstances, including the capacity to assess the usefulness of the latest lesbian and gay initiatives coming from metropolitan centres.

A core element of our strategy was a rejection of the once prevalent notion that Irish society was inherently reactionary on socio-sexual issues and that progressive change would only happen under the influence of external forces such as the European Union. For us, real and positive traditional values arose from the struggle against colonialism and for civil, religious and economic rights. We could activate them. We certainly were not going to allow reactionary forces using New Right ideology, tactics and money from the USA and Britain to hijack the deeply felt values of most Irish people. Carol Coulter (1993) makes a similar point regarding a vibrant but hidden tradition of Irish feminist politics which, since the nineteenth century, has had 'a profound, if not always amicable, relationship with Ireland's nationalist tradition'.

In addition we were not interested in just being 'right'. We deliberately set about winning a majority from all sectors of Irish society for our radical but feasible programme of equality. The building of coalitions, initially with other disadvantaged groups and organizations such as the trade unions, was an important strategy. As Bob Cant (1995), the Scottish gay activist, put it, 'Ghetto politics had no part in this scenario'.

At the height of our lobbying effort on law reform (between 1992 and 1993) we were also preparing a detailed research proposal for the state agency Combat Poverty. This study[4] examines the processes of discrimination that increase the risk of poverty for lesbians and gay men and that further disadvantage those already living in poverty. In carrying out this research we were surprised that we were not able to find evidence of similar projects in countries where the lesbian and gay movement has more resources and research facilities at its disposal. A central recommendation of this study is that we should prioritize community development, and that these efforts should be integrated into the existing Community Development Programme which is based on a (problematic) partnership between disadvantaged communities and the state.

This evolution of appropriate political projects is not inevitable. For example, writing about Brazil – another post-colonial, peripheral country – Joao Trevisan (1986) comments that

> Its cultural élite copies the latest fashions from Paris or New York, but is seldom inclined towards real change. As a result, modernity in Brazil is easily reduced to a phenomenon that simply follows the latest fashion. Gay liberation has developed along the same lines. If it arrived in Brazil at least a decade late and then entered a cul-de-sac, this is largely due to the basic conservatism, insensitivity and self-indulgence of a cultural élite which feeds on fashions in order to recycle itself.

In explaining the many defeats in this country in the past decades in terms of abortion, divorce and contraception, John Waters 'Jiving at the Crossroads' (1991) makes a similar point about an élite in Ireland, which he describes as 'Dublin 4', and which he says became synonomous with such issues:

> It did not seem to occur to them that the people of Ireland might be more open to change and progress if from time to time they were asked for an opinion or were made to feel entitled to participate in the creation of this promised land. ... Dublin 4, however, had got used to losing, and perhaps

even a little in love with it. It derived so much pleasure out of being able to berate the rest of the country for its backwardness that it had excluded the possibility of the entire country being ever able to move forward together. It was prepared to go on losing, so long as this allowed it to feel superior.

One of the basic concepts brought forward by lesbian and gay liberation was 'self-oppression' and, in this description by John Waters, I think one can see elements of such 'self-oppression', identification with the values of the dominant group and rejection of one's own positive traditions. The condescension of 'Dublin 4' echoes that of the English liberal establishment, which seems to regard this country as a charming, backward, priest-ridden and sometimes threatening place beset by the anachronistic politics of nationalism. Discordant facts are either forgotten or else, as in the case of the equality-based gay law reform and anti-discrimination legislation, regarded as merely another peculiarity of this quaint state, not requiring serious political reflection.

Tasmanian gay activist Rodney Croome makes a related point about Australia:

> Tasmania has been the nation's whipping post for 200 years. The place where Australians project all those things Australians don't like about themselves: their racism, their homophobia, their environmental pillage. The mainland media tries to portray Tasmania as being a backward place populated by rednecks to make the mainlanders feel a bit more enlightened about themselves. (Personal communication to Galbraith)

A conflict then arises because these metropolitan areas are also the source of the dominant gay and lesbian imagery, a conflict which must be resolved, because as he says: 'I can't be free as a gay man unless I'm free in that place that has shaped my sexual identity, and that place is Tasmania' (Hand, 1994). The ways in which we construct our identities as lesbians and gay men are inextricably bound up with our strategies for political action.

The problem of adapting ideologies and strategies for change developed in advanced capitalist countries is not unique to the lesbian and gay movement. The Irish labour and trades union movement has faced similar dilemmas since the nineteenth century. One labour historian (Foster, 1990) recently put the question or paradox as follows:

> Irish immigrants in England, Scotland and Wales played a leading role in Chartism, in new unionism and in the rise of socialist politics at the end of the nineteenth century. In Ireland itself, agrarian conflict repeatedly produced mass movements of epic proportions. Yet organized labour in Ireland achieved very little. (Foster, 1990, p. 67)

Different reasons have been put forward to explain this apparent contradiction. One answer relates to what has been described by Emmet O'Connor as the 'mental colonization of contemporary labour' (Howell, 1993, p. 85), whereby the Irish movement adopted the British model of labour ideology and strategy, one that proved particularly unsuitable to Irish circumstances. This has been described by Howell as 'the endorsement of a damaging form of industrial organization and the abdication from the most vital political issue of all [the National Question] moreover one that had been regarded hitherto as a labour question' (Howell, 1993, p. 64). The subsequent creation of the Irish Transport and General Workers' Union (TGWU) in the early years of this century was the first step away from that 'disastrous option', and this initiative began 'a process of modernization more relevant to native conditions'.[5]

This is not at all a call for a narrow xenophobic politics. It has been said of James Larkin[6] that 'he had always believed in the solidarity of labour the world over, but it might be that the best way to bring workers into line with the workers of the world was to organise them on Irish lines first'.

Similar problems beset the international women's movement. These are discussed in a recent article by Ethel Crowley (1991) entitled 'Third world women and the inadequacies of Western feminism'. One of her basic points is that 'Freedom certainly does not mean the same thing to all the women of the world'. She continues:

The issues around which women's demonstrations of dissent are organized are very different throughout the world and while western feminists have sometimes provided a blueprint for protest, the final plans are necessarily tailored to suit the specific needs of women world-wide.

She points out that the risks arising from overt revolutionary action by women in many Third World countries may range from social ridicule to torture to death. She describes various forms of resistance and includes a delightful quote from James C. Scott (author of *Weapons of the Weak*). He describes the everyday resistance of peasants as

> The ordinary weapons of relatively powerless groups: foot-dragging, dissimulation, false compliance, pilfering, feigned ignorance, slander, arson, sabotage and so forth ... To understand these commonplace forms of resistance is to understand what much of the peasantry does 'between revolts' to defend its interests as best it can.

Writing of the 1980s, Noam Chomsky (Said, 1993, p. 343) stated that:

> the North–South conflict will not subside, and new forms of domination will have to be devised to ensure that privileged segments of Western industrial society maintain substantial control over global resources, human and material, and benefit disproportionately from this control. ... It is an absolute requirement for the Western system of ideology that a vast gulf be established between the civilized West, with its traditional commitment to human dignity, liberty, and self-determination, and the barbaric brutality of those who for some reason – perhaps defective genes – fail to appreciate the depth of this historic commitment.

The conviction that the imperialist countries are more advanced and therefore entitled to dominate less powerful countries is a constant colonialist theme. Writing in 1910 Jules Harmand, the French Commissaire-general in Indochina observed:

> The basic legitimation of conquest over native peoples is the conviction of our superiority, not merely our mechanical, economic and military superiority, but our moral superiority. Our dignity rests on that quality, and it underlies our right to direct the rest of humanity. (Caherty *et al.*, 1992)

In the sixteenth century Edmund Spenser argued that Gaelic Brehon Law should be forbidden and the Irish must be subjugated by force so that they could be brought 'from their delight of licentiousness and barbarism into love of goodness and civility' (Curtis, 1984). Part of this civility was the criminalization of homosexuality, which was regarded non-judgementally under Gaelic law as merely a reason for divorce. Centuries later, according to Edward Said, even those elements of a (metropolitan) society we have long considered to be progressive were, so far as empire was concerned, uniformly retrograde: 'Eurocentrism penetrated to the core of the workers' movement, the women's movement, the avant-garde arts movement, leaving no one of significance untouched.' (Said, 1993, p. 268)

There is an unfortunate tendency among some gay people in Western countries to ignore the brutal realities of history and contemporary politics. I have heard activists divide the world into three categories in terms of lesbian and gay rights: at the top are countries such as Sweden and the Netherlands; next come countries such as Ireland; and finally, at the bottom, are countries such as Russia and Iran. There is, of course, a strong element of truth in such a description, but, besides being insensitive and insulting, it ignores the fact that the so-called progressive countries have often worked to destabilize the economies, the social structures, the cultures and the democracies of the supposedly 'backward' countries. The heroic and ultimately victorious struggle of the USSR against fascism is of course elided.

Iran is another prime example of this tunnel vision. A leftist and popular government of the 1950s was ousted by Western forces when their oil companies' interests were challenged. What followed might be described as Iran's 'carnival of reaction'. The brutal dictatorship of the Shah was installed and given the weapons of war and torture to oppress the Iranian people so that the economic and geo-political interests of the West could be supreme. The Shah was eventually overthrown by the combined forces of secular leftists and the fundamentalists led by Khomeni, with the latter finally winning control. Adding insult to injury and ignoring history, Iran is now demonized by the West.

However, I would suggest that it is precisely the struggles for justice and freedom of people in Iran, Nicaragua, South Africa and other beleaguered countries which will build a world order that will respect the human dignity of all people, including lesbians and gay men. Commenting on the cultural resistance of writers such as Yeats and Synge, Declan Kiberd (Caherty, 1992) writes:

> Central to all this was a healthy refusal to play the victim's part, and a generous insistence that the deformities visited by colonialism upon the Irish were as nothing compared to the repressions suffered by the British, rulers as well as ruled. In saving themselves the Irish would also save their erstwhile masters, and ultimately the whole colonial world.

Some forms of intervention such as military action are obvious. However, there are more subtle and covert forms of domination and exploitation, for example through such organizations as GATT, the World Bank and the International Monetary Fund (IMF). The Structural Adjustment Programmes implemented by the IMF and the World Bank are further impoverishing Third World countries and directly undermine the life chances of lesbians and gay men (*New Internationalist*, 1994). In his excellent international study of HIV and AIDS, Dennis Altman (1994) quotes the Inter-Church Coalition statement that the 'single greatest factor' contributing to the poor health of the developing world is the World Bank's emphasis on the diversion of resources to debt servicing and the development of export industries.

In Ireland we have long argued that economic rights and independence are of vital importance to lesbians and gay men, and that these right-wing economic programmes directly threaten such economic autonomy both in developed countries but more severely in Third World countries. The new 'global economy', we are continually warned by right-wing commentators, demands that the gains made by the labour movement in terms of wages and conditions of work, social welfare support and legal protections must be cut back if we are to compete with 'new low cost producers'. (I have often been struck by the irony that the gains we have slowly achieved in terms of labour protection legislation and trade union support could be so quickly undermined by resurgent and harsh capitalist imperatives.) This economic domination and exploitation in the absence of a strong socialist alternative encourages a fundamentalist and xenophobic reaction, which also directly threatens the lives of women, gay people and other minorities particularly, but not exclusively, in Thirld World countries such as Algeria.

We know now in Ireland that there can be no peace without justice, but we need to contribute to this perspective at an international level if we are, as lesbians and gay men, to have any secure future. I am not calling for any grandiose plan of action, merely that we should make a realistic contribution from our perspective, which includes colonization, a struggle for self-determination and an economically peripheral status.

We have already made a significant contribution to the development of the lesbian and gay communities and movements internationally. Perhaps most importantly our emigrants have helped build the communities and movements of London, New York and other metropolitan centres. But these high levels of emigration continually undermine our communities at home. An economic study of Northern Ireland argues that emigration is one of the processes by which peripheral areas remain disadvantaged and by which core areas retain their economic and political dominance. Emigration involves losses or costs to the exporting area and considerable gains and subsidies to the importing area (Dignan, Haase and Healy, 1990).

The two successful Irish cases at the European Court of Human Rights set the international precedents. Interestingly, the next major precedent has been established by another peripheral island, with the success of the Tasmanian case at the UN Committee of Human Rights. The Irish Section of Amnesty International lobbied very effectively to have Amnesty adopt lesbians and gay men as prisoners of conscience. The Irish delegate at the UN Economic and Social Committee also argued persuasively for the official recognition of the International Lesbian and Gay Association (ILGA). It seems that Ireland's status as a post-colonial and Catholic country makes our support for the rights of lesbians and gay men more acceptable to countries who would otherwise be resistant to what might be seen as the cultural and historical insensitivities of the USA or Northern Europe.

In 1994 the then Minister for Justice, Máire Geoghegan-Quinn, put on record that lesbians and gay men persecuted because of their sexuality would be granted asylum under new refugee legislation. On a lighter note, Jeff Dudgeon has written of our equality-based law reform that

> It will be both a spur and a magnet in Whitehall if the recognition grows that the UK has been upstaged by a new Ireland that is no longer given a fool's pardon for Catholic excess, but can instead swank around Brussels with a modern image.

What can our relatively small lesbian and gay movement do to advance the rights of lesbians and gay men internationally? Given the complexities of our country's history and current status, there is a great opportunity for us to make a realistic and much-needed contribution through the government and its agencies, through the non-governmental organizations (NGOs) and through ILGA. We need to encourage the government to continue its equality commitment at the UN, the International Labour Organization, the European Union, the World Health Organization and other international bodies.

There is a strong Third World solidarity movement in Ireland, and Catholic Church groups such as Trócaire are an important element in that movement. We need to continue to encourage these groups to incorporate an awareness of the needs and role of lesbian and gay communities and organizations. We also need to learn from

the analyses developed by Third World organizations and incorporate them into our work at home and internationally. We need to help
build an alternative perspective within the international lesbian and
gay movement which will benefit us all. We need to recognize the
integrity of the various struggles for peace and justice around the
world and the crucial importance of links between different peoples.
This international solidarity has been described by Tomas Borge, a
leading Sandinista, as 'the tenderness of the peoples'.

Acknowledgement

I would like to thank Joan Dooley and Íde O'Carroll, the Centre for
Women's Studies and Trinity College, Dublin for their invitation
and support.

Notes

1. This article is based on a lecture given by Kieran Rose in 1994 as
   part of the Public Lecture Series in Lesbian and Gay Studies
   organized by the Centre for Women's Studies, Trinity College,
   Dublin.
2. This song was made popular by Christy Moore during the
   widespread protests against the visit of President Reagan to
   Ireland in 1984
3. Writing in 1914 regarding the proposed Partition of this country,
   James Connolly stated that such a scheme 'would be a betrayal of
   the National Democracy of industrial Ulster, would mean a
   carnival of reaction both North and South, and would set back
   the wheels of progress, would destroy the oncoming unity of the
   Irish labour movement and paralyse all advanced movements
   while it endured'. See 'Labour and the proposed partition of
   Ireland', *Irish Worker*, 14 March 1914, republished in P.
   Berresford Ellis (ed.), *James Connolly, Selected Writing*
   Harmondsworth: (Penguin, 1973).
4. Eoin Collins and Íde O'Carroll, *Poverty, Lesbians and Gay Men:
   The Economic and Social Effects of Discrimination* (GLEN
   Combat Poverty Study). Dublin: Combat Poverty Agency.
5. The imitative nature of Irish society is a central obstacle to
   economic development according to many commentators. In the
   view of Peadar Kirby, the greatest development challenge facing
   us now, as at the turn of the century, is to find a contemporary
   alternative to the assimilationist and neo-traditionalist options.

The assimilationist model sees the answer to our ills in integrating us ever more firmly as a dependent element into multinational capitalism and the European Union. The neo-traditionalist 'alternative' proposes turning aside from the outside world and its polluting influences back to some illusory native, utopian, religious past. See 'Challenging passivity, a pre-condition for Irish development', *Irish Reporter*, no. 12, fourth quarter, pp. 27–30.

6.   James Larkin (1876–1947) was born in Liverpool of Irish parentage. He organized the National Union of Dock Labourers, reformed the Irish branch of the Independent Labour Party and in 1908 founded the Irish Transport and General Workers Union. Imprisoned in the USA in 1920 for 'criminal syndacilism', later Labour T.D. (member of parliament). His statue is in O'Connell Street, Dublin. (Foster, 1989: 438)

References

Altman, Dennis (1994). *Power and Community: Organizational and Cultural Responses to AIDS*. London: Taylor and Francis.

Breen, Richard *et al.* (1990). *Understanding Contemporary Ireland: State, Class and Development in the Republic of Ireland*. Dublin: Gill and Macmillan.

Caherty, Therese *et al.* (eds.) (1992). *Is Ireland a Third World Country?* Belfast: Beyond the Pale Publications.

Cant, Bob (1995). 'Small earthquake in Ireland. Not many hurt'. *Gay Scotland*, issue 89, February, p. 10.

Coulter, Carol (1993). *The Hidden Tradition: Feminism, Women and Nationalism in Ireland*. Cork: Cork University Press.

Crowley, Ethel (1991). 'Third World women and the inadequacies of Western feminism'. *Trocaire Development Review*, Dublin, pp. 43–56.

Curtis, Liz (1984). *Nothing but the Same Old Story: The Roots of Anti-Irish Racism, Information on Ireland*. London.

Dignan, Haase and Healy (1990). 'Planned migration as regional policy'. NIERC Working Paper, quoted in Mike Tomlinson, 'Outbreeding the Unionists: emigration and the Northern Ireland State'. *Irish Reporter*, no 1, first quarter, 1991.

Foster, John (1990). 'Completing the first task: Irish labour in the Nineteenth Century'. *Saothar: Journal of the Irish Labour History Society*, 15, pp. 65–69.

Foster, Roy (1989). *Modern Ireland, 1600–1972*. London: Penguin.

Hand, Derek (1994). 'An island to itself'. *Rouge*, issue 18, pp. 15–17.

Howell, David (1993). 'Irish labour: an exceptional case'. *Saothar: Journal of the Irish Labour History Society*, 18, pp. 63–74.

Lee, J.J. (1989). *Ireland 1912–1985: Politics and Society.* Cambridge: Cambridge University Press.

New Internationalist (1994). *Squeezing the South*, no. 257, July.

Said, Edward (1993). *Culture and Imperialism.* London: Chatto & Windus.

Trevisan, Joao (1986). *Perverts in Paradise.* London: GMP.

Waters, John (1991). *Jiving at the Crossroads.* Belfast: Blackstaff.

Waters, John (1994). 'Confronting the ghost of our past'. *Irish Times*, 11 October.

Living Visions

Ger Moane

THURSDAY, 7–9 p.m., Dublin Lesbian Line, 6613777. As soon as we connect the phone starts to ring. Quiet, sad, confused, fearful voices. Cheerful, chatty, curious, confident voices. Apprehensive, hopeful, relieved, uplifted voices. Sometimes no voices, long long silences, tears, whispers, voices that dare not say the word. Or voices that love the word, live the word, defiantly joyously declare – LESBIAN.

Phone calls to Dublin Lesbian Line highlight the diversity of lesbian existence, and include young lesbians, lesbians returning from abroad, lesbian mothers and married lesbians. The majority of calls are from women – of all ages – dealing with their lesbian feelings for the first time. Some are openly curious and excited. But the pain and anxiety expressed by many callers contrasts sharply with the exhilaration that can be experienced upon finally embracing lesbian sexuality. Coming out can be ecstatic release, joyful abandonment, passionate embracing, sexual surging, a plunging into new consciousness, a journey of discovery. But where lives are deprived of support, of positive lesbian images and identities, coming out can be fraught with internal turmoil, and enmeshed in hateful anti-lesbian rhetoric, with wilful suppression and censoring by family and friends, and exposure to taunts and physical attacks (Byrne and Larkin, 1994).

These difficulties are related primarily to prejudice and hatred against lesbians and gays – 'homophobia'. The manifestations of homophobia include ignorance and fear, anger and rejection, and even extreme violence, as exemplified by the murder of an Irish man in 1982, and the killings of homosexuals in many countries that have been uncovered by Amnesty International (1994). This essay adopts a double-edged view, acknowledging the damage caused by homophobia and its links to other oppressions while also embracing a celebratory and perhaps idealistic vision of the future.

Homophobia in Irish society

Even in the relatively liberated 1990s, homophobia still imposes tremendous burdens on lesbians and gay men in Ireland. Phone calls to Lesbian Lines and discussions in coming-out groups continue to reveal shame, ignorance, fear and self-hatred. Workers on Lesbian Lines hear the stories of many lesbians who live in total secrecy and isolation, deprived of access to their children, or prevented from being with their lover during illness. In 1994 alone, countless lesbians and gay men were intimidated by the news that two activists, Suzy Byrne and Junior Larkin, had been physically assaulted after appearing on the *Late Late Show*, and by the sacking of Donna McEnellan for allegedly kissing another woman at her workplace. Stories continue to circulate through gay and lesbian networks of young men and women being forced to leave home, or even committing suicide. Positive attitudes in the media and among legislators do not easily erase homophobia, and it remains deeply embedded in Irish culture and psychology.

Up until the 1990s, most people growing up in Ireland rarely heard reference to homosexuality or lesbianism; they remained taboo subjects. *Webster's Dictionary* defines taboo as a 'prohibition put upon certain people, things or acts which mark them untouchable, unmentionable etc'. A taboo word is not a neutral word, but one laden with anxiety, disgust, guilt, shame and repression. The word 'lesbian' is powerful; it arouses strong emotions within a whole system of prohibition. One of the reasons for the adoption of the word 'homophobia' to describe the oppression of lesbians (and gay men) was because it encompassed the violent emotional reactions that people have to a taboo, and to the breaking of a taboo.

Homophobia is not just a set of attitudes which creates psychological and social problems for lesbians and gay men. It creates a climate of fear even for those lesbians who have overcome their internalized homophobia, and who are fully accepting of and positive about their sexuality. It is damaging to all women because homophobia involves extreme negative images and views of women, and induces fear in heterosexual women about their own feelings of affection for other women. The label 'lesbian' has been used as a weapon to silence and intimidate women who speak out assertively or defiantly, and as a label to express an anti-feminist position.

Homophobia also manifests itself materially in Irish lesbian and gay lives through economic, social and legal discrimination. This has been documented in the recent GLEN survey of lesbians and gays (Collins and O'Carroll, 1995), as well as informally through Lesbian Lines and other contact groups. Lesbian partnerships do not have the legal status of marriage, and therefore cannot take advantage of the legal and economic benefits of married persons, for example in relation to mortgages, taxation, insurance, pensions and inheritance (ICCL, 1990). Lesbian partners have no rights of access or decision-making in the case of illness or death, and have even been prevented from visiting their long-term partners in hospital. They do not have any say in the medical treatment their partner may be receiving, and no one is obliged to consult them about funeral arrangements. Lesbians are excluded from adopting children, and the threat of losing custody is frequently used to intimidate and control lesbian mothers.

The Catholic Church remains the primary and most vocal source of condemnatory views of homosexuality, and has provided the main justification for discrimination against, and hatred of, homosexual men and lesbians. Recently the Vatican not only reiterated its view that homosexuality was a moral disorder, that is, unnatural and immoral (a view also publicly endorsed by the Archbishop of Dublin), but went so far as to state that this could be grounds for discrimination against homosexuals, especially in areas of employment involving young people. Ironically, in the recent publicity about paedophiliac Irish priests, there were few calls to similarly exclude priests from positions involving contact with young people.

Homophobia and control of sexuality

An understanding of the pervasiveness and potency of homophobia can be gained by viewing it as one element in the systems of domination which characterize our society. Society can be seen as a pyramid, the top occupied by a wealthy few (mostly men) who have access to political and other types of power (for example, mass media). Elsewhere I have tried to briefly summarize feminist and other radical analyses by proposing that there are six mechanisms of control which support this pyramid and maintain the patterns of inequality characteristic of modern society (Moane, 1994). These mechanisms are violence, economic exploitation, sexual exploitation, exclusion from political power, control of ideology and culture, and fragmentation (or divide and conquer). All of these are involved in the control and oppression of lesbians and gay men, as well as travellers, unemployed people, people with disabilities and other minority groups.

Irish society is typical of modern Western societies – it is male dominated and capitalist, but is relatively unique in its colonial history. Legacies of colonization include very narrow definitions of womanhood, phrased almost exclusively in terms of maternity, and a distrust and fear of women and of sexuality (Meaney, 1991; Nandy, 1983). These concerns are enshrined in Article 44 of the Constitution, which defines a woman's place as in the home, and which equates the life of a foetus with that of its mother[1]. Meaney (1991, p.4) refers to 'the Irish obsession with the control of women's bodies', an obsession manifested in religious, medical, legal and educational institutions.

There can be little doubt that sexuality, and particularly women's sexuality, has been rigidly controlled in Irish society. Numerous examples testify to the lengths to which our society has gone, largely under the influence of the Catholic Church, to restrict women's sexual expression to the confines of a single heterosexual marriage, and to equate sexual activity with reproduction and heterosexual intercourse. Punishment of women who transgressed, particularly unmarried mothers, included confinement to church-run 'Magdalen' laundries, where they laboured as unpaid cleaners of priestly garments, or to psychiatric hospitals. This has led to a litany of tragedies, such as the death of Anne Lovett, a fifteen-year-old who died alone in childbirth at a grotto of the Virgin Mary. Women have been deprived of access to contraception, and even today only the contraceptive pill is available on a medical card. As recently as 1992, a young girl of fourteen, pregnant and suicidal as a result of rape, was prevented from leaving the country to have an abortion.

Catholic teaching that equates sexuality with reproduction has also meant that approved sexual activity meant heterosexual intercourse without contraception, in effect forcing women to become pregnant. This equation of sexual activity with reproduction actually contradicts the facts of women's sexual anatomy, since the main source of women's sexual pleasure and of orgasm, the clitoris, is positioned outside the vagina. It ignores the fact that for women sexual pleasure is totally independent of reproduction. It not only forces women to become pregnant, but as Brenda Maddox (1991) points out, it is actually a form of gynocide (killing of women). She argues that throughout the world many women die in pregnancy and childbirth, and that some of these deaths could have been prevented by the use of contraception, which the Catholic Church vigorously opposes worldwide. Another example of the lethal implications of its teaching arises over the Catholic Church's opposition to public education about AIDS.

Adrienne Rich (1980) provides the most well-known feminist analysis of the way in which sexuality, particularly heterosexuality, is constructed and experienced in society. She asks why it is that sexuality is so rigidly confined to a particular form of heterosexuality, one which equates sex with vaginal penetration and which enforces women's emotional and erotic loyalty and subservience to men. She and other feminists, such as Janice Raymond (1986) and Sheila Jeffreys (1990), argue that relations between the sexes are heavily controlled by society, which regulates the sexual, emotional, political and economic relations that are possible between men and women. Of course, individual women and men may resist or transcend these regulations. The point is that society has institutionalized a particular form of heterosexuality.

Women's sexuality is not only controlled in the sense of being restricted and sanctioned, but also in the sense of being conditioned and moulded. As a result, many women believe that heterosexuality as they experience it, however unsatisfactory, is natural, and that their own sexuality must fit the mould of heterosexuality presented to them. Modern surveys, however, show that more women than men express dissatisfaction with their sexual relationships. Such was the extent of the repression of women's sexuality that it was only in the 1960s and 1970s that the possibility of women's orgasm, and the role of the clitoris, was fully acknowledged. Even in the 1990s, women's sexual anatomy is not fully understood, as recent research on the G spot and female ejaculation has shown (Masters and Johnson, 1993).

This analysis of heterosexuality offers a radical challenge to the construction of heterosexuality. It sees both men and women as restricted in their possible sexual expression, and regards heterosexuality as a vehicle for maintaining male domination. In addition, feminists argue that this construction of sexuality completely suppresses and distorts the possibility of lesbian sexuality, a sexuality which is completely independent of men. Feminists such as Janice Raymond and Adrienne Rich further argue that institutionalized heterosexuality not only precludes lesbian sexuality but also distorts and denies the strength and importance of woman-to-woman bonds of kinship, friendship and political solidarity. Lesbian existence presents a threat because it rejects prescribed forms of sexuality, and offers a viable alternative sexuality for women.

Lesbian political organizing

In the discussion so far, I have linked homophobia and the oppression of lesbians to the maintenance of a hierarchical society, and to the control of sexuality and of women. Lesbian activism has been informed by a recognition of these interconnections from the early days of the Women's Movement, if not before (Crone, 1989). Lesbian activists have recognized that because lesbians and bisexual women can be raped and sexually assaulted, violence against women is a lesbian issue. Because lesbians and bisexual women can get pregnant, then access to contraception and the right to choose are lesbian issues. Because lesbian mothers are often alone, then lone parenthood is a lesbian issue. Because women may marry and then later realize that they are lesbian, divorce is a lesbian issue. Because poverty hits women hardest, poverty is a lesbian issue. Because some prostitutes are lesbian, prostitution is a lesbian issue.

In short, lesbians have been active in every area of concern to the Women's Movement, as well as in trade unions, nationalism, socialism, travellers' rights, disability rights, the environment, and other progressive movements. Conversely, the Women's Movement, together with these other progressive movements, provides a vital background and context for progress for lesbians and gays. It is no accident that we had a woman Minister of Justice and a woman President in this country when the legislative victory for an equal age of consent was won. The Women's Movement has had a huge impact on attitudes around sexuality in this country. It would be impossible in this brief account to detail the extent of lesbian political activism, or even the interconnections and alliances between lesbian groups and others.

For lesbians active specifically on behalf of lesbians, the main priorities have been firstly to diminish the immediate impact of homophobia by providing support for lesbians who want to come out, and secondly to build a supportive and celebratory community. Fortunately, there has been considerable activity in these areas all over Ireland, particularly in the last few years, with the proliferation of Lesbian Lines and coming-out discussion groups; campaigns for legislative protection for lesbians and gay men; the education of the public through outreach, publishing and media work; the provision of resources and social spaces for lesbians; and the development of lesbian culture through writing, art, music and a whole range of other activities.

The diversity of activities in the 1990s – which I will refer to collectively as lesbian organizing – demonstrates a wonderful flowering of lesbian pride, and displays a heartening willingness to act on behalf of lesbians. Until the 1990s, Lesbian Lines were the only groups in Ireland organizing specifically on behalf of lesbians on an ongoing basis. They provided the cornerstones, along with social and cultural events, for the lesbian comunity. Dublin Lesbian Line and Cork Lesbian Line delegates have been very active in the Council for the Status of Women. Council motions urging the government to introduce anti-discrimination legislation were passed in 1987, 1988 and 1989, and the Council was active in lobbying for the law reform passed in 1993. Lesbian Lines now exist in Dublin, Waterford, Cork, Limerick, Galway, Derry, Belfast and Drogheda. The tradition of cross-border co-operation between Lesbian Lines provides a basis for other cross-border activities which we hope will contribute to the peace process.

In 1991, Dublin Lesbian Line, Dublin Lesbian Discussion Group (now First Out) and Cork Lesbian Line made written submissions to the second Commission on the Status of Women. This was followed by an oral presentation to the Commission by Dublin Lesbian Line. In its submission, Dublin Lesbian Line asserted the right of lesbians to participate as full and equal members in all areas of society. Our proposals for change involved four broad areas:

1. The provision of resources, in particular funding for an office and meeting place.

2. Legislative reforms, especially the inclusion of lesbians in anti-discrimination legislation (and, of course, the decriminalization of homosexuality).

3. An education programme which would include realistic portrayals of lesbians in all areas of education and training (including the training of youth, education and health professionals).

4. Positive action to promote out lesbians into positions of power in the private and public sectors.

It is amazing to see how much has been achieved since 1991. This has been helped greatly by the formation in 1991 of Lesbians Organizing Together (LOT), a co-ordinating group for lesbian activists, which now has an office in Dublin staffed by eleven women. Groups affiliated with LOT include Dublin Lesbian Line and First Out. Lesbian Equality Network (LEN) monitors developments in the legislative area; it made a detailed submission to the Department of Equality and Law Reform on their proposals for anti-discrimination legislation. The LOT finance group focuses on raising funds through grant applications, and works closely with the social and entertainment group, which organizes discos and other events. The publishing group concentrates primarily on producing documents and articles, especially in *Gay Community News*. The outreach group provides speakers for schools and other groups, and the PR group handles media and information. Many other groups are active at national and local levels with social, cultural and political projects which cannot be detailed here.

Explicitly feminist ideals do not necessarily inform lesbian organizing in the 1990s to the same extent as they did in the 1970s and 1980s. There is an increasing diversity of values and motives. However, the concepts and ideals of equality and of community remain central, and are, in my view, the key elements of future visions.

Visions for liberation

Lesbian writers have addressed questions concerning the kind of community that lesbians want or aspire to, the difficulties involved and the values and ideals for such a community and culture, especially the values of equality and inclusiveness. These ideals have been expressed in lesbian culture, including romantic fiction, music and music festivals, art, poetry, literature, celebratory events and woman-centred spirituality. In Ireland, events such as the Irish (formerly Galway) Women's Camp, the Cork Fun Weekend and the Dublin Wild and Wonderful Women's Weekend aim explicitly to enact these ideals.

Equality and inclusiveness are interconnected, and are linked with lesbian pride and ideals about lesbian relationships and sexuality. Equality implies that all individuals are valued equally, and value each other equally, while at the same time acknowledging and giving expression to difference. The ideal of equality challenges traditional concepts of power and domination. It is related to empowerment, the process whereby individuals acquire skill and self-confidence through involvement in the community. Inclusiveness implies that all individuals will feel part of a community and have a place within it. Fundamental to inclusiveness is accessibility:

the idea that all lesbians, regardless of class, income, ethnicity, ability, or background, can participate in community events. Tolerance and respect are crucial in the enactment of these values.

Both equality and inclusiveness require new ways of organizing, as hierarchial structures and inaccessibility through financial and other barriers reproduce inequality and exclusivity. The structures which have evolved to incorporate these ideals include collective organization, decision-making by consensus, and rotation of responsibilities. Lesbian Lines in Ireland have been organized in this way since their foundation. At present, LOT is undergoing expansion, while maintaining a commitment to equality and inclusiveness. A fundamental belief remains: the structures and processes which are used in organizing are crucial to the creation of community.

I would argue that the main problems which arise in the implementation of these ideals are personal, (the internalized patterns of oppression) and political (the patterns of inequality and exploitation in society). The feminist slogan 'The personal is political' makes this connection. Equality and inclusiveness are completely at odds with a society based on domination and subordination. Their attainment involves radical transformation, since almost every aspect of society, as well as our interpersonal relationships and our psychological patterns, are permeated by domination and subordination. Changes must occur at the personal, interpersonal and political levels, since all are interrelated. We cannot have an egalitarian community or society when there is economic and social inequality. Yet we cannot have economic and social equality when we have internalized patterns of domination and subordination, and when we enact these patterns in our relationships and in our communities.

'Internalized oppression' describes the psychological patterns which people tend to develop under conditions of subjugation. These patterns have been identified by writers on women's psychology, on racism, on colonialism and on other systems of oppression (Moane, 1994). Self-hatred, low self-esteem, a sense of inferiority, feelings of alienation, hopelessness and despair, and ambivalence towards one's peers, are among such patterns. Personal change involves tackling these patterns by developing a strong sense of self, building solidarity and forging a political analysis which will facilitate hope (Moane, 1991).

At the interpersonal level, there is a need to address patterns of domination such as aggression, élitism and competition (Hoagland, 1988). Additionally, a major focus of lesbian-feminist writings has been on sexuality and relationships, with a central theme of broadening our concept of the erotic. Adrienne Rich (1980, p. 53), expressing this wish, writes

> As we deepen and broaden the range of what we define as lesbian existence, as we delineate a lesbian continuum, we begin to discover the erotic in female terms: as that which is unconfined to any single part of the body or solely to the body itself.

Rich and other feminists, such as Janice Raymond, Lillian Faderman, Mary Dorcey, Mary Daly and Audre Lorde, extend our vision of woman-to-woman sexuality, sensuality, passion and emotional bonding. They believe that in a patriarchal society women's relationships with each other have been distorted and destroyed. Janice Raymond (1986) draws on the work of Lillian Faderman (1981) and others to document women's often heroic commitment to each other in different cultures, to highlight the loyalty, passion, honesty, caring and joy that are possible between women. Mary Dorcey (1989) writes of lyrical sensuality and passion between women, while Mary Daly (1984) celebrates the special energy, 'gynergy', that women create between them in the process of Be-Friending. Audre Lorde (1984) describes how 'the erotic offers a well of replenishing and provocative force to the woman who does not fear its revelation, nor succumbs to the belief that sensation is enough' (p. 54).

At the political level, a society based on equality will involve challenging its hierarchical structuring and the mechanisms of control which accompany this, including restrictions on sexuality. The variety of areas where lesbians and others have been politically active have already been touched on in the previous section: violence, poverty, health, education, anti-discrimination legislation and community building. Much of this organizing is informed by the ideal of a fully egalitarian society which may never be completely attainable. However, as I hope the above analysis has shown, the ideals of such a society can inform personal, interpersonal and political actions in the here and now, and result in communities which show far greater levels of equality and inclusiveness than we at present experience in society. As Alice Walker (1984 p. 91) says. 'Keep in mind always the present you are constructing. It should be the future you want.'

Lesbian existence has the potential to be fundamentally and radically revolutionary. It is, in so far as it is resistance, refusal and nay-saying, taboo breaking and rebellious. It is, in so far as it is woman-centred, placing women at the centre of affectional and sexual existence. It is, in so far as it has a separate and identifiable culture and politics, an articulation of a radical and revolutionary set of values and practices. If these values and practices can inform our current political activism and community building, then it is my hope that we can build a community which will be a microcosm of an egalitarian society, and a fundamental challenge to the status quo, rather than a reflection of our current oppressive and exploitative society.

Note

1.   The eighth amendment (to Article 44 of the Constitution) states: 'The State acknowledges the right to life of the unborn child, and, with due regard to the equal right to life of the mother, guarantees by its laws to respect, and as far as practicable, by its laws to defend and vindicate that right.'

References

Amnesty International (1994). *Breaking the Silence: Human Rights Violations Based on Sexual Orientation*. New York: Amnesty International.

Byrne, S. and Larkin J. (1994). *Coming Out*. Dublin: Martello.

Collins, E. and O'Carroll I. (1995). *Poverty, Lesbians and Gay Men: The Economic and Social Effects of Discrimination* (GLEN Combat Poverty Study). Dublin: Combat Poverty Agency.

Crone, J. (1989). 'Lesbianism in Ireland: the hidden face of prejudice'. *Co-options: Journal of the Community Workers Co-op.*

Daly, M. (1984). *Pure Lust: Elemental Feminist Philosophy*. Boston: Beacon Press.

Dorcey, M. (1989). *A Noise from the Woodshed*. London: Onlywomen Press.

Dublin Lesbian and Gay Men's Collective (1986). *Out for Ourselves: The Lives of Irish Lesbians and Gay Men*. Dublin: Women's Community Press.

Dublin Lesbian Line (1991). *Submission to the Second Commission on the Status of Women*. Dublin: Dublin Lesbian Line

Faderman, L. (1984). *Surpassing the Love of Men*. New York: Quill.

Hoagland, S. (1988). *Lesbian Ethics: Toward New Value*. Palo Alto, CA: Institute of Lesbian Studies.

ICCL (1990). *Equality Now for Lesbians and Gay Men*. Dublin: Irish Council for Civil Liberties.

Jeffreys, S. (1990). *Anticlimax: A Feminist Perspective on the Sexual Revolution*. London: The Women's Press.

Lorde, A. (1984). 'Uses of the erotic: the erotic as power', in *Sister Outsider*. New York: The Crossing Press.

LOT (1994). *Annual Report*. Dublin: Lesbians Organizing Together.

Maddox, B. (1991). *The Pope and Contraception: The Diabolical Doctrine*. London: Chattus & Windus.

Masters, and Johnson (1993). *Human Sexuality*. New York: Collins.

Meaney, G. (1991). *Sex and Nation: Women in Irish Culture and Politics*. Dublin: Attic Press.

Moane, G. (1991). 'Gender and colonialism: towards a psychology of oppression and liberation'. Paper presented to Women's Education Research and Resource Centre (WERRC). University College Dublin.

Moane, G. (1994). 'A psychological analysis of colonialism in an Irish context'. *Irish Journal of Psychology*, 15, pp. 250–65.

Nandy, A. (1983). *The Intimate Enemy: Loss and Recovery of Self under Colonialism*. Delhi: Oxford University Press.

Raymond, J. (1986). *A Passion for Friends: Toward a Philosophy of Female Affection*. London: The Women's Press.

Rich, A. (1980). 'Compulsory heterosexuality and lesbian existence'. *Signs: Journal of Women in Culture and Society*, 15, pp. 459–65.

Walker, A. (1984). *In Search of My Mother's Garden*. New York: Harcourt Brace Jovanovich.

Identity, Existence and Passionate Politics

Joan McCarthy

WHAT I will attempt to do in this article is to draw a distinction between lesbian *identity* and lesbian *existence* placing an emphasis on *existence* as the ground from which the story of a life unfolds. I believe that through our attempts to analyse the realities of oppression we have generated political and social identities which have forced us to fragment ourselves and our experiences in the name of theoretical consistency and political commitment. This theoretical and political focus on identity has obscured our primary human project which is to *be* in the world.[1]

Saying that 'I am a lesbian' shatters the 'self' psychologically, emotionally, logically. It places me outside of human and woman, and raises the question of what identity in general might mean. A lot of work has been done in an attempt to come to grips with the question of identity, and my exploration of this body of work, together with my own experience over the past number of years, has given me tools for understanding and a language in which to articulate my 'self'.

Postmodernism and identity

Against the background of the nature versus nurture debate and the impossiblity of resolving it, contemporary theorists have rephrased the argument in terms of essentialism versus anti-essentialism. What's at issue about identity, for them, is the degree of certainty we claim to have about it. What are called essentialist positions involve the claim that irrespective of whether our human identity is constructed in nature or culture there are still some basic truths that we know about ourselves, for example Freud's claim that we are primarily sexual beings. One anti-essentialist (or postmodernist) position articulated by Michel Foucault rejects this strong claim to truth. He believed that every truth-claim about humanity is made by *some one* and so must inevitably come from the perspective defined by the history, language and politics of that someone. A vision of 'humanity' always comes from a particular view. What this means is that there is no 'human nature', no 'women', no 'men', no 'lesbians', 'homosexuals', 'bisexuals' or 'heterosexuals'. For Foucault, sexual identity has no sexual essence, unconscious or otherwise, which needs to be liberated, no normal or abnormal sexuality. Sexual identity is constructed in history and in the context of a whole range of political social and economic forces.[2]

Two models of lesbian identity

To begin with I'll have to say I agree with Foucault: we can have no certainty about our definitions of humanity or sexuality. This position has implications for definitions of identity including lesbian identity. Two models of the latter which have emerged in the past sixty-odd years have had a particular impact on me. The first, which was developed in the 1970s, derives largely from feminist writings about women. Theorists like Mary Daly and Susan Griffin argued that men's Truth about women's nature must be replaced by women's Truth. They rejected men's classification of women, and claimed that women's real nature exists underneath or alongside patriarchal classifications and must be liberated. In this sense, they are essentialists, because they believe that there are 'real' women and that it is possible for the theorist to make universal, trans-historical or trans-geographic claims about them. Judith Butler (1987, p. 142) asks a very basic question of this position.

What happens when individual women do not recognize themselves in the theories that explain their unsurpassable essences to them? When the essential feminine is finally articulated, and what we have been calling 'women' cannot see themselves in its terms, what then are we to conclude? That these women are deluded, or that they are not women at all?

The model of lesbian identity which derives from this essentialist view of women is that it is the inevitable choice in the face of the reality of male domination in patriarchy:

> Feminism at heart is a massive complaint. Lesbianism is the solution. Which is another way of putting what Ti-Grace Atkinson once described as feminism being a theory and lesbianism the practice. When theory and practice come together we'll have the revolution. Until all women are lesbians there will be no true political revolution. No feminist *per se* has advanced a solution outside of accommodation to the man. ... Feminists who still sleep with the man are delivering their most vital energies to the oppressor. (Johnston, 1973)

This view offers a very positive lesbian identity. In doing so, however, it alienated heterosexual feminists, who felt they were getting it wrong, and intimidated those of us who felt we were 'queer' whether the patriarchy existed or not. As with the category of woman: what happens to the lesbians who do not recognize themselves as the militants of feminist theory? Joan Nestle in *A Restricted Country* (1987, pp. 111–12) sees her lesbian identity in terms of her membership of an oppressed minority, not as the battle-cry of the sisterhood:

> I need to keep alive the memory of passing women and their wives, the memory of Lesbians who because they 'looked like men' were ridiculed, beaten, locked up, hidden away. These women presented gender challenges at a time when only the

deviants questioned gender destiny. I need to keep alive the memory that in the 1940s doctors measured the clitorises and nipples of Lesbians to prove our biological strangeness. When transvestites and transsexuals are beaten by the police, as they were at Blues [a New York City bar], this history calls me to action. I cannot turn away from it. My roots lie in the history of a people who were called freaks.

This second model of lesbian identity is generated not out of the pain of women's oppression but out of the pain of the sexual outcast of either gender. This queer identity finds its root in sexual and not gender oppression. The political agenda which comes out of this analysis is a libertarian approach to sex.[3] In short, sex is good any old way, any old how, as long as it's consensual. My experience tells me otherwise. Sex and desire for me are not so simple. Desire is neither a spirtual experience nor a box of cornflakes. Sex is not a pure experience which requires no political analysis. My experience of my body is politicized. My body is flesh which is wont to expand, or fall, or disappear. Pock marks, the absence of decay, the number of gold or white fillings, what we eat, how we stand, our experience of shame from molestation or rape, our height, the colour of our hair, the way we smell or sweat, all locate our body in class and race and gender. What and how I desire is mediated through my own story, through my social and historical place in the world. In many ways I didn't invent my fantasies. I learned them. I am not interested in making moral judgements about all of this, not for others and not for myself – I am saying that we bring ourselves to sex.

The tension that exists between the political agendas of radical feminist and queer theorists is there because both are making too strong a claim for their version of identity. What is essentialist about the radical feminist approach is its claim that *gender is identity*. What is essentialist about the approach of queer theorists is the claim that *sexuality is identity*. I would argue that membership of an oppressed group, be it of women or sexual dissidents, is not the measure of who we are, that patriarchy is beginning to blur at the edges, revealing itself as a framework among others and that identity cannot be fixed solidly in it, anymore than anywhere else.

Coming from Outside

When you come from the outside, and from a place of silence, the experience of coming home, of finding a language, a community, a morality, a reality that makes you feel safe, is something that's difficult to relinquish. The discovery that radical feminism and subsequently queer politics do not offer all of the answers is hard to accept. A contemporary American novel which tells the harrowing story of a woman coming out in a small town in the 1950s reflects my experience in 1980s Ireland: 'But I always wanted all of us who were different to be the same'. (Feinberg, 1993, p. 271)

The anti-essentialist approach to identify is used in a very radical way by contemporary lesbian theorists to challenge the monopoly which 'lesbian identity' has had in any analysis of the political and social forces of oppression.[4] 'Lesbian identity' exists as a category only because 'heterosexuality' and 'homosexuality' exist as categories, only because *sexuality* is considered a key to personal identity. And in general, we are 'women' because there are 'men', 'Irish' because there are 'English'.

But simply because gender and sexual identity are not as stable as we thought they were does not make them less real.[5] The facts are that we are born, feel pain and joy, and then die. It is bodies that experience these things not theoretical constructs, whether these constructs emphasize gender or sexual practice. While I agree, for instance, that all sexualities are constructed, it is inappropriate to consider 'lesbian' as a construct in the same way as 'heterosexual' is a construct. Using the same term for both equalizes them, as if the range of economic, linguistic, religious, social, cultural and political forces which underpin them both were one and the same thing. They may both be constructs but the resonance of the meaning is the difference between the silence and the storm.

Recently, I went to Dublin to hear Adrienne Rich read from her latest work, *What is Found There: Notebooks on Poetry and Politics* (1993). I was immediately struck by her humanity. Through her work this woman has extended the boundaries of reality for so many women and men, and yet she offered her audience such sincere respect. In her book, Rich identifies one aspect of the framework of oppression as a 'system that depends on our viewing our lives as random and meaningless or at best unserious'. (p. 227) Talk of constructs confirms this view. Elsewhere she comments 'Politics is imagination or it is a treadmill – disintegratable, stifling, finally brutalizing – or ineffectual.' (p. 49) I favour the term 'lesbian existence' when it comes to explorations or expressions of our own created and creative lives.[6] To talk about lesbian *existence* rather than lesbian *identity* allows me to talk about my life as I am trying to live it, rather than to talk about the theory of my life. My lesbian existence is interpreted, lived through, and experienced in the context of other identities. For me, these are working class, Catholic, woman, Irish, thirties. My life is informed by those, and is manifested through those. And all of these identities are not all there is. For me they change with each day, each moment, each face I meet. I *am* in the world in a concrete and holistic way, not in terms of membership of fragmentary and fragmenting theories. When I sit in a room alone with no lover to hold, mother to love, friends to meet, job to go to, the social/political categories of woman/lesbian/class do not have the significance they have on the street. And when I move out into the street, I take on my multiple identities as I would my hat and coat: these are the things we wear when the wind is blowing.

Passionate politics, coats and hats

Sarah Hoagland in *Lesbian Ethics* (1988) concludes that it is our fear of change and uncertainty which fuels our need to establish stable fixed identities:

> It is a fear of change, I think, a fear of things being in flux, that fuels the struggle to create meaning in this way: we seek an objective standard for all time against which we can be judged, against which we can – with certainty – measure ourselves and our actions, within which we can find ourselves, and by means of which we can feel secure about making judgements of others. Yet this objectivity is nothing but a collection of perceptions which agree.

Yes, it is a fear of change which informs us, but I would also suggest that my confusion comes from a mistaken belief that, somehow, all of my 'self' is explicable in terms of political categories of oppression and my revolt against them. In truth it was personal pain which informed the anger of my separatism from heterosexual women and men. Resentment and jealousy fuelled my years on the barricades. I realize now that my mad rush toward the future was in fact a very frenzied rush away from the past. This does not mean that there is no oppression, that there is no injustice. It does mean that it is possible to deal with it in a different way. The personal and the political are like lovers, they hang out together, ideally they embrace, they argue, they sometimes hold hands and walk side by side. When they merge, there is blood on the walls.

Is it possible that once we have moved outside in a very fundamental way from *reality* that we might also have found the room and the courage to look at our own names for describing politics, oppression and self-hood? To assume the name of lesbian is to stand outside and to ask all the questions. That includes asking about our own category. It is to go all the way down:

> To be a lesbian, to act and name oneself as a lover of women, presents an unmitigated challenge to the belief system that structures reality. ... If, instead, we challenge the belief systems that sustain reality, that is, if we take the underlying beliefs to be arbitrary, we begin to understand reality itself as changeable. It is then that we contribute a new structure to reality, rather than argue for the inclusion of our experience in the dominated reality. (Hart, 1990, p. 295)

There is an historical arrogance about a political movement which declares a single generation capable of colonizing the past (how many lesbians can we find in 1853?) and forecasting the future (into the twenty-first century), as if we were the centre of history and that this time is the moment from which the past and the future derive their meaning. But history has lessons to teach us. How many revolutions have there been, how much fine rhetoric, how many lives devoted to 'the cause'? Personal investment in causes helps us to avoid our responsibility for ourselves. We join a cause to validate human existence as worthwhile. But whose life are we establishing as worth living? How long do we wait for the life that is worth living to be lived?

The revolution will not begin tomorrow, or next week, it is already taking place and we are already on the barricades. All of us live our lives quietly, creatively, in calm and storm, etching our way, creating new value, ensuring our survival. That is our revolution. We need not be afraid that 'nothing is happening', that we have 'given up', retreated from the world. We are always in the world as long as we are in it. My lesbian existence is less a focus of oppression than it is a ground for creating new possibilities for living my life. From living this life, I know that fear, self-hatred, pain and poverty are not exclusive to lesbians. I haven't met a single soul who has been exempted from any of these on the grounds of heterosexuality, class or skin privilege. When you can no longer justify the walls you have built and the ghetto you have created, politics informed by anger becomes compassionate. Anger is replaced by passion, pride by humility, strategy by heart, cynicism by hope. Adrienne Rich (1993, p. 250) again, 'The revolutionary poet loves people, rivers, other creatures, stones, trees inseparably from art, is not ashamed of any of these loves, and for them conjures a language that is public, intimate, inviting, terrifying, and beloved.'

Change comes so slowly, as we from the perspective of our lifetimes perceive it, and yet in so many ways and in so many dimensions my world has been recreated, and created again, with possibilities, choices, realities I could not have imagined. I have found a community of honest women and men in which I can imagine my dreams. In which I can try to tell the truth honestly about myself. In which I can take responsibility for myself. It is from this place that my politics begins. For me, it is not my job to stay alive; it is my job to *be* alive. I do not want to be a lesbian hero, I want to take off my coat and hat and feel the wind on my skin.

Notes

1. The phrase 'being in the world' is associated with Heidegger, who used the term *da-sein* (there-being) to describe a self-conscious as distinct from an unconscious existence in the world. See the Introduction to *Being and Time*, trans. by John Macquarrie and Edward Robinson (New York: Harper & Row, 1962).

2. Foucault offers a warning to the political movements which consider sex a hidden essence to be liberated: 'We are often reminded of the countless procedures which Christianity once employed to make us detest the body; but let us ponder all the ruses that were employed for centuries to make us love sex, to make the knowledge of it desirable and everything said about it precious. Let us consider the strategems by which we were induced to apply all our skills to discovering its secrets, by which we were attached to the obligation to draw out its truth ... ' M. Foucault, *The History of Sexuality*, (Harmondsworth: Penguin, 1978), vol. 1, p. 159.

    One contemporary thesis which uses Foucault's anti-essentialist approach was developed by Noreen O'Connor and Joanna Ryan to dismantle the psychoanalytic weight of theory depicting lesbian sexuality as either innate or chosen as a reaction to a dysfunctional family upbringing. I am indebted to their radical argument for the existence of diverse sexualities as an alternative to the necessity of having a single and absolute truth about human sexuality. See Noreen O'Connor and Joanna Ryan, *Wild Desires and Mistaken Identities, Lesbianism and Psychoanalysis* (London: Virago, 1993), p. 22.

3. In her article, 'Sex war: the debate between radical and libertarian feminists', Ann Ferguson distinguishes libertarian from radical feminist agendas. For the libertarians, sexuality involves a liberatory aspect: sexual practice is the exchange of pleasure between consenting partners. For the radicals, sexuality in a male-dominant society involves danger: sexual practice can perpetuate violence against women. The first identifies sexual oppression, the second male violence as the place from which to challenge the patriarchy. *Signs*, vol. 10, no. 1, 1984.

4. Jacquelyn N. Zita, in her article 'Lesbian body journeys' presents a very brilliant and clear analysis of identity: 'I use this word "self" cautiously, since I do not want to imply that there is a hidden self to be discovered in "the search for identity". Rather I believe that we construct "partial coherencies" in and through our daily interactions which have the semblance of a "self", as a locatable and embodied reference for first-person pronouns.

This embodied "self" is relationally and interactively constructed, continuously constituted through memory, principles of coherency, rules of meaning and value, and materialities which set limits and opportunities for individuation and experience.' Jeffner, Allen (ed.), *Lesbian Philosophies and Cultures* (Buffalo: SUNY Press, 1990), p. 343.

5. For an exploration of this view, see Carol Vance and Ann Barr Snitow: 'But if careless generalization about women's experience is dangerous and mystifying, so too is avoidance of generalization in the belief that each woman's experience is so unique and conditioned by multiple social influence that larger patterns are impossible to discern, that to attempt to generalize is to do violence to individual experience. Feminist work on sexuality must confront the dialectic between specificity and generalization and endure its ongoing tension.' 'Toward a conversation about sex in feminism: a modest proposal', *Signs*, vol. 10, no. 1, 1984.

6. Adrienne Rich used this term in her pioneering article, 'compulsory heterosexuality and Lesbian existance', to describe both the historical presence of lesbians and the possibility that we continue to contribute to the meaning of the term. Responding to later criticism of her position, Rich stated that it was neither separatist nor a gay rights plea for openness to an alternative lifestyle. My own thesis advocates an even wider meaning for *existence* in order to accommodate what I believe is left out of rationalist theoretical debates (be they essentialist or otherwise) and that is the knowledges I have of my 'self' which cannot be assimilated or explained by the conscious mind. Rather than talk of the 'mind/body', or the 'embodied mind', I suggest the term 'mindful body'. This shifts the emphasis from the mind to the body as being central to the process of 'knowing'. *Signs*, vol 5, no. 4, 1980.

References

Butler, Judith (1987). 'Variations on sex and gender: Beauvoir, Wittig and Foucault', in S. Benhabib and D. Cornell (eds.), *Feminism as Critique*. London: Polity Press.

Feinberg, Leslie (1993). *Stone Butch Blues*. New York: Firebrand Books.

Hart, Nett (1990). 'Lesbian desire as social action', in Jeffner Allen (ed.), *Lesbian Philosophies and Cultures*. Buffalo: SUNY Press.

Hoagland, Sarah Lucia (1988). *Lesbian Ethics*. Palo Alto. CA Institute of Lesbian Studies.

Johnston, Jill (1973). *Lesbian Nation: The Feminist Solution*. New York: Simon and Schuster.

Nestle, Joan (1987). *A Restricted Country*. New York: Firebrand Press.
Rich, Adrienne (1993). *What is Found There: Notebooks on Poetry and Politics*. New York: Norton.

'I Used To Be an Activist, But I'm Alright Now'

Izzy Kamikaze

Dear Íde,

What an exciting opportunity you've offered – a chance to expound a vision of the future, no less! However, my mind keeps straining in the opposite direction. But as Confucius said, and every Irish bar-stool philosopher would agree: 'Study the past, if you would divine the future.' If I've learned anything from the past it's this: speculation about the future is pointless, nothing ever works out as you expect. Still, crystal-ball gazing is an educational game for all the (pretended) family. So, gaily forward into the past ...

My 'past' begins in 1982, the year I came out. Before then, I couldn't even have imagined a lesbian or gay future. There was no precedent for it. The words themselves were familiar only from 'dirty' jokes and nasty rumours which would occasionally blaze through my school (often about me, funnily enough).

I was born in 1963, so when I was in secondary school Ireland not only had a 'scene' but also a developing network of groups and services – a fledgling lesbian and gay movement. Most of this was happening in Dublin, only fifty miles away from me, but (and this must be the biggest change of all) it was *almost completely invisible* from the outside. One consolation of being called a 'lezzer' by gangs of marauding ten-year-olds – as I often am these days – is the knowledge that at least children today recognize a lesbian when they see one. I, at a much more advanced age, would not have recognized a lesbian even if she'd jumped up in plaid shirt, jeans, Doc Martens and crewcut and shaken her labyris at me. I was almost seventeen before I even saw a lesbian on television (I almost died of embarrassment), and I never met anyone who was 'out' until after I came out myself at nineteen. I did encounter a few self-hating closet cases (like myself), but frankly that wasn't much help. So, before I bashed my own way out of the closet, it was simply impossible to imagine a future that was lesbian or gay. In the beginning there was no 'lesbian' or 'gay'. In the beginning there was only 'queer'.

'Queer: differing from the ordinary or normal, peculiar, droll, strange.' I was pushing twenty before I could get my mouth around 'lesbian' or 'gay' (without blushing anyway), but I must have been queer, in every conceivable sense, from the day I was born. I always was (and felt) 'peculiar'. It seems that I was reading and writing (and otherwise escaping reality) almost as soon as I could talk, and I must have come out of the womb talking. I grew up in a small town, in an upwardly mobile new housing estate. Nothing much happened. I didn't have many friends, just girls I went to school with. 'Everyone' wanted to be mammies or teachers or nurses, but I never did. Sometimes I wanted to be a boy, because they had more fun and more freedom (and because girls fancied them, but that was a very buried, secret thought). But mostly I just wanted to grow up and get the hell out of there.

The day after I left school I came to Dublin. Not for work or college like 'everyone' did, just to get away. (Straight) people would ask me, 'What brought you to Dublin?' 'Gravity', I'd answer, but it took another couple of years before I could say *why* smalltown life was unbearable for me.

Coming out of the closet was like finding the entrance to some magic cave or secret garden: 'Abracadabra' and a whole new world opened up. I didn't feel any fear or guilt or shame, just relief. If I had stopped to think about the future (which of course I didn't) it would have been a happy-ever-after future with all my beautiful, newly discovered sisters and brothers in the wonderful secret garden where everything was perfect and I'd never have to feel lonely or crazy or queer again as long as I lived. I don't think it even occurred to me that there might be snakes in the grass ...

Here's a prediction: due to the increased visibility of lesbians and gays, long-term languishing in the closet will soon be almost a thing of the past. More young people will come out, become more visible in our communities, and maybe, in time, even be taken more seriously. As a prediction it's a bit of a dud, because it's already happened – there are so many young faces on the scene (hanging out with their mates, looking decidedly unfazed by their sexuality), that sometimes it's easy to forget it wasn't always that way. Even young gay men seemed a lot thinner on the ground when I came out, but dykes my age were a rarity. In my first couple of years out of the closet I only met three – one I only ever said 'Hi' to, another for whom my first lover left me (which rather put me off her for a while) and one I hung out with for a bit but she emigrated.

Towards the end of my first year out I remember realizing I had to choose between being twenty and being a lesbian. I chose to be a lesbian (which probably sounds a bit sad, unless you know that later, when I might reasonably have been expected to settle down a bit – I decided to be an adolescent and have since steadfastly resisted every encouragement to grow up).

Nineteen eighty-two and nineteen eighty-three are a blur. I lurched like a drunken flea through that first year, falling madly in love for the first time, getting dumped for the first time, falling apart for – well not quite the first time. Even apart from the emotional rollercoaster, it was an exciting time. 'Progressive' forces in Ireland were united – or at least less divided than usual – behind the Anti-Amendment Campaign in opposition to the so-called 'Pro-Life' Amendment. In the feminist circles in which I suddenly surfaced, it was a time of intense activity and great hope. Close up, in the heat of the battle, the God Squad didn't look so unbeatable. I did what any naïve, politically motivated, hyperactive teenager would do – I joined everything. The Dublin Women's Centre, the National Gay Federation (NGF), Liberation for Irish Lesbians, the Dublin Gay Collective, Women for Disarmament, the Women's Right to Choose campaign . . . you name it, I joined it.

This politicized environment dominated 'the scene' way back then, especially for women. The Women's Centre in Dame Street was a social (as well as political) focus of many dykes' lives. Even the gay men's scene was relatively uncommercialized, revolving around the nearby Hirschfeld Centre (which despite its many failings was run and staffed by volunteers and not entirely money-driven). The NGF had a large membership – it controlled the only gay disco in town and members got in cheaper – but no discernible political agenda. The other groups were mostly short of members and heavy on politics. I hung around them all, making myself useful at times, a nuisance at others and learning lots along the way. There were so few young queers on the scene (it often took years just to *find* the scene) that there was little tolerance for youth and inexperience. (As I recall, people of twenty-six or twenty-seven were by far the most patronizing. Older people weren't too bad.) One group met secretly to agree to throw me out for bad behaviour (under the influence of alcohol and a broken heart), but most gave me time to find out for myself that it wasn't all roses in the secret garden.

It took a while. That first year I was indiscriminately in love with it all. Luckily, I picked a good year – I experienced some of the most exciting moments in Quare history, like the Fairview Park march against violence against gays and women, organized by the Dublin Gay Collective, which called in every conceivable old debt to mobilize women's organizations, anti-amendment groups, and others to ensure an unprecedented attendance for a lesbian and gay event. It would have felt brilliant, except that we were there because a man had been killed and his queerbashing killers had been freed.

The 1983 Pride march was a more joyful occasion. The sun shone as we pranced through Dublin with pink carnations, pink dungarees and even pink hair. No drag, of course – nothing too flamboyant – but someone threw dye into the fountain on Dame Street (the one they call 'Urination Once Again'), turning it pink for one glorious instant. There were enough of us for it not to feel scary, as we shouted ourselves hoarse in a merry band of queers, claiming the Saturday streets of Dublin's Quare City. God, what a buzz! To this day nothing intoxicates me like Pride. Imagine – a day devoted to public expression of our delight in ourselves. 'We came through the flames!', it tells the world. 'You brought us up to hate ourselves and we don't!' I'm pretty sure now *that* was the day I first enjoyed the luxury of a vision of our future.

A vision of the future is not a prediction – which is just as well. There was so much I couldn't have predicted. If any of us had known half of what lay ahead, we might have been too paralysed to dream, and then what would have kept us going? I dreamed that we who had grown up queer and had experienced the miracle of finding each other would create communities with room for all of us. We were different from each other in almost every possible way, but we had all been 'outsiders'. We wouldn't do that to each other. In our world nobody would be 'queer'. None of us knew what loomed ahead, but lots of us dreamt of communities which would sustain us, come what might.

Emigration was one thing that crept up on us. For obvious reasons, Irish queers had always been at the top of the queue for the boat or the plane, but the trickle soon became a flood, taking with it some of the people most needed here. The 'New Irish Emigrant' stereotype is just another crock of manure. People are still being starved out of this country, but many also leave because they're sick of being pushed around – which is bloody good news for upholders of the *status quo* inside the lesbian and gay communities, as well as outside.

The energy of radical Irish queers has exploded onto an international stage, breathing life into moribund movements elsewhere, as in ILGO's (Irish Lesbian and Gay Organization) battles with the AOH (Archaic Oirish Homophobes). I hope that at least some of that energy will find its way home. Hurry back, gang. The new 'liberal' Ireland has a pain in the Árus burning candles for your return. Incidentally, so many foreign queers (especially dykes) are settling here now, that unless some of you come back to keep up the numbers we could become 'a minority within a minority' over here too!

Quare times alright, and a far cry from 1983 ... I had heard of AIDS then, but only from reading the Yankee gay papers in the Women's Centre library. Everybody said it wouldn't happen here, but it's happening everywhere and everything has changed for ever. Now a future without AIDS is almost impossible to imagine. Our traumatized personal lives will shape our politics for decades in ways we cannot yet envisage. Each community, each *individual* will experience it differently. The full story will not be told until every voice is heard.

These huge forces rocked our communities. We struggled to deal with them, and with the more local disasters like closure of the Women's Centre and the Hirschfeld Centre fire. But hard times don't kill dreams, hard times deepen our *need* for dreams. None of us had ever dreamt that queers would have an easy ride – we always knew there would be tough times, even if we never suspected quite how tough they would be.

If I now find it easier to look back than forward, it's not because of AIDS, emigration or homophobia (though all of these have hit me where it hurts). It's because so many of us have also been profoundly damaged by involvement in the lesbian and gay movement itself and in the AIDS movement which developed from it. We have been disempowered, marginalized and silenced within the movements which we worked so hard to build. A bitter example: AIDS, the disease itself and the movement which has responded to it, has been part of my life for a long time now. I can't write that story: the voices which claim lesbians' lives are 'unaffected' are stronger than mine. I fight their generalizations – on a factual basis – every chance I get, but I refuse to justify my 'right' to feel affected. This competitive attitude to grief is disgusting and sick. Our movements are not yet places where every voice can be heard. Somebody owns this boat – whoever rocks it is a 'dangerous radical'.

Lesbians and working-class or radical gay men have done most of the dog-work of building our communities. We didn't mortgage our houses to fund projects, we gave our time instead. We didn't have houses to mortgage, but we had plenty of time – life being what it is, most of us were on the dole. But no matter how much time we invested, it never brought us the right to speak for ourselves.

We tried to build a movement which would represent all of us, but the lesbian and gay movement got hijacked. It became the personal property of an élite who have *bought* the right to speak for all of us. The rest of us are expected to know our place. If we're lucky – and prepared to play that game – they may adopt some of us as tokens in an effort to appear more representative. Otherwise we are only good for cannon-fodder. If we speak for ourselves, we are 'radicals' bent (oops) on taking over 'their' movement. If we dare to set up structures they cannot control, they resort to sabotage. This has happened to our movement in every country, in almost every organization, and, despite what many of us once thought, it is never going to change.

The use of 'radical' as a term of abuse is hilarious. For a pervert to have any pride is radical. A lesbian and gay movement which is not radical is no fit place for any self-respecting queer. But the lesbian and gay movement everywhere, including Ireland, is infested with cliques of privileged men and their co-opted cronies who systematically exclude the rest of us, making us queers and outcasts all over again. Let me give you an example, a little local example, of how this whole set-up works ...

It seems reasonable to suppose that lesbians and gays, having survived the bullshit we were force-fed in our closets, might be a pretty radical bunch. I believe this is actually true. But in Dublin, as elsewhere, a small group, dominated by well-heeled gay men, emerged which assumed the right to speak for everyone in what they did not even bother to call the *lesbian and* gay communities. They named their baby the National Gay Federation although even in its heyday it was neither national nor a federation but – bugger the facts – it had a nice, butch, authorative ring to it. Even in the late 1970s this name was slightly presumptuous. Today, when the most exciting developments are coming from what they would call 'the country', it's just plain offensive.

They 'ran' the Hirschfeld Centre, but real control rested with an even smaller group. Mick Quinlan called them The 'Three Musketeers' – the major shareholders in 'Hirschfeld Enterprises' who'd had sufficient means to persuade a bank to cough up the money for the premises.[1] They were the legal owners, with an investment to protect, and they felt they were entitled to overall control (which in legal terms they were). Everyone called the Hirschfeld Centre a 'community centre', but it wasn't controlled by 'the community' or even by the NGF. Somebody else was calling the shots. Many members (at the time there *were* many members) questioned this arrangement, but the bottom line was always that the bank had to be paid before the centre could come under 'community control'. It never happened. Even if the Hirschfeld Centre had not been destroyed, it always seemed unlikely, because when people have that kind of power they don't give it up easily.

('The Hirsch' wasn't the only place where a mortgage was used to whip us into line!) Anyway, these people really seemed to believe that the community was exclusively composed of people like themselves. I wonder (not really) what their version of 'community control' would have looked like?

'There is a basic distrust of politically active lesbians and gay men within the NGF hierarchy. They seem to be scared shitless by working-class, republican and activist lesbians and gay men. Why is this?' Mick Quinlan asked in 1986.[2] The answer is simple. Like their counterparts everywhere, they were obsessed with projecting a 'respectable' image of homosexuality. They were (barely) prepared to tolerate women with feminist politics if they confined themselves to LIL (Liberation for Irish Lesbians, an autonomous women's group linked with NGF) and did not attempt to influence NGF policy. But they had a fear bordering on paranoia of socialist, republican or otherwise radical activists who might contaminate their cosy arrangements. Essentially they feared anyone they could not control, anyone who might question their 'right', as well-off males, to rule the roost.

The NGF often seemed to make a virtue of stupidity. They fought, often with as much passion as if there'd been a principle involved, to keep the word 'lesbian' out of the name of their organization for many years. They even refused to support the Fairview Park March, of all things, until eventually they realized that every dog and divil in town (and its mother) was solidly behind it. And they went on seeing themselves as 'leaders' of a community which had passed them out years ago.

The kindest thing to say about the NGF would be that it was irrelevant. Not only would it be possible to write a history of Irish lesbian and gay politics without mentioning it at all – it has already been done.[3] They avoided political action like poison. But everything is political, so they were political too. Let's put a name on their politics. They were conservative. In the context of lesbian and gay politics a 'conservative' is someone who thinks they can solve our problems by re-defining normality to include some of us (themselves). This group is composed mainly of middle-class men. A 'radical' is someone who realizes that the very *idea* of normality caused our problems, made us queer. Radicals are different from each other and think that is OK, yet conservatives somehow delude themselves that *they* are more 'representative'!

Sadly, the NGF was a fairly typical example of what, world-wide, pretends to be the leadership of what they *now* call the lesbian and gay movement. (NGF finally became NLGF in 1990 when there were hardly any women left in the organization. Hardly any men either. On at least one occasion they had to drag people in off the street to make up a quorum for their AGM.[4] Just whose leaders do they think they are?) There have been changes of personnel, of course, but the problem is that this type of structure is unrepresenta-tive. Our communities are diverse, but the people who run the lesbian and gay movement only make room for those who play the game by their rules. They represent themselves as selfless martyrs, claiming that 'the community' is 'too apolitical' to support them. Who? Us? The NLGF is understandably coy about membership figures, but I bet I could introduce you to three times that number of queers who would never join its ranks precisely because *it's* too apolitical to support *us*!

The only reason that the NLGF is not yet completely irrele-vant is that it owns the only lesbian and gay newspaper with national distribution. *Gay Community News* (*GCN*) is produced from the burned-out shell of the Hirschfeld Centre by FÁS scheme workers (unemployed people who work for little more than the dole on government-funded schemes used to fiddle the unemployment figures). With its windowless rooms, stinking toilets and falling masonry the centre is a worthy successor to the sweatshops which once dominated the (now trendy) area in which it is located. *GCN* (still bravely holding out against the 'L') is what the NLGF uses to maintain its pretence to be an active organization, and to sabotage anything that does not have its seal of approval. This is our local version of a weapon used by the gay élite everywhere to protect their interests.

This is neither paranoia nor ancient history. A recent exam-ple. In 1992 a handful of activists organised a Pride Parade in Dublin for the first time in seven years. We were not members of the gay establishment. We were from AIDS services and ACT UP. We weren't trying to threaten anybody's position. We needed Pride. It felt like a long time since we'd had anything to celebrate.

We didn't exclude the gay hierarchy; in fact, we did everything we could to encourage them to get involved. We were open to everyone. Over the next couple of years, people from every section of the community got involved *except* the gay establishment. No matter how many invitations we issued, the organizations which claim to represent us refused to get involved. If they could not control us, they would not work with us.

That first year, GCN (our only available means of publicity, apart from a few photocopied posters) 'supported' community activism by claiming that the parade probably would not take place because it was so badly organized. Talk about the pot calling the kettle black! We had worked our arses off actually, and we got the turn-out to prove it. Needless to say, the NLGF was there too, on the day – they have to take each other's pictures to plaster all over the paper. Despite GCN's ecstatic coverage of Pride events abroad, we had to fight, cajole and beg for every inch of space we got over the next couple of years. But we kept on doing it, more people became involved (many of whom had never been involved in any lesbian and gay organization), and it grew.

In 1994 more stones were thrown from the NLGF's glasshouse, and we were again attacked in GCN by Anthony McGrath.[5] Despite the traditional hostilities, this outburst was puzzling. First, the pretext was the use of supposedly offensive language in the Pride programme. Crusades against obscenity are rare in gay publications, aware as they are of their own position at the margins of public tolerance. (GCN itself had suffered censorship at the hands of its printer during the same month in which our programme had appeared.) Second, the writer was someone with an established interest in free speech, his own column being GCN's most complained about feature (no mean achievement). Many have prayed for confiscation of his crayon, but in vain – he's on the NLGF Committee. Personally, although I've often been offended by his ill-informed ramblings (as when he defined the difference between a lesbian and a gay woman as 'the latter doesn't have an attitude problem' GCN, March 1994), I respect his right to hold odious opinions and the NLGF's right to publish them. Call me a dangerous radical, but it's just the way I am! Even so, I have stopped reading GCN as I also respect my digestive system. Our attacker created the impression that he had received numerous complaints about the Pride programme, and of widespread community outrage – an impression strangely unsupported by a full-page *vox pop* on the same issue.

Fair enough so far. Obscenity, as queers know well, is very much a matter of opinion and Mr McGrath is entitled to his. But he did not leave it at that. Piling innuendo on innuendo (in an attack which would almost certainly be found libellous, if any of us had been of a litigious frame of mind) he smeared us as commies, provos, radicals, all the old bogies – everything the old-style NGF had ever feared. The more things change, the more they stay the same. The problem wasn't what we *did*, the problem was what we (allegedly) *were*. We didn't just use dirty words, we were the *wrong kind of people*.

Imagine how Pride's visible diversity threatens those who believe that any difference, however trivial, indicates an 'attitude problem'! This ragbag of 'radicals' had, for the third year running, brought cheering crowds of queers onto Dublin's streets, while NLGF's showpiece (participation in the Paddy's Day Parade) had barely mustered a dozen.

This story is no big deal, just another chapter of the same old story. There are NLGFs all over the world. The visible face of the international lesbian and gay movement is a lie, a conspiracy to hide the diversity of queers and to unfairly weigh the balance in favour of conservatives. Queers who don't fit the mould have no power in it, even though we did most of the work building it. The Stonewall Riots, now hypocritically mythologized by the movement, they were not the queens' tea party ... I bet plenty of bourgeois faggots at the time reckoned the rioters were 'giving us all a bad name'.

This Uncle Tom-osexual Movement has become a major league queerbasher. We should all abandon it and see how long it lasts without us. 'They' should watch out – their victims may eventually fight back. I'm finished with it anyway, count me out of organizing Pride or anything featuring the words 'lesbian and gay' from now on. Someone else owns it, even if we build it from nothing but our blood, sweat and tears. If I ever get involved with something queer again, it'll be called something 'filthy' enough to keep the leeches at a distance.

I hope the other Pride stalwarts don't give up yet, though (lots of them didn't know they were 'radical', some thought they weren't even political), because I still want us all, at least once a year, to have the right not to be censored out of the picture of our community. That's what Pride is about and that's RADICAL!

And the future? I still have my vision of room for all of us. If the gay élite won't move over, we'll just have to make room for ourselves (again!). The so-called lesbian and gay movement is in its death throes. In the future we might get to hear from the rest of the queers. Who knows? Your book might even be the start of it! Give my love to the grass-roots everywhere ...

Love, Izzy

Notes

1. Mick Quinlan, 'Some class of a scene', in *Out for Ourselves* (Dublin: Women's Community Press and Dublin Lesbian and Gay Collectives, 1986).
2. Ibid.
3. Kieran Rose, *Diverse Communities: The Evolution of Lesbian and Gay Politics in Ireland*, a pamplet in the Undercurrents Series (Cork: Cork University Press, 1994).
4. According to former NLGF member, Donal Traynor, who thinks the quorum was ten people.
5. Anthony McGrath, 'Postcards', *Gay Community News*, August 1994.

Letter from a Gay Republican: H–Block 5

Brendí McClenaghan

Dear Eoin and Íde

I am writing this letter in my prison cell in the H–Blocks of Long Kesh. I've been in prison seventeen years, since I was twenty years old. For me, prison has been very much a mirror of my life, for I have witnessed oppression, torture, sadness and even death inside and outside these prison walls. I was sentenced in March 1979, and shortly afterwards joined my comrades on the 'Blanket protest' for political status as a prisoner of war.[1] I spent over three years naked in a cell in this prison to prove that I was not a 'criminal' but a 'political prisoner'. It hasn't been easy to be a gay Republican, in or out of prison.

When I was asked if I would write something for this collection I was very apprehensive about what I could or should write. I realize that just as there are many gays and lesbians who do not share my view of the Republican struggle here, there are also many Republicans who do not share my view on the gay/lesbian struggle. So, I found myself in a bit of a dilemma. I thought long and hard about this and decided that I had two options: one, to decline the offer, which would be to deny the existence of homosexuals within the Republican movement, and two, to present the links that exist between the Republican and gay/lesbian struggles.

1994 was a year of great significance for the Irish lesbian and gay community. It marked twenty years since the struggle for lesbian and gay rights began here, but it was also the twenty-fifth anniversary of the Stonewall Riots, which gave birth to the modern lesbian and gay movement. The Republican in me also remembers that it marked another anniversary: the 'reintroduction' of heavily armed British troops onto the streets of our country.

While quite a few well-aimed sticks, stones and high heels were being thrown in the direction of police from the Stonewall bar in June 1969, I, like many from my home area (Ardoyne, in the city of Belfast), was witnessing similar scenes (albeit without the high heels) as running battles were fought with the RUC and B Specials (the exclusively Protestant militia) in most Nationalist areas of the North. At that time I wasn't aware of the Stonewall Riots, nor for that matter of my own sexuality. What I was aware of was the desire on the part of people here to protest against the denial of civil rights by a brutal state.

The struggle that developed from Stonewall in 1969 involved gays and lesbians confronting the state of America, and here in the Six Counties people were also taking on the state. There are many similarities within both these struggles. In America it was about rights and liberties denied on the basis of sexuality. Here, the struggle was being waged by a people discriminated against in every aspect of their lives because they were Catholic/Nationalist.

Within the Republican movement the position on lesbians and gays has been pretty dismal. It was only in 1980, a full six years after the emergence of a lesbian and gay movement in Ireland, that Sinn Féin adopted a motion at its *Ard Fheis* (party conference) in relation to lesbians and gays. Why wasn't there support before this? Two reasons. Republicans were involved in a multitude of campaigns, none of which appeared to have the remotest connection with gays or lesbians. And there were 'no gays or lesbians in the Republican movement' (well, that was the myth at least). So there was no focus on gay/lesbian issues. Yet at the same time, gays and lesbians were visible in their support of various aspects of the Republican struggle during those years. I can remember when my comrades and I were 'On the Blanket', word came into the prison about the thousands of people who were marching in support of us and our women comrades in Armagh prison. Those who marched were members of trade unions, Gaelic Athletic Associations and so on, but a number of gays and lesbians walked behind the banner, 'Gays and Lesbians Against Imperialism'.

That was many years ago now, but there have been opportunities for Republicans since then to show their support for, and belief in, the gay/lesbian struggle. Sadly that support has been in short supply. At the same time, I would acknowledge that messages of support have been sent by Sinn Féin to a number of gay/lesbian events over the years; that Sinn Féin has marched on Gay Pride Day in Dublin; and also that *An Phoblacht/Republican News* (the weekly newspaper of the Republican movement) has covered issues relating to gay/lesbian rights.

I have no doubt that there were Republicans who were lesbian or gay both before and after 1969. They just weren't visible, either out of fear or from choice. While 'choice' may have been a luxury, 'fear' was the greater force (and possibly still is for many). To understand this fear you have to realize not only the nature of the movement at that time but also the history of Republicanism during those years since 1969. The perception was that to be a Republican was to be Catholic, Nationalist and very much the upholder of 'traditional family values' as dictated by the Catholic Church. Homophobia has always been a factor in Catholic teachings, so it is no surprise that many (if not most) Republicans up until the 1980s, held those teachings to be 'right', irrespective of the fact that they were and are most definitely prejudiced, oppressive and blatantly anti-Republican. My experience of being gay within the Republican movement is one that is common to many – I hid, lied and pretended. I felt unable to deal with the consequences of coming out within the Republican struggle.

Today I can look back and understand why I was involved in the Republican movement: I wanted a better society, one that would guarantee freedom, equality, justice and peace for all its citizens. Growing up in Ardoyne, and like many of that community, I witnessed firsthand the oppression of the state against my people. My family was a traditional Republican family. Stories were told of the 1916 Rising, songs were sung about Irish history. My heroes were those men (typical of the sexist nature of my environment then) who had died glorious deaths for the Republic. I was brought up to believe that to become like these men I had to be a 'traditional' Irish Republican, and to be that, all I had to do really was to be a 'good Catholic' and I was 90 per cent there.

Yet, from about the age of twelve, I knew there was something going on that I was unable to put words on or understand clearly. My sexuality was developing, even though the only expression of sexuality that I could see around me was heterosexuality. There didn't appear to be any alternative. With a loaded sense of heterosexuality (but no real sex education either from family, teachers or the clergy) I have to admit I was becoming a very confused and worried young boy. I had two choices. I could tell my family and friends that I had feelings which were far removed from wanting to see one of the local girls after the the weekly disco (I wanted to see their brothers). Or I could suppress and deny the reality of my feelings and allow my confusion and frustration to rule my future. I chose the latter because I was unable to articulate, even to myself, what my feelings meant. Also, it was 1969 with plenty of excitement and just enough distraction in the daily riots and marches to take my mind off my own hormonal riots.

So, while I was fighting my own personal and political battles, the men and women who fought in 1969 at Stonewall sought to be treated as equals, to enjoy the same basic civil and human rights as everyone else in America. They were not prepared to accept merely minor reform of the law that had for so long been detrimental to their lives. They sought to achieve full and equal rights for their community. In the intervening years many people have struggled and some have even gone to prison. Although there is still work to be done, the accomplishments of gay and lesbian groups throughout the world is a testimony to courage, resilience and sacrifice. And just as those men and women at Stonewall took both history and their destiny into their own hands, so too did the men and women on the streets of my part of Ireland.

My life has been dramatically affected by both struggles. While I knew some of the background history of the Republican struggle, I was ignorant of lesbian/gay history. Indeed my involvement with gay/lesbian politics only began when I was in prison, after

I had been arrested, interrogated and charged with being involved in military operations as a member of the Irish Republican Army.

In prison I knew for sure that I was gay, yet I was afraid of the response of my family, my comrades and my friends to such a revelation. It was much easier to hide behind a façade of being 'one of the lads'. No one questioned heterosexuality, whereas homosexuality was, at best, frowned upon, and at worst, actively opposed (to put it mildly). I've learned much during my years in prison, and while I wouldn't recommend prison as an ideal place to learn, it did provide me with an opportunity to see the truth within myself. I realized that I must make the attempt not only to come out of the closet but, just as importantly, to discover and articulate the relevance of gay/lesbian liberation within the struggle for Irish national liberation. I began to read any gay/lesbian material I could get my hands on, and during this period came across an article in a magazine about Stonewall and the riots. I couldn't help but relate what I was reading to the struggle here in Ireland. It seemed to me that I could realistically argue for and articulate the right of gays and lesbians to be visible within the Irish struggle.

My coming-out was not an easy or smooth process. For a long time I had hidden my sexuality in prison. I became very close to a friend who was going through a sexual identity crisis. The nature of the prison environment did not allow for privacy or space. The prevailing mentality was to 'do your whack', 'big boys don't cry', and 'fruits and queers are sick'. As time went by, our friendship developed into a relationship of sorts. I was very much afraid and worried about the reaction of the other prisoners. There was a very real fear in my head that we would be put off the Republican wings of the prison if we were discovered.

I came under pressure within the prison – the whispers and nods from one person to the other; the innuendo; the accusations of 'touching up' other guys on the wing, of 'screwing' every new guy. I felt the stares, and recognized the whispers and smirks. Sometimes I cried alone in my cell. Eventually, a close comrade called me to his cell one day and asked me if I was gay. I looked at him and said 'Yes, I am'. Tears of fear and relief ran down my face. His reaction was 'Jesus, Brendí, I'm sorry. I didn't know. Why didn't you tell someone before now?' He was sorry that I had had no one to turn to in a situation that was both hostile and homophobic. He wasn't sure how to help. This was something 'new' to him.

Over the next two years or so things gradually became worse. I felt more and more isolated in the wing, even ostracized by some people. I would go down to the 'ablutions area', and men would leave their sinks, showers or urinals and stand a bit up the wing until I had left. Or I would drop into a cell and some of those already there would walk out. In desperation I contemplated suicide, or leaving the Republican wings of my own accord. Two options that I dreaded most and wanted least. When the camp OC (a prisoner appointed by other prisoners to act on their behalf) was made aware of the situation he gave me every support. I am extremely indebted to him and to the camp leadership since that period who have shown me respect and support. From then on other comrades began to challenge the homophobia within the wings.

Maybe one day I will thank my protagonists, as their actions forced me to stand up for myself and to actively promote and develop my view that the Irish struggle must, if it is to fully succeed, incorporate gay/lesbian liberation. I knew from my experience that there were those within the broad Republican family who would not subscribe to such a view. But I felt that as a member of that family I had a responsibility and obligation to myself and to other (invisible) comrades to fight for and speak out about gay/lesbian issues and the links I saw between them and the overall Irish struggle. So, I set out on a road of discovery and challenge.

I saw a letter in *An Phoblacht* from a group of gay men in Dublin and Cork, one of whom was Kieran Rose. I gained a lot from this initial contact. Kieran and others began to write and visit regularly, and they sent books, magazines and newspapers to the prison on a regular basis. I could develop my thinking a bit further, understand more clearly the links between the Irish struggle and the gay/lesbian struggle at home and abroad.

I wrote my first article, 'Hidden comrades: gays and lesbians in the struggle', with a lot of help and support from friends within the gay community and many comrades in the H-Block and Maghaberry prisons. It appeared in the winter 1991 issue of *An Glór Gafa* (Prisoner's Voice), the quarterly magazine written exclusively by Republican prisoners. It was the first time that a Republican, and a prisoner, had come out publicly as gay and put across the view that 'national liberation by its very nature incorporates gay/lesbian liberation'. The article gave me great satisfaction, and also pain. But I was delighted that at last the debate could start within the Republican family about gay/lesbian issues.[2]

Reactions to the piece were many and varied, ranging from blatant homophobia to solid support. I learned to challenge and overcome the homophobia, and to harness and develop strong support. The pain the article caused me came from a piece published in a Sunday tabloid which set out to vilify me. Insulting, derogatory graffiti appeared on walls near my family home, causing many problems for me with my family, most of whom were unaware that I was gay. But to have buckled under or retreated would have led to a life of self-pity and misery. As it is, I am now a more confident person in relation to my sexuality, and seek to further raise the cause of gay/lesbian liberation within the struggle in Ireland.

In the light of my experience with that article, I set out to try and move the issue further within the Republican movement. As a first step I felt that it was necessary to try and get a change in policy. The 1980 position (which was basically a one-sentence statement of support for gay/lesbian rights) was totally inadequate. Naïvely, I thought that it would be easy to get the support of enough men within the prison Sinn Féin Cumann (branch) to pass a motion to go forward at the following Ard Fheis. This was not possible. There were a lot of people still very fearful of anything that was seen to be a dramatic change from the norm, and to them gay/lesbian issues were not a great way to gain support for the movement. Indeed some felt that to take on the issue at all could mean the loss of support. In the end, after eighteen months or so, we did send a motion which was passed and adopted by the party. Some people did say to me that while they agreed in principle with the spirit of what I was proposing, they did not feel that the time was 'right'.

At the time of writing this article, the struggle in Ireland has entered a new and exciting phase. For the first time in our history a genuine opportunity exists to realize 'liberty, equality and justice' for all our people. It is my hope that in any new constitution which must be drawn up to prepare for this new era, articles will be incorporated which guarantee in law full rights and protection in all aspects of life for gays and lesbians in Ireland: from areas such as education to full and proper recognition of partnerships. We have seen the new South Africa set out on this road, and we must ensure that it becomes our reality as we move ever closer to the twenty-first century.

Although the struggle for gay/lesbian rights, like the struggle for Irish national self-determination, did not just start in the summer of 1969, it did lay building blocks for future gay/lesbian and Republican activists. Today both struggles are continuing, but there is a sense that real liberation is no longer just a dream, it is a visible reality that is almost within our grasp. The men and women who stood up for their rights in Ireland and in the Stonewall Bar can be proud that by demanding justice in 1969 they lit a flame which inspired and motivated many into action. Now, twenty-five years later, that motivation and spirit has given me and many others the courage and desire to play an active role in the cause of gay/lesbian liberation.[3]

Editors' note

The individuals whom we contacted to present the Unionist position were unable, because of time constraints, to contribute to this collection.

Notes

1.   From 1971–76 all prisoners held in relation to the conflict in the North were given 'political status', i.e. they were held in special compounds in Long Kesh Prison, wore their own clothes and had free association with each other. Their own command structures, were recognized by the prison administration and the British government. They were also not required to do any type of prison work. This situation was changed by the British government in March 1976 when all prisoners arrested and charged with any action on or after that date were/are now classed as criminals. The reason for this move was that the British had embarked on a policy of 'Ulsterization, Normalization and Criminalization'. Criminalization was to have a dramatic effect on those who considered themselves political prisoners and were now labelled criminals. Irish Republicans took the decision to challenge this denial of political status, and rather than wear the criminal

uniform demanded by the state they embarked on a protest in which they refused to comply with all and any rules of the prison which attempted to criminalize them. The result was that hundreds of Irish Republicans were confined to their cells naked, so they wrapped the rough prison blanket around their bodies: hence the term, 'On the Blanket'. Republican women who were in Armagh prison during this same period faced the same attempts to criminalize them, and they too participated in a similar protest for political status. These protests culminated in the hunger strikes of 1980 and 1981, in which ten of our comrades died.

2. This article was removed from the copies of *An Glór Gafa* sent to Republican supporters in the USA.

3. Though Brendí McClenaghan was originally sentenced to life imprisonment, he was released from prison on licence in December 1994.

Ghetto-blasting

Marie Mulholland

I RECENTLY took part in a radio debate with a gay male
activist from the North who contended that sectarianism does not
exist between lesbians and gays here. His rationale was that our
experience of sexual oppression, and the need to band together as
queers to survive it, made us somehow 'better than the rest of
society'. My radio protagonist was certain that, by virtue of our
non-conformist sexuality, we automatically held the freehold to
some acre of moral high ground. Hence, Northern Irish lesbians and
gays are immune to sectarianism. If this is the case, then perhaps
those who frequent some of the Belfast gay venues whose taste in
tattoos runs to primitive tribal slogans and logos such as 'Fuck the
Pope', 'Rem 1690', and Union Jacks proclaiming 'For God and
Ulster' would say they are merely asserting their cultural identity.
(Unfortunately for them, recent cases brought under the Flags and
Emblems Act have found these same symbols when displayed in the
workplace to be threatening, intimidating and sectarian.)

Yet, his belief in the infallibility of the oppressed is one which
I have heard in different circumstances on several occasions (framed
a little more subtly perhaps) since the cease-fire began in the North.
It can be condensed to: those who suffer are, because of that
experience, morally superior to those who inflict the suffering. This
blanket analysis provides a convenient evasion for all our individual
and collective responsibilities in perpetuating the oppression of
others. Such quick-fix arguments are the product of insular ghetto
politics, and indicate that we are transfixed by our pain, unable or
unwilling to broaden the context of our own experiences to include

the realities of others. It is a consequence of mutating the concept of community to a narrow one-dimensional view of who we are.

Community versus ghetto

Community plays a vital role in our survival. It is a coming together to consolidate energies. A nurturing place where we can draw comfort from one another, gain strength, formulate collective strategies for fighting back and gain the confidence and pride to be who we are. However, the flipside of community is the sole channelling of those energies inwardly and the directing of effort into defensively sealing ourselves off. Initially, this sometimes happens as a means of preventing assaults on our sensibilities and in some cases our lives. The desire is to protect ourselves, but the effect is to separate. With separation, comes an irresistible, unchallenged pull to see ourselves as a breed apart, disowning the society that views our difference as a disease, as a criminal act or a treacherous presence. Once we delude ourselves into the notion of being 'apart', we collude with all the efforts of the status quo to marginalize us, and then justify it by presenting our disconnection from an offending and offensive society as evidence of our moral superiority.

Ghetto-fever

As a Catholic-raised, working-class woman from the North, I have lived too long in imposed ghettos – economic, geographic and political corrals, controlled, censored and marginalized. As a lesbian, I have been made invisible – shunned and silenced in a hetero-patriarchal world. I have had two choices, if they can be called so, for neither of them is to my liking. I can remain in the constructed socio-political ghetto with other working-class Catholics, and be defined by my religious and cultural identity. Or I can immerse myself in a lesbian and gay ghetto to be defined by my sexuality.

Some years ago, I approached the gay owner of what was once the only lesbian and gay venue in Belfast about introducing live music performances to the monthly lesbian bop, only to be told that he would consider it, but that I was not to bring any 'rebel fiddle' music on to the premises. As a lesbian I was tolerated there, but God help me if I tried to be anything else. As a product of several ghettos, I can recognize the symptoms of ghetto-fever when they strike. When the social, political, economic and sometimes physical confines are so thickly enmeshed, and the holding of that little piece of ground which those restraints define becomes all-consuming, they give birth to the siege mentality. Full-blown, it stunts personal growth, imagination and the desire to soar beyond imposed boundaries. The struggle for survival degenerates into a rejection of anyone who is not one of 'us' and an obsession with apportioning blame, which overwhelms the impetus to engage in constructive strategies for change. Locked in our own company, stockpiling grievances, consumed by self-righteous anger and defensiveness, we scramble only as far as the top of the ghetto walls to hurl accusations and spurn the tedious, trying processes towards negotiation and bridge-building.

Suppressing difference

Community is further soured when, in order to maintain unity in the face of widespread vilification, we respond by insisting on uniformity, suppressing differences among ourselves in the mistaken belief that any dissent is a weakness in our collective armour. Suppressing those differences which exist is the same as actively discriminating against those who are different. It is a reality which the gay activist on the radio show refused to acknowledge. The early Women's Movement perpetuated the same offence when it attempted to define all women, regardless of class, race and sexuality, as an homogenous mass. We have also seen the tactic used by lesbians against those among us who would not conform to a prerequisite pattern of sexual practices.

It is an understandable fear that dissent will be manipulated by other forces to undermine our sense of unity. We are plagued by the evidence of past history and that of contemporary politics, which aptly demonstrates how powerful interests will always seek to divide and rule. But we make that possible by supporting the view that difference and dissent are something to be feared rather than embraced. Taken to its extreme, it results in the kind of homicidal purge witnessed in the mid-1970s when dissenters within the official Republican movement who attempted to create a new political platform for their Republican Socialist views were hunted down and assassinated by their former comrades. A more contemporary example, albeit less fatal (but within its own context, nonetheless vicious), is the feud between OutRage! and Stonewall in Britain. Both groups represent commendable initiatives to highlight the extent of homophobia in Britain. Given the task which they have to tackle, using very different but equally valid tactics, it is distressing to see them attack, deride and attempt to undermine one another with such venom in the gay press.

In the North today, the removal of a confining, violent backdrop has allowed people to shed some of their defensiveness and look beyond the besieged space we occupy. Voices of healthy dissent are gaining strength. Women in the North, who have been to the fore of anti-imperialist and pro-Republican activism, are clearly making independent demands of the peace process, redefining the politicians' cliched remarks about 'inclusion' to embrace a much more fundamental concept of equality for *all* marginalized and minority groups, including lesbians and gays. The need to align in 'one camp' or the other in the midst of adversity is no longer the pressing precondition to our survival here that it once was. We have shared an experience of inestimable pain together, we have given each other strength and clung together in fear, in desperation, in faith and in hope. Now that we can turn our faces to an open window, we must not be afraid to look in more than one direction.

The politics of the ghetto are not designed to extend beyond an immediate form of existence, because they are based upon a one-dimensional view of identity. It can only cater to a single uniform concept of who we are. By persisting with those politics we are recreating the very conditions which marginalized us to begin with, and in so doing we reduce human experience to the lowest common denominator, whether that be Catholic, Protestant or lesbian and gay.

In the North, the unity of a shared oppression within my culturally-defined community may have been enough to help us survive the onslaught of the last twenty-five years, but that alone is not enough of a basis on which to build a future with those of other communities. It is the conclusions we draw from our experience of struggle which will dictate the principles on which we base our future practice. That struggle has essentially been to have the same respect and value placed upon our needs and aspirations as is available to the majority in Northern Ireland. (Republicanism contends that this cannot fully be delivered within the confines of a statelet which was constructed to preserve the disparity of status between two communities.) We cannot, having struggled so long for something so precious and essential, then deny it to anyone else who suffers from its absence. There is no justification for withholding the same rights that we would have for ourselves because of perceived and or tangible differences between us and others. If we are to effect meaningful change which benefits more than the few, we must have a clear vision of the future we want to create. Vagueness only results in short-term, exclusive and essentially superficial privileges; the 'right' to shop till I drop in Soho may be the gay consumer's idea of heaven, but it is no utopia for the rest of us.

Justice and equality only become a reality when they are shared by everyone. Anything else is inequality and injustice. That is the conclusion which must be drawn from our own experience of oppression and struggle if it is to lead to a future built on real change. We can only achieve that if we are prepared to embrace the struggle of others who have yet to gain any ground or receive any recognition for their rights. And we can only do that effectively when we begin to address the issue of how we collude in oppressing others. We do it when we reject others who will not conform to our perceived notions of acceptability; when we adhere to political programmes which are not fully inclusive of the diversity throughout our community; when we insist upon the predominance of one oppression over another; and when we impose definitions on others not of their choosing.

Community: a vision of the twenty-first century

And watch that 'our', – make it as big as you can, it ain't got nothing to do with the barred room. The our must include everybody you have to include in order for you to survive.

Bernice Johnson–Reagon

I do not want to exist in a barred room or a series of barred rooms where only parts of me are welcomed and other parts are, at best, ignored, at worst, rejected. I do not want my cultural or political heritage to be ignored or denied within the lesbian or gay movement, nor do I want my sexuality regarded as a defect or an embarrassment by Republicans. I want to be part of an 'our' where all of who I am is not just accepted, but wanted. If I am to have that for myself, then I must contribute to creating the conditions which make every person with whom I choose to align myself feel wanted too.

Recent coverage of lesbians and lesbianism in the contemporary press and media has been applauded as progress into mainstream visibility. But far from presenting us as a natural part of society, the coverage has compounded the image of lesbians as an exotic phenomena, slightly risque and apart. The effect has been to pamper our presence as a chic addition to the fashion garden, but the underlying message is that we are best kept at a distance, lest we pollinate and breed unpredictable hybrids. Despite our new-found popularity in the glossy magazines and on Channel 4, the ghetto walls are still visible and unchallenged. We are newsworthy because of our apartness, not because we belong.

When we talk about fighting against the oppression which dominates our lives as lesbians and gay men, how compatible are our aspirations? Do we simply want the burden off our back, unconcerned about who else is weighed down? There are those who apart from their 'unconventional' sexuality would happily, once that stigma was removed, conform to all the other dictates of a society which is based upon the marginalization of those without power and who are classed as different. For many white gay men, in particular, their sexual proclivities present the only glitch in their otherwise conformist, conservative path through life. We may share a similar oppression, but our vision of the future may be at total variance. It is the presence of a shared vision which creates community on a scale wider than the ghetto-boundaries.

And the community I envisage is a community where we belong in totality. A community that is greater than the sum of its parts, because it embraces not only who we are but what we want to become. A community cemented by hope rather than adversity, engaged in communicating between itself and beyond. A community that learns from each other, listens to one another and is sensitive to the needs of all its constituent parts, that celebrates its diversity and which has the capacity to embrace dissent, not force compliance. My vision of the twenty-first century is of an Ireland of fertile ground where unpredictable hybrids bloom.

Glimpses

Suzy Byrne

AS the eldest of four children, I lived a very sheltered child-hood. I was shy and didn't make friends easily. I was bullied a lot because of my size, and because I was considered a 'know all'. I was also deeply unhappy at home and ran away when I was seven years old, only to be returned again in a squad car. At school I stayed a loner, and did not enjoy being young. I spent a lot of time at home because of my illnesses, and enjoyed watching TV and reading. In a house where the words 'that's not suitable' echoed loudly, I was not allowed to see the first Irish lesbian to appear on the *Late Late Show*.

In an attempt to escape my unhappiness I became very involved in my parish. I read at masses and became a minister of the Eucharist. It was a relief to get out of the house. I became attached to the rituals and feeling of belonging of the Catholic Church: it was somewhere I felt safe from the hatred and discomfort of home.

Leaving Ireland when I was eighteen was a daunting experi-ence. But it was exciting to be in control of my life for the first time, and London was, as expected, big, dirty and impersonal – perfect for getting lost in. I enjoyed my studies, made a few friends, but still didn't know what, if anything, was wrong with me. I was, I think, in a state of denial. I knew what I was when I read about other lesbians, but was troubled by what I knew to be Church teaching, and didn't feel that it was right. Compulsory heterosexuality was the order of the day, and I didn't know any lesbians.

I became involved in a lesbian and gay youth group and went for counselling, but still, like a typical Irish Catholic, I felt guilty. I did allow myself to fall in love though, a relationship which was to last for several years.

When I came home to Ireland, I went back into the closet. I was happy to be back, even if there was a secret in my life. I got involved in youth and church work, travelling to Lourdes with the sick on Dublin diocesan pilgrimages. I was slowly losing my attachment to the Church, but having difficulty finding something to replace it. The youth organization I belonged to in Dublin was under the patronage of the Archbishop. I pretended to be straight, but although I felt repressed living in Ireland, I couldn't leave. I was involved in two relationships at once – one with a boyfriend and the other with Cathy. I was still struggling with what was going on in my head and heart.

My involvement with youth politics happened almost by fluke. Seeing a leaflet about a National Youth Parliament, I went off to a weekend conference, which turned out to be a hot debate on many issues. I became absorbed in the topics that interested me, got elected to the governing body of the National Youth Parliament, and slowly separated myself from Catholic youth work. From this base I finally felt strong enough to question the Catholic Church on issues surrounding sexuality, divorce and the right to choose. I joined the Labour Party and worked on Mary Robinson's campaign. Thereafter, I became a political animal. To be honest, I had little else to do, being out of work because of a blood disorder later diagnosed as lupus. The illness had a strange effect: it sapped my energy, but made me more determined to make my mark.

I gradually became more and more comfortable with my lesbianism as my relationship with Cathy deepened. The word 'lesbian' rolled off my tongue, and I wasn't struck by lightning. Initially I watched the lesbian and gay movement from afar, reading *Gay Community News* (the national lesbian and gay newspaper) between the pages of the *Irish Times* on the way home on the bus. However, after attending a meeting of a lesbian and gay youth group as chair of the National Youth Parliament, I returned to the group the following week to declare my lesbianism.

Glimpses of a fairly silent revolution

There has been quite a bit written about the campaign for the decriminalization of homosexuality. I'm not old enough to remember how the situation prior to decriminalization really affected people's lives, in terms of arrests and suicides, but I was aware that criminalization did breed contempt and hatred among many. The small right-wing groups which had controlled the government line in the constitutional amendment campaigns of the 1980s frightened off any attempts to change 130 years of discrimination in relation to sexual relations between men.

I became involved in lesbian and gay politics when I joined the Gay and Lesbian Equality Network (GLEN), which was campaigning to repeal the criminal laws which affected gay men. Some think it strange that as a woman I should have prioritized this as a political issue. I have been told more than once that my so-called talents could be better used working solely on lesbian issues. My response was that this was an issue of human rights, and lesbian lives were being affected. Lesbians were less visible, hidden behind even bigger waves of lesbophobia and ignorance. Though I am a feminist, and proud of the term, my decision to work with gay men was not a rejection of my feminism. Things had to change for all of us.

Joining GLEN was like finding a 'home'. I saw real commitment and a belief in equality for all. There was a high level of professionalism in relation to the campaign, and no infighting (which was a rarity in my experience of Irish politics). Writing for *Gay Community News* and working with GLEN was part of my 'coming-out'. Walking off the streets into the heart of the campaign for law reform was a stroke of luck. I wanted to see things change, and felt that Irish people had shown by the election of Mary Robinson as President that they could think for themselves. The Church was losing its grip over people's lives.

After the general election campaign in 1992, in which the Labour Party won thirty-three seats, there was a new sense of hope. Standing in the National Concert Hall at a special conference convened to decide whether Labour would join a coalition government, I came out to the party but opposed the impending coalition on the basis of the poor track record of our prospective partner, Fianna Fáil. I invited Dick Spring, (Leader of the Labour Party and currently Minister for Foreign Affairs) to a meal, where I declared that I would eat my hat if decriminalization of homosexual acts was supported by Fianna Fáil deputies. It was an invitation I have yet to live down.

When the Labour Party entered a coalition with Fianna Fáil, I was hugely relieved to discover that the new programme for government contained a strong commitment to equality which was inclusive of lesbians and gay men. This relief changed to excitement in 1993, when the bill to repeal the laws based on the principle was introduced to the Dáil by the Fianna Fáil Minister for Justice, Maire Geoghegan-Quinn. The days of the debates in the Dáil and the Seanad still conjure up very happy memories, as we watched politicians speak in favour of full decriminalization, often employing phrases from the briefing notes we had supplied them.

On the first day of these debates, fundamentalists gathered outside the gates of the Dáil, reciting the rosary and imploring the legislators to save them from 'Sodom and Gomorrah'. Meanwhile we were inside, having drinks with two government ministers who had invited us into the bar to celebrate. After the bill was passed in the Dáil, Ruairi Quinn, Deputy Leader of the Labour Party and a Cabinet minister, turned to us cheering in the gallery and raised his fist in victory. Afterwards, I sent the Minister my hat with an offer to eat it.

Glimpses of the microphone

My evolution into a 'media dyke' was all part of my coming out at this time. There was no getting used to things, no gradual coming out or staying behind the scenes. I just went on the radio to declare myself as a lesbian and decided that I would use my full name. I was fed up with the pretence.

In many ways, my role as a media spokesperson involves steering the media hacks away from the myths and stereotypes. However, to get the message across, you have to respond quickly when stories break and to engage in debate with calmness and humour, even when you are dealing with some right-wing lunatic.

Not surprisingly, my decision to come out so publicly has involved a certain amount of personal cost. My relationship with my family has suffered because of my visibility, and I have experienced a lot of verbal, and some physical, abuse from homophobes. After an appearance on the *Late Late Show* (Ireland's leading TV talk show), I was kicked to the ground by three lads who recognized me and decided to 'teach the lezzer a lesson'. I also received a death threat, which has simply added to the mental anguish I felt after the attack.

A battle against time

While coming out as a lesbian, I have also had to face adversity brought about by illness. Recognizing the fact that I am a disabled person, and allowing myself to live with my disability instead of fighting against it, has proved harder than accepting my sexuality. However, meeting other lesbians and gay men with disabilities has led me to realize that all is not perfect in the lesbian and gay community. While lesbian and gay invisibility is slowly becoming a thing of the past, the invisibility of lesbians and gay men with disabilities is very much a reality of the present. What we are talking about here is double, or even triple, disadvantage, where lesbians and gay men with disabilities face prejudice from other gay people on the basis of their disability, and then face prejudice from some of the disabled people's movements in relation to their sexuality.

Glimpses of the future

Many lesbians and gay activists ponder whether a lesbian and gay community exists or not. Getting involved in gay community groups and organizations so soon after coming out, I suppose I do have a very clear sense that a community does exist. With the very positive changes in the law in Ireland, I feel this community will expand very quickly in the future. However, there is still a lot to be achieved. The lesbian and gay community is very diverse, and every effort needs to be made to ensure that difference is respected and diverse needs are met. Visitors to the country often express frustration at the small lesbian and gay scene, and wonder if anything has really changed on the ground. Yet things are changing rapidly and, with the law reforms in place, a huge energy is now being focused on building up our communities throughout the country.

My *wish list*

This book is about visions of the twenty-first century. I don't have a vision, but I do have wishes, and here they are in no particular order. I hope there will be no more distressed young people and that every young person will be educated to respect difference. I want to see a lesbian feminist elected to the Dáil. I want to walk safely in the streets with my partner. I want to see an Ireland where lesbians will not appear on the *Late Late Show* only to talk about being lesbian, but will appear to talk of all the other wonderful things they have done. I want 'out' lesbian politicians, judges, journalists, newsreaders and athletes. I want woman-owned and woman-run social venues. I want a lesbian Pope.

Part III
Arts and Culture

Oscar's Mirror

Eibhear Walshe

IF the personal is indeed political, then it follows that I reclaim the living presence of a lesbian and gay imagination in Irish writing precisely through those moments where, for me, literature and life collided. There is a powerfully inviting succession of homoerotic or 'queer' archetypes and images alive within Irish literature, but the process by which these archetypes and images revealed themselves to me was a gradual one. In this essay, I propose to explore these images by retracing the context in which I came to realize my affinity with them. I call this essay 'Oscar's Mirror', firstly because of an autobiographical incident of unconscious self-revelation and, secondly, to acknowledge how, in coming out, the meanings that stared out at me from the mirrors of Irish writing only then became fully intelligible and discernible. These meanings, the outline of Oscar Wilde's face in the mirror of Irish literature, will be my focus in this essay.

Without realizing why, I'd always been attracted to stories about people who were without power, marginal people who none-theless, in a spirit of crazy, doomed defiance, remade that very powerlessness into acts of resistance. Antigone, Quentin Crisp, Joan of Arc, Tosca, Oscar Wilde. Therefore, during frenzied last-minute Christmas shopping, one December afternoon, the sight of a brass mirror, with Oscar Wilde's face traced in the glass, seemed like a godsend. So I bought it and duly presented it to one or other of my bemused siblings, fondly imagining them to be both touched and honoured by the act. For some reason, the Oscar Wilde mirror has survived the ravages of time and now stands on a bookcase in my parents' house, a monument to unimaginative Christmas shopping.

However, in the course of coming out to my brothers and sisters some years later, it transpired that they took the purchasing of this mirror to be a heavy hint. They saw it as an encoded message that I, like Oscar, experienced loves that 'dared not speak their names' but, instead, was forced to buy kitsch little gifts, covert symbols of allegiance and affinity. I laughed it off at the time and told them that they were reading far too much into it, but now I'm not so sure.

Having decided to spend my time studying literature, and Irish literature in particular, I immediately ran up against problems of identification and of identity. What exactly was Irish writing? Writers like Swift, Goldsmith, Edgeworth, Somerville and Ross, Bowen, Shaw and Wilde were somehow not exactly Irish, more Ascendancy or even something called Anglo-Irish. The area of research I chose to work in was called Anglo-Irish literature, even though all of the writers had been born and bred in Ireland and wrote in Hiberno-English on predominantly Irish themes. It seemed to me that, for the Irish writer, there was a fundamental dilemma – what precisely do you call yourself, or, even more fundamental than that, what exactly were you? Elizabeth Bowen, born in Ireland into a family that had been in Co. Cork for over two hundred years, said that she felt English in Ireland but Irish in England, and that it was only while sailing across the Irish Sea that she felt at home. Lady Morgan, her predecessor, went one better and told everyone that she had been *born* on the Irish Sea! It was hardly surprising, therefore, that Joyce called Irish literature the 'cracked looking glass of a servant' (p. 25).

So where could the Irish lesbian or gay reader find reflection or even representation in the cracked looking-glass of Irish writing? Irish literature falls into two distinct historical periods, pre- and post-Celtic revival, and the period before Yeats and his cultural revolution is a barren place for the Irish lesbian or gay reader. Swift refers sarcastically, in *Gulliver's Travels*, to 'Those Politer Pleasures', while Maria Edgeworth, Sheridan Le Fanu and George Moore all feature lesbian characters in their novels, albeit as freaks, cripples and vampires!

It is only with the project of cultural nationalism (and the simultaneous emergence of the emblematic figure of Oscar Wilde) that the homoerotic become more possible, and at the same time, more threatening in the formulation of an indigenous Irish literary identity. Artists like Yeats, seeking to free Ireland from the control of the colonizing power, sought an independent and autonomous self-image, in opposition to the imperial culture. Therefore, Irish writing became vitalized by the challenge for renewed self-definition, and so did the lesbian and gay sensibility living within Irish culture. Yet post-colonial countries, like Ireland, have particular difficulty with the real presence of the homoerotic, because colonialism itself has a gendered power relation and, inevitably, casts the colonizing power as masculine and dominant and the colonized as feminine and passive. Because the homosexual is assumed to be a transgendered 'pretend' woman and the lesbian to be an unsexed 'pretend' man, lesbian and gay identity is acutely threatening and unsettling within a post-colonial culture like Ireland. The emergent post-colonial nation perceives the sexually different as destabilizing and enfeebling, and thus the lesbian and gay sensibility is edited out, silenced. So, in my studies of Irish literature from the late nineteenth century to the present day, I found little or no trace of lesbian and gay writing, little sense of a past or a present, or even a future, for a sexuality and a sensibility like mine.

Apart, that is, from Oscar Wilde. And there were two problems with Oscar Wilde, as far as I could see. Firstly, he seemed to be more English than Irish in his writing and, secondly, what he wrote was mainly light and frothy, Coward-like in its luminous, delicate irrelevancy. (This was before I read *De Profundis*, and before I began to reinterpret *The Picture of Dorian Gray* and to understand something of the true nature of Dorian's double life.) Wilde's significance, his meaning for me was, as yet, blurred and unclear.

Yet, as I began to discover from my reading of Irish history, lesbians and gay men were not exactly excluded from the formulation of cultural revolution, quite the opposite in fact. Close to the source of national pride and identity, the creation of an Irish Republic, there also existed traces of lesbian and gay writing, albeit veiled, screened and barely discernible.

In my primary school, a reproduction of the proclamation of the Irish Republic was placed above the blackboard in every classroom, next to the crucifix, and pen-portraits of the leaders of the

1916 Rising, key figures in the pantheon of Irish nationalism, encircled the text of the proclamation. Roger Casement, whose handsome features stood out in the ring of portraits, was also the author of something called *The Black Diaries*, a copy of which I found in our local library. This book caught my eye because the usual covers had been removed and replaced by heavy black cardboard, with an ominous-looking, handwritten card proclaiming the title. Intrigued, I took the book to the librarian to check it out, but she confiscated it, informing me that it was out of bounds for younger readers, and thus the book disappeared off the shelf. Only years later did I discover that these diaries contained a frank and, in many ways, disarmingly honest account of Casement's life, with daily expenditure and sexual encounters all accounted for in the same business-like manner.

Casement, knighted for his services to the British Foreign Office, was converted to Irish Republicanism after his experiences of Belgian atrocities in the Congo. His involvement with the 1916 Rising led to his arrest and trial for treason. It was during this trial that his diaries, dubbed *The Black Diaries*, were circulated by the British government. This was a strategy to ensure his conviction and execution by exposing the 'black' and unwholesome nature of his sexuality. Casement was subsequently executed and since then, controversy has raged over the authenticity of these diaries, with Irish Republicans expressing unhappiness with the notion that one of the bravest, most heroic leaders of the 1916 Rising might also have preferred, and even enjoyed (as the diaries tell us), sex with other men. From my point of view, Roger Casement, brave, enlightened, resolute, an idealist, is a gay forefather well worth reclaiming and celebrating.

Eva Gore-Booth, sister of the dynamic Constance Gore-Booth (revolutionary and government minister), was another suppressed figure from these stirring times, a lone voice that found expression for a lesbian sensibility through the dominant tropes of the Celtic Revival. The critic and novelist, Emma Donoghue, in her essay, 'How could I fear and hold thee by the hand' (Walshe, 1995), traces the course of Gore-Booth's life and her writing, and argues persuasively that she subverts and lesbianizes the poetry of her friend and admirer, Yeats, in poems such as her 1905 work, 'The Perilous Light'.

> The Eternal Beauty Smiled at me
> From the long lily's curv'd form,
> She laughed in the wave of the sea,
> She flashed on white wings through the storm.
> In the bulb of a daffodil
> She made a joyful little stir,
> And the white cabin on the hill
> Was my heart's home because of her.

Crucially, others of these revolutionaries were just as capable of expressing same-sex desire, even the most revered of the 1916 leaders, as the following poem by Padraic Pearse reveals.

> There is a fragrance in your kiss
> that I have not found yet
> in the kisses of women
> or in the honey of their bodies.
>
> Lad of the grey eyes
> that flush in thy cheek
> would be white with dread of me
> could you read my secrets.

'Little Lad of the Tricks'

Yet Ruth Dudley–Edwards (1977), Pearse's biographer, in her study *The Triumph of Failure* writes:

> he knew nothing of homosexuality. When he wrote of beauty he was inspired by the descriptions, so frequent and so elaborate, of characters in the old Irish sagas ... Pearse was an innocent and his lifetime quest for innocence, purity, chastity and perfection had blinded him to the instincts reflected in his poetry. (p. 127)

Compare this thinking with Ulick O'Connor's (1972) forthright assessment of that other Republican writer, Brendan Behan:

> He was also known to have bi-sexual tastes. John Ryan remembers he was quite open about this, defining the type he liked best: 'clean-skinned, fresh lads'. And Desmond MacNamara remembers that he would usually add to the statement 'Preferably working-class'. Brendan used to boast about it almost as if it was a new discovery he had made at borstal. He would refer to it mockingly as his 'Hellenism'. 'Brendan would get up on anything in those years', an IRA man put it to me. Another IRA officer remembers the shock he got when walking down Fleet Street after an IRA meeting in Jury's Hotel in the centre of Dublin and came across Brendan in an alley kissing a man they both knew well, a composer with left-wing sympathies, though he was not a member of the IRA. (p. 96)

All of these moments of discovery were important for me, the realization that nationalism, creativity and sexual dissidence were not always incompatible or excluding terms. But the most profound moment of connection, or even epiphany if you want to call it that, happened for me while I was pursuing post-graduate studies in Anglo-Irish literature and drama. As part of my study requirements, I had to take a course on the modern Irish novels, reading such writers as Sean O'Faoláin, Francis Stuart, Flann O'Brien and John Banville. Searching one afternoon for a Flann O'Brien novel, I happened to notice some old Heinemann editions of another novelist called O'Brien, one not studied or even mentioned in that absolute document of literary validation, our course booklist. The titles of her novels were beguiling in their almost excessive romanticism: *The Last of Summer, Farewell Spain, As Music and Splendour, The Land of Spices*. The last title in particular attracted me, so I checked it out and, instead of working on Flann O'Brien as I had been told to do, I spent the weekend reading my first Kate O'Brien novel.

Because I had never heard of her in lectures and seminars, I began reading the novel with a sense of unease and guilt, maybe she was a pulp novelist, the Patricia Scanlon of her day, far beneath the lofty heights achieved by 'real' novelists of the likes of Flann O'Brien and Banville. But as I read on, any sense of unease was soon dispelled, as the quality of Kate O'Brien's writing began to reveal itself: her cool detached control of narrative, the perception of interior life, her measured insight into the nature of desire. And then I read this passage: '*Two people were there. But neither felt her shadow as it froze across the sun. She saw her father and Etienne, in the embrace of love.*' (O'Brien, 1988, p. 157) That sentence, unexpected and unheralded in this cultivated, poised novel, hit me like a blow or a kiss. Here, at last, was a moment of homoerotic reality, an unequivocal recognition of my own truth. It was the shock, not of the unknown, but of the familiar, submerged.

Anger and curiosity drove me on to find out more about Kate O'Brien; anger because her work had been judged unworthy of inclusion in a course of studies on the modern Irish novel and thus kept from me; and curiosity to know more about the kind of writer who could produce such work. Throughout my time researching a doctoral thesis on contemporary Irish drama, Kate O'Brien's fiction became, to borrow David Hare's phrase, 'my secret rapture'.

I read her other novels, finding, again and again, subversion and dissidence within these clearly paced, civilized narratives. I searched out her critical writings, her essays, her biographical writings and grew to like very much this quirky, shrewd sentimentalist. I discovered that she was from Limerick (born in 1897), coming from a provincial, middle-class merchant milieu much like my own; that she had struck out early from Ireland, after university, working as a journalist for the *Manchester Guardian* and then as a governess or 'Miss' in Northern Spain; that she had married and then ended that marriage herself, after which she had become a novelist. I discovered, in addition, that she was quite a well-known figure in Ireland with people older than me, because of her broadcasting work and also because her novels had been banned. In 1941, the banning of one novel had led to a heated debate and wrangle in the Irish Parliament, the Dáil. The novel was *The Land of Spices*, and it was banned because of one offending sentence. That sentence was, I was delighted to discover: 'she saw her father and Etienne, in the embrace of love'. I was delighted because the Irish Censorship Board and I agreed on one crucial point – the overwhelming significance of that one sentence.

As I read more about her life and her writing, I discovered that battling against censorship and against silencing became something of a lifelong task for O'Brien. She loved Spain dearly, choosing a Spanish setting for her first banned novel *Mary Lavelle* (1936), and therefore, when the Spanish Civil War broke out in 1935, O'Brien had little difficulty in recognizing Franco and his Nationalists for what they were, enemies of personal liberty and of all she loved of Spain's courageous, solitary heart. Her attack on Franco took the form of a travelogue, *Farewell Spain* (1937), an imaginative journey, returning to all her best-loved places, historical figures, paintings and music, and wresting them from the appropriating clutches of Franco. She fought him with the only weapons available to her – memory, evocation and proud, possessive love. For her pains, she was barred from entering Spain by Franco when he emerged victorious at the end of the Civil War. *Farewell Spain* was also censored and O'Brien was now silenced in two Catholic, paternalistic cultures.

However her 1946 novel, *That Lady*, perhaps her most profound work, can be regarded as an ultimate repudiation of all these attempts to marginalize and silence her. A historical novel, set in sixteenth-century Spain, *That Lady* takes the real historical figure, Ana De Mendoza, as protagonist and sets her up in opposition to the authoritarian ruler, Philip II. Philip, in accord with his belief in the absolute power of the monarch, interferes in a matter of private morality concerning Ana, an influential noblewoman and his lifelong friend. The central scene in the novel concerns Ana's refutation of Philip's rule and her counter-assertion of personal liberty:

> There have been, Philip, as long as I can remember, thoughts and even acts in that private life, which, presented to the world, would seem to injure this or that. If I do wrong in it, that wrong is between me and heaven. But here below, so long as I don't try to change it into public life, I insist that I own it. (O'Brien, 1946, p. 236)

'I insist that I own it'. The essential freedom, the one basic require-
ment for any Irish lesbian or gay man, and already, in 1946, this
Irish writer had perfectly articulated this primal, necessary right
and, yet, her's had become a lost voice. O'Brien's later life, the loss
of earnings from her writing, her loss of critical and popular interest,
the novels, one by one, going out of print, the lack of interest in her
last, most openly lesbian novel of 1958, *As Music and Splendour*
(still out of print!), all of these facts depress any lover of O'Brien's
writings. The current popular and critical revival, although somewhat more encouraging, is long overdue.

My anger at being deprived of this voice, this mind, these
writings, pushed me towards finding out as much as I could about
our other Irish lesbian and gay literary forebears. And this led me to
that delightful confection called Micheál MacLiammóir. A friend of
Kate O'Brien, a leading figure in Irish theatre for over forty years,
actor, dramatist, writer and stage designer, Micheál MacLiammóir
was also, with his partner, Hilton Edwards, Ireland's only publicly
acknowledged homosexual. A strikingly beautiful man in his youth,
MacLiammóir kept his beauty alive (Dorian-like) with paint and
powder, and his face became a familiar, exotic presence on the
streets of Dublin, the avenues of St Stephen's Green and in the
drawing-rooms of the Shelbourne and Gresham hotels. When
MacLiammóir died in 1978, the President of Ireland attended his
funeral and offered his condolences to Hilton Edwards, as chief
mourner, and this in a state which criminalized homosexuality and
continued to do so for another fifteen years.

Yet MacLiammóir was, as I say, a confection, a name and an
Irish identity invented by an English actor, Alfred Willmore, who
had fled from Britain and British intolerance of 'Wildean Unspeak-
ableness' in the wake of the Wilde trials. Alfred Willmore reinvented
himself as Micheál MacLiammóir, learned Irish, conjured up a Cork
ancestry and childhood and carried off this, his greatest acting role,
successfully for the rest of his life. MacLiammóir and Edwards
founded the Dublin Gate Theatre, a theatre dedicated to the presentation of European experimental drama to a city dominated by
the Abbey Theatre, and, among other innovations, staged the first
Irish production of Wilde's *Salome*.

Wilde was to be an important figure in MacLiammóir's creative life, the subject of his one-man show, *The Importance of Being Oscar* and his volume of autobiography, *An Oscar of No Importance*. In many ways, Wilde provided MacLiammóir with a dramatic persona by which the carefully masked homoerotic within MacLiammóir's own imagination could express itself. After reading MacLiammóir's autobiographies, it seems to me that Wilde essentially empowered MacLiammóir in his gayness, gave him a mask, a persona in which to accommodate his dissident, differing sexuality. The achievement of MacLiammóir, the assuming of another identity and the successful living of an adopted dramatic role, is perhaps a more heartening story than that of his friend Kate O'Brien.

With the discovery of MacLiammóir came the discovery of other writers of his circle, novelists like Paul Smith and John Broderick, men who wrote of sex or love or loss between men at a point when our culture denied the existence of such sex or love, and institutionalized those who dared to make such matters public.

Side by side with this reclamation of lost voices from previous lesbian and gay lives is the living presence of a gay sensibility within contemporary Irish literature. Starting with Frank McGuinness's play, *Observe the Sons of Ulster Marching Towards the Somme*, numerous texts produced by contemporary Irish writers have emerged, articulating visions and imaginings of same-sex desire. Mary Dorcey's *A Noise from the Woodshed*, the *Tangles* project from the Theatre-in-Education company, Wet Paint, Emma Donoghue's *Stir-Fry*, Tom Lennon's *When Love Comes to Town*, the Muted Cupid lesbian and gay theatre project. All of these creative projects reflect a new confidence, a claiming of space and of expression for the contemporary Irish lesbian and gay imagination. Perhaps, above all, it is in the poetry of the Irish-language writer, Cathal Ó'Searcaigh (1993), that we see Oscar's face most strikingly reflected in the imaginative idiom of the contemporary. Ó'Searcaigh, using the Irish language, too long the whipping-post of reproachful cultural nationalism, imbues the homoerotic with the unexpected, fruitful resources of Irish poetry. It is with his poem, 'Ceann Dubh Dílis' that I look towards the twenty-first century, aware that the variety and vitality of our Irish lesbian and gay literary past survives and endures, paralleled by the living presence of our contemporary imaginings.

> A cheann dílis dílis dílis
> d'fhoscail ar bpóga créachtaí Chríosta arís;
> ach ná foscail do bhéal, ná sceith uait an scéal:
> tá ár ngrá ar taobh thuathal den tsoiscéal.

> My blackhaired love, my dear, dear, dear,
> our kiss re-opens Christ's wounds here;
> but close your mouth, don't spread the word:
> we offend the Gospels with our love.

'Ceann Dubh Dílis'/'My Blackhaired Love'
(trans. Gabriel Fitzmaurice)

References

Dudley-Edwards, Ruth (1977). *The Triumph of Failure*. London: Faber and Faber.

Gore-Booth, Eva (1929). *Collected Poems*. London: Longmans.

Joyce, James (1992). *Ulysses*. London: Penguin.

O'Brien, Kate (1946). *That Lady*. London: Heinemann.

O'Brien, Kate (1988). *The Land of Spices*. London: Virago.

O'Connor, Ulick (1972). *Brendan Behan*. London: Coronet.

Ó'Searcaigh, Cathal (1993). *An Bealach'na Bhaile*. Connemara: Clo Iar-Chonnachta.

Pearse, Padraic (1917). *Plays, Stories, Poems*. Dublin and London: Maunsel and Co.

Swift, Jonathan (1940). *Gulliver's Travels*. London: J. M. Dent.

Walshe, Eibhear (1995). *Sex, Nation and Dissent: Essays*. Cork: Cork University Press.

Noises from Woodsheds: Tales of Irish Lesbians, 1886–1989

Emma Donoghue

BROWSING in a second-hand bookshop in a Dublin suburb at the age of fourteen, I picked up a paperback with the word *Interlude* (Richards, 1982) in lurid pink letters on the cover. The first page began, 'Suddenly Martha realized that the assistant's hand was touching her breast'. It was not the first lesbian sex scene I had ever read; the sentence that shocked me was, 'Luckily, Grafton Street's old established stores still had decent fitting rooms, solidly made, with full length mirrored doors.' (pp. 13–14) Grafton Street? Not San Francisco or Berlin or some well-known city of sin, but the Dublin shopping street where I walked every other Saturday? I remember staggering out of the bookshop, weak at the knees, just as the book's heroine staggered from her cubicle. Suddenly anything seemed possible.

I could not buy the book, of course, because what if someone saw me, or if in this small city the bookseller happened to know my mother? In fact, I didn't come across it again till I had burst my last closet door at twenty-one, and this time I cackled my way through the novel's bra-bursting frenzies. But it remains an important book because it was written, it was published by an Irish press, and it was goggled at by fourteen-year-old Irish lesbians who could find nothing else that told them they existed. You take what you can get. What this memory teaches me is the importance of home-grown literature. Lesbian poetry and novels published by American and British feminist presses are sold in the occasional bookshop in Irish cities, but their impact can be rather deadened by the cultural distance they have to travel. *Patience and Sarah*, *Rubyfruit Jungle*, *The Work of a Common Woman*, *Légende*, *Oranges Are Not the Only Fruit* – I found these books early and gladly, and they suggested possibilities for lesbian escapades in other times and other places, but where was there to escape to on this cramped island? Foreign savours stimulated my appetite, but I hungered for the local. The wonderful surveys of lesbian literature I tracked down (by Jeannette Foster, Jane Rule, Lillian Faderman, Barbara Grier, Bonnie Zimmerman) had next to nothing to say about Ireland; they told me about the novels of Mary Renault, but not of Kate O'Brien. 'Irish lesbian' still had the ring of a contradiction in terms: how was I to conceive of myself as a practising Catholic and a furious lesbian feminist, a sweet colleen and a salty sinner?

This essay attempts to sketch out just one path along the terrain of Irish lesbian literature: fiction by Irish writers about love between women in Ireland. The poetic tradition – from Charlotte MacCarthy in the mid eighteenth century, to Eva Gore-Booth (1870–1926), to the modern work produced by (to name but a few) Nuala Archer, Nuala Ní Dhomhnaill, Susan Connolly, Máighréad Medbh, Mary Dorcey and Cherry Smyth – is not covered. Nor are plays by, for example, Honour Molloy, Louise Callaghan, Claire Ní Measc, and myself.

Being more concerned with the books we read than with their writers, this essay does not include those Irish women writers who were lovers of women (in varying senses), such as Anna Brownell Jameson (1794–1860), Frances Power Cobbe (1822–1904), Emily Lawless (1845–1913), Sarah Grand (1854–1943), Edith Somerville (1858–1949) and Martin Ross (1862–1915). Focusing as it does on Irish characters, this essay does not include the English, sexually ambiguous cross-dresser created by Maria Edgeworth (1768–1849) in *Belinda*, or the androgynous New Women that 'George Egerton'

(Mary Chavelita Dunne, 1859–1945) described in just about all her stories except the Irish ones. Nor can it make room for Joseph Sheridan Le Fanu's vampire *Carmilla* (1872), Maeve Binchy's hapless heroine in London's 'Holland Park' (1980), or Edna O'Brien's exile discovering erotic bliss with her Spanish chambermaid in *The High Road* (1988).

The reason I list everything I am *not* going to discuss is to show that – happily for us – there is quite a lot of Irish lesbian literature about, if we scratch beneath the surface of the canon represented by the Great Dead Irish Males who glower at us from mugs and T-shirts. All this essay attempts to cover is a century of fiction that in some way answers the question that haunted my teenage years: how is a woman who loves women to live as an Irishwoman?

At University College Dublin, after dragging myself along to the GaySoc's coffee mornings, I finally found some lesbian content on my English course. George Moore's *A Drama in Muslin* is about five well-off girls from Galway, who are about to leave their convent school to become the muslin-dressed martyrs of the over-stocked marriage market. Our sensible heroine Alice Barton's best friend is the fastidiously virginal and hunchbacked Lady Cecilia Cullen.

Influenced by the French tradition of lesbians as 'carnivorous flowers', Moore's characterization of Cecilia is hostile and lurid, but it is also refreshingly frank. From the beginning we are told that Cecilia's love for Alice is 'wild and visionary, and perhaps scarcely sane', and that even in their schooldays 'the intensity of this affection had given rise to conjecturing' (p. 3). 'Lover was never more anxious to meet mistress than this little deformed girl to see her friend.' (p. 53) Moore's explanation of lesbianism presents a rather frantic combination of theories: Cecilia's father was old and feeble when he begot her; her mother hated her father; feminism turned Cecilia against men; and, of course, her 'misshapen body' made her bitter (pp. 195–6, 187).

But Cecilia insists that she would never marry even if she were physically attractive to men, and that her devotion to Alice represents an informed choice. Metaphors of filth and damnation are used not by the narrator about the lesbian, but by the lesbian about heterosexuality. She begs Alice not to 'soil' herself (p. 185): 'your love for that man hangs about you like an odour; to me it is a visible presence and it revolts me.' (p. 301). When Alice starts getting to know men, Cecilia becomes paranoid with jealousy, and – with gnawing teeth and flaming eyes – insists that if Alice leaves her she will die (p. 185). In her final scene she admits the truth: 'Yes, Alice, I had desired more than God had willed to give me, for I desired you. I desired to possess you wholly and entirely.' (pp. 298–9) In giving up that desire, and doing penance for it, Cecilia is redeemed as a character, and allowed to become a nun and fade back into convent life.

George Moore was ahead of his time in seeing dangerous possibilities in female 'romantic friendship' in 1886, but by 1928, when Radclyffe Hall was taken to court over *The Well of Loneliness*, this suspicious attitude was the norm. For those Anglo-Irish novelists who looked to London as their barometer, lesbianism had a certain cachet as a theme, if carefully handled.

Typical is Molly Keane, whose novels (as M. J. Farrell) of the 1930s, 1940s, and (under her own name, after a long silence) 1980s, are sprinkled with lesbian moments. In *Good Behaviour*, which I read with great unease in my teens, the governess Mrs Brock conceives a 'senseless, star-struck passion' for her distant mistress, and stays up all night to knit her an exquisite wrap, feeling a 'raving desire for the moment when Lady Grizel's thanks and delight would overwhelm and satisfy her'. Bursting in at dead of night to announce 'I love you', Mrs Brock is told coldly, 'You must be over-tired.' (pp. 20, 38) Keane's men have sexual identities, several of them in each book being definitely and exclusively gay; her women, however, just have pathetic crushes, and lesbian sex never happens in Ireland. The only clearly lesbian character, the demonic Jessica of *Devoted Ladies* (1934), who expresses her passion by throwing bottles at her girlfriend's head, is a visitor from England.

Elizabeth Bowen treats the specifics of sexual identity rather more seriously than her friend Molly Keane, but only in one novel, *The Last September* (1929), does Bowen bring Ireland and lesbian attraction together. Hanging round her parents' country house on the eve of the Irish War of Independence, our school-leaver heroine Lois loses no time in falling for the glamorous English visitor, Marda

Norton (pp. 144, 146). She tries on Marda's mink coat, flirts with her, and stares at her long mannish back (pp. 112–7). When Lois hears about Marda's engagement she is disgusted: 'I hate women' (p. 146), she declares, but a little while later admits in confusion that she will always be 'a woman's woman' (p. 149). To avoid a troublesome suitor, Marda runs into an old mill, pulling Lois round the waist, and 'in an ecstasy at this compulsion' Lois follows (p. 185). But there is nowhere safe for them, no privacy for their exploratory conversation; the mill is held by a soldier of the Republican Army who shoots Marda in the hand. Soon Marda departs to civilized England, and Lois is left in the crumbling ruins of Anglo-Ireland, stroking the outline of Marda in the bed, 'as though since last night the pillow had not forgotten the feel of her head' (p. 210).

It cannot be a coincidence that on the two occasions when Kate O'Brien wrote clearly about lesbians, the stories were set at a distance, on the Continent. *Mary Lavelle* (1936) was one of her two novels to be banned as 'obscene' by the Irish Censorship Board; it has been presumed that the offending passage occurred at the point where the Irish governess, Mary, demands that the married son of her Spanish employer should deflower her, but O'Brien's explicit validation of Agatha Conlon's love for Mary must have scandalized the Board too.

Agatha is introduced as 'queer' (p. 84), acidic and blunt, with the fanatical, noble, boyish face of your average sexual deviant. She is thirty-eight, having escaped from Ireland when she was twenty-one; unlike the other 'Misses', she has not clung to her Irish identity, but has learned Spanish and blended into the culture which offers her more freedom than Co. Wexford did. She is still a pious Catholic and is several times described as 'nunnish' (pp. 97, 100), which seems to operate as a code word for lesbian; what keeps her from being a nun, she explains vaguely, is her 'evil nature' (p. 207). But this is not a rerun of *A Drama in Muslin*, with the frustrated lesbian being absorbed into the Church. What Agatha is fanatical about is not Catholicism, but the bullring. Invited along, Mary is exhilarated but revolted by it; when she says it must be a sin to watch a bullfight, Agatha laughs and says, 'Not for me, until the Church says so.' (p. 119) This may be a hint that on some level she is aware of her queerness, but unwilling to feel guilty about it until the Church specifically tells her to. But finally, in the confession box, a priest tears away her illusions. Hearing that Mary is about to go home to Ireland, Agatha blurts out her new-found knowledge as they sit opposite the cathedral steps:

> I like you the way a man would, you see. I never can see you without – without wanting to touch you. I could look at your face forever . . . I knew it was wrong; but lately I've been told explicitly about it in confession. It's a very ancient and terrible vice.

Mary reacts without horror; she says she is sorry, and tries to comfort Agatha's conscience by telling her, 'Oh, everything's a sin!'

Agatha ends the novel in quite a strong position. Though her passion for Mary is unfulfilled, and she is planning to 'settle into old age' (at thirty-eight!), she has decided not to take the Church's word for everything, especially not about what her priest calls 'the sin of Sodom'. She asks Mary for a photograph as a keepsake, explaining. 'It can't be such a ghastly crime to – to think about you.' (pp. 297–8) So Agatha doesn't get the girl, but she doesn't end up dangling from a lightbulb either.

At the end of her career, when Irish censorship was easing up, Kate O'Brien allowed herself to return to a lesbian theme. Her last novel, *As Music and Splendour* (1958, and due to be reprinted by Virago in their Modern Classics list), is set at a safe distance in place and time, but is more celebratory than *Mary Lavelle* in the central place it gives to a lesbian relationship. We meet Clare and Rose at sixteen, in a Parisian convent of the 1880s, lonely for the families and homes they have had to leave behind in Ireland. Only more than halfway through the story, when the readers should be fully involved with both heroines as they become professional singers in Rome, does O'Brien reveal that Clare has been in love with her Spanish friend Luisa as far back as the convent in Paris.

Clare is described as cool, reserved, almost nunnish (p. 189); again, O'Brien makes 'nun' stand for 'lesbian'. Her scenes with Luisa are subtle without being coy, full of unfinished sentences and kisses on eyelids. When Clare's gloomy suitor, the failed priest

Thomas, guesses the truth, Clare explains the situation with no self-hatred or essentialist theories: 'Easily I might have loved you . . . But – she caught my heart before I knew what was happening, Thomas. And I think she's lovely, and I love her. I can't help it. It's true.' (p. 211) In her quiet lines Clare makes some extraordinarily powerful statements – even a painful, generous defence of Luisa's need for other lovers (pp. 211, 195) – not found in most lesbian fiction till the 1970s. But Thomas sees it as a schoolgirlish crush, and explains (in the language not of his pre-sexologist 1880s but of Kate O'Brien's 1950s): 'Your development has been delayed.' O'Brien makes Thomas a figure of fun by giving him ludicrously homophobic lines like, 'You pale, self-loving ass! You – you stinking lily, you!' (p. 209) Never losing her temper, Clare resists his labelling of her as 'amoral', and turns his weapons against him:

> Certainly I am a sinner in the argument of my Church. But so would I be if I were your lover. So is Rose a sinner – and she knows it – in reference to our education and faith. . . . We are so well instructed that we can decide for ourselves. (p. 207)

Clare's relationship with Luisa breaks up after a year and a half, because of the pressures of absence, Luisa's other lovers, and being closeted; but loss is not presented as a direct consequence of lesbianism. The reader is left with a vivid impression of their time together – radiant Sunday mornings peeling peaches, snatches of opera – and the heterosexual triangles in which Rose is involved sound dull by comparison. A 'Catholic agnostic' herself, according to one of her long-time companions (Reynolds, 1980 p. 118), Kate O'Brien took seriously the Catholic consciences of her heroines, but Clare comes across as no more angst-ridden than any heterosexual heroine when she accepts the life of a 'bohemian', exiled from Ireland (pp. 253, 343).

The Northern novelist Janet McNeill created a platonic lesbian character in *The Maiden Dinosaur*, a novel I am rather glad I did not come across in my teens, as it might have turned me off the whole business. Set in pre-Troubles middle-class Protestant Belfast, the 'dinosaur' of the title is Sarah, who has spent forty-five years in thrall to her exploitative friend Helen, since schooldays when 'the

sight of her leapt out across a hockey pitch or class-room' (p. 8).
Sarah is mocked by the author for her ambitions as a poet, her pupils
who have crushes on her, her bulky plainness, her bulging gloves
which make her look like 'a female impersonator' (p. 18). She has no
desire for a consummated relationship – a traumatic early glimpse of
her father and his mistress having scared her off sex (p. 49) – and so
McNeill can fuse the cliches of lesbianism and sterile virginity.
Though their more well-read friends wonder about Sarah and Helen
(p. 59), Helen wants nothing but flattery from her reliable old friend
(p. 66). There is no suggestion that they will ever turn their friendship into a fulfilling relationship, and so lesbianism is presented as a
dead-end. Even at the end of the novel, when Sarah manages to
break free from Helen, all she can think of to try is a weary affair
with Helen's last lover George. This has been read as the escape of a
sexually repressed woman into fertile life, but it makes no sense to
me except as a transparent device for pleasing the reviewers.

From the mid 1960s to the early 1980s – times of sexual
revolution in this society, so we were told – Irish fiction generally
continued to give the impression that such things never happened on
our island. In 1982 came *Interlude*, the first account I have found of
lesbian sex occurring within our borders. I forgive Maura Richards
all her inanities, her apportioning of orgasms to each character's
'furry friend', just for that. In earlier novels Ireland represents the
pure, strict heartland, and 'abroad' is where risky sexuality can be
explored. By contrast, Richards's perspective as an Irishwoman
settled in married life in England allows her to see Ireland with new
eyes, as a place for wild holidays and forbidden interludes. In this
nostalgic exile's vision – don't I know it well myself? – Ireland can be
criticized and praised simultaneously. Martha finds the atmosphere
of dirty old Dublin unique: 'The total hopelessness of its efforts to
pull itself together tugged at the heart strings.' (p. 61) Because it is
hopeless, they need not try to change it, or to challenge the hatred
they see on the faces of a young married couple who pull their
children away from the kissing women (pp. 58–9). Sheila tells
Martha, 'pretend we're foreigners here' (p. 60); by embarking on a
lesbian relationship, they have become resident aliens.

When the pressure in Dublin gets too bad, Sheila and Martha
escape to a borrowed cottage in Galway. Here they can swim in icy

lakes, rhapsodize about turf fires, glimpse an old Gaelic-speaking lesbian-feminist ghost (p. 98), and listen to trad sessions, holding hands only when the lights are down (p. 108). In one hilarious, unbearable scene, Sheila is speaking Irish to a local farmer; she reacts calmly when he admits that his only lover is his dog, but he freaks out when she says she prefers women. 'Seán Og got quickly to his feet, then there was a kind of hissing breath as he exclaimed, "*Ainm Dé*", and then he spat on the floor. "Unnatural woman!" he shouted in English.' (p. 112) What is fascinating here is the shift in languages. The mild curse 'aimn Dé' (in the name of God) can be spoken in Irish, but Seán Og the dog-fucker can find no words in Irish bad enough to name lesbians. Or perhaps it is truer to say that he will not let their terms into his native language; the unnatural women are exiled into English.

Finally, *A Noise from the Woodshed* (1989), the book of stories that won Mary Dorcey the Rooney Prize, fell into my hands like a gift the year I was coming out in college and needed to know that 'lesbian writer' was not a limiting label. Lacking the space here to analyse the precision of her imagery or the wit of her wordplay, I want to concentrate on one aspect of her stories: place.

Dorcey avoids both the geographical cliches: that lesbians can be free only in an urban subculture, or only in a picturesque cottage. 'The Husband', for example, is a meticulous account of Sunday morning in a married couple's Georgian town house, on the morning when she leaves her husband for a woman. 'A Country Dance' moves between Grafton Street and a rural hotel near the sea; 'the lads', with their mixture of drunken wheedling and lesbophobic violence, are drawn with chilling accuracy. Dorcey's women are rooted in real places and moments that are sharp with delight and danger: 'I have remembered where we are,' thinks her narrator; 'a Friday night country dance, surrounded by drunken males who have never before seen two women dance in each other's arms.' (p. 55).

The settings are most powerfully contrasted in 'Introducing Nessa', where Dorcey opposes Nessa's lesbian-feminist commune in shabby 'flatland' Ranelagh with Anna's plush nuclear-family house in the suburbs, and links both settings with the Dublin seafront where the lovers walked on their first night together. The heroine of another story, 'A Sense of Humour', plans her escape from drudgery in her parents' country pub as soon as she realizes 'the trivia of place'. All she needs to do is to hitch a lift from one of the cars 'going from here to somewhere else' (pp. 42–3).

But what happens when she gets there? Dorcey's speakers only half-believe in place; they linger in the embrace of their particular 'circle of hills' until the grip gets too tight and they have to declare their disbelief in place and come away. If there is a refuge, it is the decaying old house described in 'A Noise from the Woodshed', where one idyllic day at a time can be snatched from business and battle. This experimental story is so erotic that the lines about love-making cannot be separated from the lines about mending roofs, and are all washed into the uncounted rhythm of women's lives. Each place seems to exist on symbolic as well as literal planes, and Dorcey slides us between them with ease. No sooner have we established, for example, that the protagonist ('you') is walking across a river without galoshes, than the river turns out to be the river of life, but if we try to read the whole thing as an allegory it slips back into gritty realistic detail.

The big house the rescuer invites 'you' back to is in a shambles – half-roofed, full of animals and dirty dishes and half-written symphonies – yet it has nothing of the grim decay of Anglo-Irish novelists' Big Houses. This one is just big enough for all the love-making two women can do in it, 'raising vegetables and hell, living off the fat of the land and each other's' (pp. 13–14). At intervals throughout this odyssey, 'you' and 'she' hear a noise from the woodshed. What 'she' and 'you' finally find in the woodshed are two women making love in a sleeping bag; the sound is one 'you' suddenly recognize because 'it wasn't, after all, for the want of hearing it' (p. 16). This sound that cannot be recognized until heard from someone else's mouth being, in my own case, the voice of Irish lesbian fiction, which I could not hear until I had come out, come away, far enough away to hear what was behind me.

Since Dorcey's ground-breaking collection, fictional Irish-women have been kissing other women all over the place. Linda Cullen's *The Kiss* (1990), June Levine's *A Season of Weddings* (1992), Pádraig Standún's *Cion Mná* (1993, disappointingly watered down in the author's translation as *The Love of Women*, 1994), and my own *Stir-Fry* (1994) and *Hood* (1995). These recent publications come from women and men, writers based in Ireland and abroad, writing in both the country's languages, published by feminist, Irish, and UK-based presses. There is no one source; our well of loneliness has become a Burren full of streams, some loud and above ground, some still trickling away discreetly, but all adding to the wet.

My vision of the future for Irish lesbians, gays and bisexuals (that rarely mentioned but undoubtedly large group among us) is simple: I hope we learn by other countries' mistakes.

Haven't we all felt on occasion – especially when we come back from Britain and the USA, laden down with flashy badges and magazines – that queer Ireland is trying to catch up with elder siblings? Our Pride marches are still tiny, our numbers of out spokespersons still painfully small. But the leap from Victorian repression to a truly equal age of consent in 1993 showed that it is possible to skip the adolescent hesitance and blunders of other countries.

The first thing I'd like to see us avoid is becoming identical to other les/bi/gay cultures; I hope we hold on to our own. When I listened to Zrazy play at the Michigan Womyn's Music Festival in the summer of 1993, suddenly I was not just another tourist feasting on American 'women's culture'; I was a visitor from a faraway, distinctively flavoured lesbian nation.

The second mistake to be avoided is timidity. The slow rate of progress in other countries shows us that if we don't demand rights – as Donna MacAnallen did when she took her Cork employers to court for unfair dismissal in 1994 – we will never be offered them on a plate. All to the good if we can retain a likeable public image as a community within Irish society – but not if it means playing the happy, placid court jesters. Just as queer writers are now rejecting the pressure to churn out 'positive images', so we should not be afraid to name the negatives, show our anger, make a noise.

Mistake number three, as I see it, is the urban ghetto. Dublin has an unhealthy prominence in Irish society anyway; the last thing I'd like to see is all the queers migrating there, or to Cork, or to Belfast, just as so many of the past few generations have fled to New

York and London. We give up too much if we give up our homes. I'd like to see local Pride celebrations in every town by the end of the century. I want to read and write fiction that brings it all back home – to our villages, our suburbs, our own places.

Fourth on my personal list of don'ts is the generation gap. This is mostly an invention of the straight-dominated media: journalists love a conflict, and articles about 'Lesbian Chic', for instance, often set up a catfight between what they see as the young lipstick generation and the old dungarees generation. But many of my friends own dungarees, many wear lipstick, and several do both. Of course, there are immense differences between Irish queers – gaps of gender, class, age, politics, tolerance of the closet, sexual preferences, and styles – but I hope we won't let the media polarize us into warring camps. If we learn from each other's experiences, we will save so much time.

I was too young to stay up and watch the *Late Late Show* in 1980 when Joni Crone became the first out Irish lesbian to give a TV interview, but I heard about it later (as a kind of oral 'creation myth'!) from women who came out as a direct result. When I did a similar interview myself in 1993, and walked on rather shaky legs back into the RTE hospitality room, I was called to the phone, and it was Joni. Rarely have I felt such a connection down a phone line; I was suddenly anchored to the undersea dyke world again.

I suppose what I'm trying to say is that 'history' is not a luxury for arty types, nor just a vague feeling that we queer folk have been around a long time. It is crucial advice, passed from one generation to the next. Scrabbling around in libraries for glimpses of our history and literary heritage is just as important as the more obvious kinds of activism. Knowing our past brings confidence, wisdom, an ability to laugh at our enemies and ourselves. I want to see our crucial stories passed on, not just in academic seminars, but via newspapers, radio and TV, as well as in daily gossip. We are not a modern fashion, we are not alone in history: spread the word.

Acknowledgments

Some of this material first appeared in *Graph: The Irish Literary Review* (1991) and *Ordinary People Dancing: Essays on Kate O'Brien* (ed. by Eibhear Walshe, Cork University Press, 1993). A longer version of this essay will be published by Onlywomen Press in *Volcanoes and Pearl–Divers* (ed. by Suzanne Raitt).

I have put together a series of exerpts from the wider expanse of Irish lesbian literature for the forthcoming fourth volume of the *Field Day Anthology of Irish Literature*.

References

Bowen, E. (1928). *The Last September*. London: Constable.

Dorcey, M. (1989). *A Noise from the Woodshed*. London: Onlywomen Press.

Keane, M. (1982). *Good Behaviour*. London: Abacus.

McNeill, J. (1984). *The Maiden Dinosaur*. Dublin: Arlen House.

Moore, G. (1981). *A Drama in Muslin*. Gerrards Cross, Bucks.: Colin Smythe.

O'Brien, K. (1936). *Mary Lavelle*. London: Heinemann.

O'Brien, K. (1958). *As Music and Splendour*. New York: Harper and Brothers.

Reynolds, L. (1986). *Kate O'Brien: A Literary Portrait*. Gerrards Cross, Bucks.: Colin Smyth.

Richards, M. (1982). *Interlude*. Dublin: Ward River Press.

Artist–Activist

Louise Walsh

I WAS brought up in a small village in County Cork. As a teenager I was saved from the notion of homophobia by the appearance of Joni Crone on the *Late Late Show* in 1980. She was the first Irish lesbian to came out loud and clear on Irish national television, claiming her space with humour, honesty and dignity. Although I had no idea that I was queer myself at the time, her appearance raised questions for me regarding the negative representations of lesbians and gay men that were prevalent at the time. I'd seen one on the telly, and she was brilliant!

However, it wasn't until the following year, when I'd left my parents' house for good to go to art college in Cork City, that I met the real thing face to face. The Quay Co-op, a large building with a café and resource centre, supporting all sorts of alternative and gay-friendly activities was being established on Sullivans' Quay in the heart of the city. At the core of the Co-op at that time was the Women's Place, where the first ever lesbian group in the city formed.

That first Women's Fun Weekend happened in 1984. On that occasion the entire Quay Co-op building was given over to the event, while a large hall was hired for the Saturday-night cabaret and disco. It was a huge event for the Cork women to organize, but they pulled it off. Women travelled from all parts of the country. Like a lot of women in Cork I found the idea of going to a cabaret of all-women performers, having days of women's films, discussions, workshops and card games, totally mind-blowing! I identified as heterosexual at the time, but as I watched all these women dancing together, celebrating and flirting in this wonderful atmosphere I knew something quite important and powerful had happened. A strong open lesbian community had rooted itself in Cork, and this was a celebration that was destined to become a yearly event for the next eleven years.

I remained in Cork for the next four years to complete my studies. My life evolved around the art college, the Co-op and Loafers – a really friendly gay bar that still caters for a fine mix of queers and straights. Given this queer-positive environment it is surprising that when I left Cork to do an MA in sculpture in Belfast I still hadn't identified myself as lesbian.

When I moved to Belfast the H-Block hunger strikes and deaths were not long over and the Anglo-Irish Agreement was about to be signed. 'Ulster Says No' slogans were everywhere. I was forced to look at a lot of things that living in the South of Ireland had allowed me to ignore – Partition, colonization, occupation, majorities, minorities. I was looking at Irish identity and trying to make sense of it all. I was also finally admitting that I was a dyke, and at least that realization made a lot of sense.

Belfast seemed to be a hive of feminist groups and activities. As time went on I slowly involved myself more in the women's community there, helping to organize events like the International Women's Day celebrations; working with *Women's News* and joining the Lesbian Line Collective as a volunteer on the helpline. I found the women's community in the North welcoming and supportive. I also kept up my ties with Cork, and travelled regularly to the Women's Fun Weekend with gangs of Belfast women.

In 1988 *Women's News* applied for and received funding from Co-operation North, an organisation that supports cross-border, two-way projects to promote understanding and make links between groups North and South. The idea was that each group could travel and meet with people in a similar organization. *Women's News* had applied for money to exchange with a group of women based in the Women's Place in Cork. The aim was to share the information and expertise the Belfast women had in publishing with the Cork Women's Group.

As we set about organizing the trip, we realized that there was plenty of room in the minibus, so it was suggested that Belfast Lesbian Line use the opportunity to link with the Cork Lesbian Line. In order to make a real weekend of it, Lesbian Lines in Dublin and

Galway were also asked to participate. Derry was the only group that could not attend.

The meetings of the publishing groups and Lesbian Lines were held simultaneously in the Women's Place in the Quay Co-op. I attended the Lesbian Line gathering, which lasted the whole day – there was so much to talk about. As we spoke it became clear how isolated we all had felt as groups working on helplines in such small lesbian communities. (For instance, in Galway there were only about twenty or so out lesbians living in the city.) We discussed a range of issues: how to run volunteer training programmes; difficulties with basic funding and premises, and how draining this was; problems separating from gay men's helplines; befriending women when there were only alcohol-related events available; homophobia from other women's groups; and the biggest problem of all, letting women know we existed, when in some cities, local papers refused to even take an advertisment for the service. We made many important decisions on policy and strategies for survival during these few hours, one of which was to affiliate with the Council for the Status of Women, (the main umbrella body of women's organizations in Ireland), to avail of the support and recognition this powerful women's lobby group could give. However, Belfast Lesbian Line subsequently found that their status as a Northern Ireland group excluded them from membership. We also decided that we needed more meetings and would apply to Co-operation North for funding to facilitate further Lesbian Line exchanges. Cork and Belfast were the first two groups to begin that process.

Later on in 1988 there was another gathering of Lesbian Lines. This was based on the applications that Geraldine McCarthy and Lorraine Stefani, from the Cork and Belfast Lines respectively, had put to Co-operation North. It was decided that we'd have the first meeting in Galway to support and encourage the emerging Lesbian Line there. This meeting happened in November and went very well, with a particularly important workshop on 'Alcohol Abuse and Lesbians' that challenged everybody's perceptions of our socializing patterns and led to discussions about the practice of befriending women in pubs.

The second part of the exchange was organized to coincide

with the International Women's Day celebrations in Belfast in 1989. Remember that these women went nowhere without a party, but were working hard on improving the Lesbian Lines at the same time. Geraldine and Lorraine put together excellent reports and submitted them to Co-operation North at the end of the year. Not long after this, it was announced that Lesbian Line Exchange had won a prize to be jointly shared with a Women's Traveller Exchange under the section 'Women's Links'. We were delighted with this news as the Co-operation North prize-givings were always well covered by the media, and it seemed like a solid way to achieve public recognition, respect and further funding. It was also a valuable way to reach women with no positive images of lesbian existence or community. Unfortunately, homophobia meant that this was not allowed to happen. Other prizewinners under the community care section were Aids Alliance Helpline in Dublin, who had twinned with Carafriend (a gay men's helpline) in Derry. The fact that two of the prizewinning groups were queer or affiliated to gay groups seemed to cause major embarrassment to some at the upper levels of Co-operation North, and although certain sections of the organization had been extremely supportive, there was a big move to try and suppress the public nature of the prize-giving.

Instead of the usual launch to promote the following year's programme, which featured the award ceremony and a big press luncheon, at the last minute someone decided to hold the prize-giving in a separate closed session with no press invited. The promotional launch continued with the press in attendance and without the winning groups. The same thing happened at the Belfast launch. Some journalists discovered and commented on this hypocrisy. Mary Holland wrote an excellent article in the *Irish Times*, exposing and condemning Co-operation North's behaviour. Other newspapers made mention of it. Needless to say, it left a very bad taste in the mouths of the women who had worked on the projects.

However, travelling, networking and organizing among lesbians around the country continued to evolve and blossom. The population of 'out' lesbians all over Ireland expanded dramatically year by year. In 1989 I moved to Limerick, and was involved in setting up a Lesbian Line that is still operating there, alongside the Gay Switchboard (which was set up in 1986) and a more recent

Transvestite Line. These helplines have continued without any government funding, and are run by volunteers who have to fundraise locally in what remains a tiny queer community in Limerick. Yet since their inception, the Switchboards have logged well over 4,000 calls.

There are now small tribes of lesbians living in rural areas like West Cork, Co. Kerry and Co. Clare, and I believe that the more events and activities that exist for emerging and returning dykes to enjoy, the easier it is to remain in this country and carry on creating an environment we want to stay in.

My favourite women's event in Ireland has to be the Women's Summer Camps. These gatherings have formed the backbone of my lesbian community here, and I cherish these weeks with women and children in the Irish countryside. These annual gatherings began in 1988 as the Galway Women's Summer Camp, and gradually evolved into the Irish Women's Summer Camp, the first of which happened in Co. Limerick in 1994. It offers lesbians a safe and cheap holiday, a space where we can relax and celebrate, getting to know each other outside the pub or club atmosphere, free from the restrictions that dominate our everyday lives. We sit up at night by the fires swapping stories and songs, learning new tunes and dances for the ceili. Together we share the work of maintaining the campsite and the land and playing with the kids. There are lots of workshops and discussions, all out in the fresh air. Of course it often rains – but you get over that and build shelters.

I have been involved in all the camps in one way or another. For me it is a vital source of energy and inspiration. I love the space where children are welcomed, where rural and urban women get a chance to gather together, organize and party. It feels like the debates, connections and ideas generated here have really fed and strengthened our lesbian culture.

For me, being a dyke, making a choice to desire, and be sexual with, another woman is an active sexual decision, one which may be seen as a dangerous position to adopt in a country where even pregnancy outside marriage is seen by many as an offence. Yet for the majority of women who claim their right to sexual freedom in a climate of oppression there is a sense of solidarity between outlaws. I think to be an out sexual heterosexual woman in Ireland is almost as subversive as identifying as queer. Maybe this is why lesbian separatism is fairly uncommon in Ireland. Events that are organized by lesbians with mainly lesbians in mind are actually open to all women: for instance, the Cork Women's Fun Weekend, the Wild and Wonderful Women's Weekend in Dublin, International Women's Day celebrations in Belfast and the Women's Summer Camps. I suppose a lot of lesbians in Ireland have had experience of how other organizations try to dictate just how we should think, and act, what we should or shouldn't desire, to such an extent that many of us would not use the politics of sexuality to exclude women open enough to affiliate with us. We need each other to defend our basic rights together.

Another important aspect of the Irish lesbian community is that it manages to encompass internal differences a bit more success-fully than they do in other countries. I'm not sure why this is. It may be that by identifying as lesbian in this country we are placed so far outside, made 'other' to such an extent, that we can't afford to split off into factions. It's not as if we could describe lesbians in Ireland as a homogeneous mass; there are real rural/urban divisions, partic-ularly between Dublin and other parts of Ireland. Partition also divides us, giving us vastly different experiences, as does religious background, disability/ability, class and colour (contrary to popular belief lesbians of colour live here too). A large number of non-Irish lesbians (mostly English) live in Ireland, as do many dykes with kids, and of course women who identify as bisexual.

I was trained as a sculptor and for a while made a series of large sculptures from wood and found objects which were a series of half horse, half female figures. I found that after a while, I needed to change that formula, to communicate more succinctly and directly. I decided to work with photography, installations and video, while still using sculptural techniques if it seemed appropriate.

My artwork deals directly with the experiences of being female in Ireland. These experiences are diverse and shifting, but when making art the primary need for me seems to be to bear witness. My subject would often be my feelings, perceptions and beliefs. Being lesbian is part of my identity and informs my creativity, but isn't the constant subject or sum of all of my work. Creativity is a kind of present you give to yourself and to others. It is a re-presentation of something. It can give joy or be confronting, hopefully making the viewer really feel or connect with some emotion, provoking someone to think or discover something that they hadn't experienced in that way before.

In 1987 I collaborated on a visual art project with Pauline Cummins, whom I'd met via WAAG (Women Artists' Action Group). What started out as a small performance project between the two of us ended up involving two years of work together and led to an installation entitled 'Sounding the Depths'. It was first shown in the Irish Museum of Modern Art in Dublin. We knew we wanted to work on the feelings we shared as women trying to live in Ireland. We had always found ourselves to be in defensive positions. But now we wanted our work to have a space in which we were free to explore ourselves – not to be held in, just trying to survive – a space where we could thrive.

The installation existed as a journey through three rooms. It's hard to describe this work. It was meant to be experienced as a progression that went from a hard, closed off place, through fear of opening, and finally into the room that expressed the power of being open. Working entirely collaboratively, we used images of our mouths projected onto our naked bodies, like a wound. In the video the wound/mouth opens, but with difficulty. It's scared. Then it begins to open wider and to laugh. The final images are of large female figures finding, exposing and discovering, then letting loose their power. A soundtrack of women's laughter reverberates around the room.

Pauline, an artist who also works in mixed media, lives in the country with her husband and children. Working with somebody whose lifestyle is so different from my own was a very affirming and positive experience. We laughed so much while collaborating on this work, yet the images we made together were very sexual, describing a human being evolving for herself, reclaiming her body and her wild power. She is not shown as an object for the consumption of the viewer, but busy about her own desire.

In 1989 I won a commission from the Department of the

Environment in Belfast for a figurative sculpture on the theme of prostitution in the city. The brief they provided for the artists was awful, suggesting the use of caricature in the approach to the subject. In developing my own submission, I came up with what I thought was the solution to a very offensive brief: I would use a mother and daughter theme to explore the issue of women and low pay. The mother would be represented as a house-wife, the daughter as an unskilled low-paid worker (given that the ten lowest paid jobs in Northern Ireland are done by women). The figures would be cast in bronze, each one having everyday objects symbolizing their work embedded into the surface. Babies' dummies for earrings, shopping baskets as stomachs, scissors, typewriters and hairdryers. Details about rates of pay and other statistics about women and low pay would be embossed onto the surface.

Instead of producing a ridiculous sculpture that insulted women who work in the sex industry, my aim was to link issues concerning the oppression of women to prostitution. I entitled the piece, 'Monument to the Unknown Woman Worker', as a joke on all the sculptures dedicated to men and war. Unfortunately, a politician interpreted the piece as a monument to prostitution and contacted the media to voice his disapproval. The sculpture was misrepresented before it was even made, and due to a complicated set of manoeuvres involving the Department of the Environment in Belfast and the Belfast City Council, the commission was withdrawn just as I was beginning work. However, it was later re-commissioned by a private company and now stands in a more public spot overlooking Amelia Street in the centre of Belfast city.

The first artwork I made which specifically explored lesbian and gay themes was completed in 1991 when I was asked to take part in an exhibition to be held in Kilmainham Gaol, the site of the execution of the 1916 rebels by the British. The aim of this exhibition was to commemorate the seventy-fifth anniversary of the 1916 Rising. Artists were asked to explore the theme of national identity.

Part of the 1916 proclamation of independence 'Guarantees religious and civil liberty, equal rights and equal opportunities to all its citizens. ... Cherishing all the children of the nation equally.' Over the entrance of Kilmainham Gaol is a Celtic knot of snakes representing the serpents of crime restrained by the chains of justice and law. Yet the Irish government continued to break the European Convention of Human Rights as the Irish state upheld antiquated English laws that criminalized and oppressed Irish gay men and lesbians. I found snakes to be an interesting metaphor while exploring notions of Irish identity. The serpent is the ancient symbol for creativity, rebirth, sexuality and power, but more recent Irish legend denies their existence, depicting snakes as banished, ugly things, squashed under saints' feet.

I found myself thinking about those chains, about punishment, of snakes, of struggles for personal as well as political freedom both past and present, and of visions of the future. I made a light box featuring photographs of two men kissing and two women kissing, and projected snakes onto their faces like tattoos. The light box was hung in a cell. I also made a series of floor tiles using an entwined snake pattern outlined in relief, which I placed under glass at the threshold to the room. Although my snakes were under the surface I wanted them to be visible, numerous, struggling and unchained.

In my artwork and in my experience of teaching at art college, I identify strongly as an Irish woman who wants things to change for us. As a lesbian I demand to be heard, respected and accepted for who I am. As an artist I want to express, explore and reflect the lives we live. The situation has changed so much in the last few years. I experience excitement and anticipation rather than fear when I talk with my gay and lesbian friends about the future. I am always interested in the stories people have: it's both important and inspiring to hear and celebrate these lives and to commemorate them in some way.

One of my visions for the future is that we would have a lesbian archive and oral history project. Lesbian lives have not been recorded because there has been so much institutionalized oppression of women and of our sexuality. Even if women had been in a position where they didn't feel threatened by disclosure or discovery, there was nowhere to lodge or collect their experience. I want a place where this information can be housed and made available. Irish lesbian culture is expanding. It is an important, exciting and evolving phenomenon. I want it to be honoured and kept safe for the future generations to build on. Our present and future should be respected and given the space it deserves to develop and grow as a valued part of Irish heritage and culture.

Part of my vision of Ireland is already happening as I write this. We have a continuing cease-fire, and the hope for peace has never been so strong. One cannot talk of visions for the future without cherishing peace in our island as the starting point for an Irish utopia. Lesbians in Ireland have been networking across the border for quite a while, struggling to evolve private and public solutions to imposed boundaries against our national identities and to see a possible end to a war that has inflicted a collective wound.

Recently during the Women's Camp held in Co. Limerick there was a discussion about setting up land for lesbians and women in this country. This is something that I am interested in working on for the future. There are so many women, all with different visions, who are determined to make this land come into being. A group has been set up called Talamh na mBan (Land of Women) which is in the process of obtaining charitable status. The primary aim of the group is to secure a site for the Irish Women's Camp, as it's been a hard slog every year to find space that is safe for women and children.

I've always been committed to staying in Ireland. I've never really considered emigrating. There is something really strong and hopeful holding me here, even if sometimes Irish society and aspects of the culture drives me crazy. I feel plain stubborn about it. If people who have a strong commitment to justice and equality for women and lesbians stay here, I believe we can effect positive change. Lately I feel that this position has been paying off in terms of real social change.

Lesbian culture in Ireland is rich, and it's alive and kicking. Through travelling together we have formed strong organizational structures throughout the country which have evolved out of an atmosphere of exuberance and pride. I look forward to more of the same.

Acknowledgement

I would like to thank Geraldine McCarthy for helping with the Cork Lesbian Line's chronology.

Part IV
AIDS

Prelude to a Vision:

The Impact of AIDS on the Political Legitimacy and Political Mobilization of Gay Men in Ireland

William O'Connor

THE uncertainty of AIDS provokes many a vision, ultimately based on a subjective relationship to the epidemic. Such visions have their usefulness, but I feel that any conception of the future of AIDS and its relevance for the gay community must be of a more pragmatic nature. It is for this reason that I have declined the opportunity to speculate here on the future of AIDS. Instead, I have examined what we know about the impact AIDS has had on the Irish gay community up to this time. Even in this, the restrictions of space have required that I confine my analysis to the political impact of the epidemic. To this end, I hope to elucidate some of the ways in which AIDS has affected both the political legitimacy and the political mobilization of gay men in Ireland. Such an analysis is not unrelated to the creation of visions, for in order to envision the future we must first understand what has already gone before.

AIDS and political legitimacy

Others have outlined the growth of gay community throughout the West in the latter half of this century (Weeks, 1977; D'Emilio, 1983; Adam, 1987). Crucial to such development has been what Weeks (1988) has described as 'a secularization of moral attitudes', 'a liberalization of popular beliefs and behaviours' and 'a greater readiness to value and respect social, cultural and sexual diversity' (p. 12). In societies such as the UK or the USA, where these trends have been widely experienced, the rise of the gay community has been relatively less arduous than in other societies such as Ireland, where social change, at least until the late 1970s, was remarkable only for its tardiness. Up until the 1980s, Ireland had successfully fought off the tide of social change which swept through other Western countries. For gay men – and the possibility of a gay community – this had the effect of maintaining attitudes and beliefs which were, for the most part, incompatible with recognizing and accepting sexual diversity.

Rose (1994) has pointed out that 'it was the fundamental economic and social changes that had taken place in Ireland since the 1960s that allowed social movements such as the lesbian and gay movement to establish themselves' (p. 10). However, while significant groundwork was done in the 1970s, through the establishment of groups like the Irish Gay Rights Movement (IGRM), it was the rapid social changes of the 1980s which forced Ireland to finally abandon its protectionist stance and accept, mainly for economic reasons, that its future lay within the bounds of pluralism, when any real potential for an open and out gay community and open and out gay men began to emerge.[1] Thus, while the Criminal Law (Sexual Offences) Act 1993, combined with other legislative provisions,[2] represents one of the more enlightened laws in Europe pertaining to homosexuality or sexual orientation, the journey to this stage has been somewhat different to other Western countries. By the late 1970s, gay men in most Western countries had achieved some sort of sexual citizenship, and many were by that time campaigning to extend this to include civil, political and social rights for gay men. In Ireland, however, gay men still lived under the spectre of draconian legislation which criminalized sex between men, and we were thus confined to the level of fighting for the repeal of laws which forbade us the right to demonstrate our affection for, and attraction to, other men.

When AIDS first emerged, and media coverage and public opinion zoomed in on the presumed connection between the epidemic and homosexuality, gay men in jurisdictions which had awarded them some class of sexual rights were fearful that AIDS could prompt a retrenchment of their sexual citizenship and force them to return to the furtive and surreptitious existence which had characterized much of gay life in previous eras. Their efforts, then, were concerned with sustaining the sexual rights won before the emergence of AIDS. In Ireland, however, where no such sexual citizenship had been awarded to gay men, the implications of AIDS were of a different nature. It was likely that AIDS could have been used to preclude the attainment of sexual citizenship in Ireland, for why would a society decriminalize an activity which it perceived as responsible for spreading a 'fatal' disease? Why would the Irish government abolish the 1861 Offences Against the Person Act and the 1885 Criminal Law Amendment Act, when in other countries such laws were being touted by conservative elements as exactly the type of regulatory public health policy that was needed to protect the 'general population' from AIDS?

With these questions in mind, the subsequent repeal of both the 1861 and 1885 Acts is indeed an extraordinary event. The successful decriminalization of gay sex, during a time when presumably hostility towards gay men has been at its greatest,[3] offers an insight into how AIDS has affected the legitimacy of the gay movement in Ireland. It can hardly be argued that AIDS has had an adverse impact on the gay movement, when many of the legislative gains have been accomplished during the time of AIDS. However, neither is the impact of AIDS so uncomplicated as to allow one to assume that it has had a purely positive influence on gay legitimacy. There are numerous examples from other countries which show how AIDS has been used against the gay movement, especially in campaigns for the decriminalization of gay sex. For example, in *Bowers* v. *Hardwick*, a Federal civil rights challenge against the Georgia State Sodomy Law in the USA, AIDS was used to justify the criminalization of homosexual sex in the State of Georgia. In this case, the Attorney General of Georgia, Michael J. Bowers, argued that the Georgia State Sodomy Law was legitimate because of 'the relationship of homosexual sodomy in the transmission of Acquired Immune Deficiency Syndrome . . . and the concomitant effects of this relationship on the general public health and welfare'. Also, in a similar case to repeal the Texas Sodomy Law, an amicus brief filed by 'Dallas Doctors against AIDS' argued that the statute be upheld because 'sexual activity in homosexuals produces much more disease ... than ... among heterosexuals' (Barnes, 1989, p. 708).

Why then, given that the USA has a far better record on gay rights than other Western countries, did Irish legislators not make better use of AIDS in an effort to avoid decriminalization or, once compelled by the European Court of Human Rights to change its legislation on homosexuality, to shape the type of legislation enacted? There are certain aspects of the epidemic in Ireland which could have prevented the government from using AIDS in an effort to avert decriminalization. Firstly, public anxiety about AIDS, while wholesale in Ireland, had not reached the level of moral panic which characterized much of the public response in the USA and other Western countries. Moral panic is often used to justify drastic policy decisions, especially where private behaviour is curtailed in the interest of 'public health'. Perhaps public reaction to AIDS in Ireland was not strong enough to justify the use of AIDS to retain the laws which criminalized gay sex.[4] Secondly, it may have been unjustifiable for the government to invoke AIDS in an attempt to prevent decriminalization due to the substantial differences that existed between the epidemiology of AIDS in Ireland and its manifestation in the USA. The proportion of gay men infected with HIV in the USA has, on occasion, been used to rationalize the breach of personal liberty, for example when gay bathhouses were closed in San Francisco in October 1984. The differing epidemiological pattern of the epidemic in Ireland, in contrast, offered little justification for using AIDS to avert decriminalization.

In addition, there was sufficient research available which pointed to the role which decriminalization could play in preventing the further spread of HIV among gay men in Ireland. The Gay and Lesbian Equality Network (GLEN), which led the campaign for decriminalization, was quick to employ AIDS 'as another reason for abolition, not retention, of our laws' (Robson, 1991). The group based its claim on international research, such as that conducted by Kippax *et al.* (1992), on the importance of gay community in the prevention of HIV transmission among gay men in Australia, which demonstrated that 'men in contact with others, via attachment to gay community – sexual, social or cultural/political – are most likely to have changed their sexual practice' (p. 116). GLEN argued that rather than precipitating the further spread of HIV, decriminalization would facilitate better education on HIV among gay men, by making it easier for men to be more open about their sexual behaviour and identity.[5] On this point GLEN also had the support of the World Health Organization, which had recommended that governments abolish all oppressive laws relating to homosexuality to expedite the easier delivery of HIV education to men who have sex with men (Resolutions of the World Health Assembly, 13 May 1988 and 19 May 1989, in Robson, 1991).

Allied to these issues was the positive effect AIDS has had on the visibility of gay men and the recognition of the gay community, a phenomenon acknowledged by Altman (1988):

> Although the AIDS epidemic has occurred in a period when social conservatives have been politically dominant in most Western societies – increasing the stigma against homosexuals and homosexuality – it has also translated into much greater recognition of the homosexual community and a homosexual movement, in most Western democracies. (p. 301)

There is considerable evidence to support this hypothesis. Firstly, as noted earlier, media coverage of the epidemic has frequently promoted a link between homosexuality and AIDS. While such publicity has on occasion been injurious, inciting hatred of, and violence against, gay men, it has also, enigmatically, produced a greater recognition of homosexuality (however 'abnormal' or 'diseased'). Secondly, the cultural response of the gay communities of the West to AIDS, *vis-à-vis* film, art, theatre, literature and music has also played an important role in increasing the visibility of gay men and of the issues affecting gay men in the time of AIDS. Thirdly, and perhaps most importantly, the commandeering of the multifarious roles of education, prevention, care, support and activism by gay men and lesbians[6] in the development of AIDS service organizations has brought us into contact with government agencies in a manner which would have been inconceivable in previous eras. Altman (1992) has pointed out that such contacts have enhanced both gay visibility and gay legitimacy by forcing 'governments to deal with gay movements and openly gay individuals to an unprecedented extent' (p. 38). Together these factors have led to increased visibility for the gay community in Ireland which, in some circles, has also led to increased legitimacy for the community and our campaign for equal status.

I don't wish, however, to infer that AIDS has provided the sole motivation for the government to decriminalize gay sex but, rather, to clarify the influence AIDS can sometimes have on the achievement of gay political objectives. AIDS has, at best, assisted gay law reform. At the very least it has not hindered Irish gay men in our campaign for equal status. What is important here is that we as gay men do not shy away from AIDS in our struggle for political legitimacy. However difficult it is for us personally, politically it can be useful. There will always be bigots who will attempt to use this epidemic against us. Understanding the way in which the epidemic can benefit us could give us the upper hand in future political endeavours.

AIDS and political mobilization

AIDS has created the impetus for the mobilization of gay men throughout the West (Altman, 1986; Kayal, 1993; King, 1993). Especially in the larger urban centres, AIDS has led to a proliferation of community involvement in AIDS service organizations and AIDS political endeavours by men concerned that something was happening to their bodies and their communities. In a climate of inveterate government indifference towards AIDS, gay men have attempted to fill the 'caregiving void' (Padgug and Oppenheimer 1992, p. 261) by setting up community-based organizations to deal with the epidemic. Through these organizations, gay men have translated confusing epidemiological reports into successful safer-sex campaigns to help prevent further spread of HIV. In addition, they have successfully nurtured and supported people with HIV and AIDS, when many who were trained to do so declined because of fear or ignorance. As Roger McFarlane, Executive Director of Gay Men's Health Crisis (New York) in the mid 1980s, recalled:

We started off trying to find services to which we could refer people with AIDS ... we discovered that we had to create them for ourselves ... we were forced to take care of ourselves, because we learned, that if you have certain diseases, certain lifestyles, you can't expect the same services as other parts of society. (Altman, 1986, pp. 84–85)

In Ireland too, AIDS has led to the growth of community-based organizations to deal with the epidemic. Beginning with Gay Health Action (GHA) in 1985, lesbians and gay men spearheaded the Irish fight against AIDS. With paltry financial resources, GHA provided a comprehensive range of services, in addition to lobbying political parties and monitoring media coverage of AIDS issues. However, while GHA remained in existence until 1990, from 1987 much of the energy of the gay community went into the creation of more generic AIDS service organizations, such as the AIDS Alliances or Cáirde, which provided services both to the gay community as well as to the wider population.[7] In addition, particular events like the Irish Quilt tour have depended heavily on the energy and support of the lesbian and gay community.

However, while there has been substantial involvement by Irish lesbians and gay men in the fight against AIDS, one should not conclude from this that AIDS has led to widespread political mobilization of the gay community in Ireland. It is true that a section of the community has confronted the challenges posed by AIDS, but it is also undeniable that the vast majority of gay men have been quite apathetic to the demands of the epidemic. As with the campaign for law reform, which depended on a band of committed and identifiable individuals for its success, the response to AIDS has relied heavily on a small proportion of the Irish gay community. Especially outside Dublin, the feeling that it is the same men who constantly rise to community tasks is not uncommon. While community-based endeavours of all types face recruitment problems, the response of Irish gay men to AIDS is particularly disappointing, especially when compared to the response of gay men in other Western countries. Some characterize this lack of involvement as a simple 'failure to act' (Philpott, 1994), but I believe that there are particular reasons why

AIDS has not produced, in Ireland, the same level of political mobilization which it has in other countries.

Central to any comprehension of why Irish gay men have been relatively politically unmotivated by AIDS is an understanding of how both gay identity and gay community are socially constructed. While this article does not afford any in-depth analysis of the social constructionist thesis, the following argument is based on the theory that the development of a gay identity and community in any society is dependent on specific social, cultural and historical forces within that society. Thus, it is unfair to compare political mobilization in one society with another without examining the particular factors which influence the political mobilization of gay men in either society.

One such factor relates to the state of political mobilization among Irish gay men before the onset of AIDS. While gay organizations did exist, the numbers involved were quite low, primarily because of the great stigma attached to homosexuality in Ireland (due, in large part, to the teachings of the Catholic Church). In addition, although the laws which criminalized gay sex did not relate to 'being homosexual', they were surely a source of discouragement for those who had considered becoming more politically active. Compared to other Western countries, gay community infrastructure in Ireland at the onset of AIDS was quite underdeveloped, and while this has improved significantly during the epidemic, we still have quite a limited gay infrastructure, especially outside Dublin.

The second factor relates more to the physical impact of the epidemic in Ireland, that is, the numbers of gay men either living with HIV or AIDS or who have died of an AIDS-related illness. The number of gay men directly affected by AIDS in Ireland is considerably lower than in other Western countries and it is the sheer number of gay men affected in other countries that perhaps constitutes the prime motive for political mobilization. Furthermore, the changing status of the disease, from one which killed very quickly to one with which people affected could live for several years, has also influenced the potential for political mobilization. Wachter (1992) has highlighted that, in the USA, the discovery of HIV as the likely cause of AIDS and the subsequent availability of the HIV antibody test 'provided tens of thousands of men with evidence of their impending mortality'. He points out that 'people with newly diagnosed HIV seropositivity, who were usually asymptomatic, were imbued with a passion that comes only from seeing oneself at proximate risk' (p. 129). Epstein (1991) echoes Wachter's theory and argues that

> People who test positive on HIV antibody tests know that they have several years of outwardly normal health – years in which activism is not only feasible from a physical standpoint, but seems eminently practical from a political or psychological standpoint. (p. 42)

Taking such arguments into account, it is understandable why the motivation for political action is far greater in societies such as the USA than in Ireland. In the USA, the numbers directly and indirectly affected by HIV and AIDS has led to the bridging of 'the gulf between the movement and the subculture' (D'Emilio, 1992, p. 262), a dichotomy which has been central to the problem of recruitment of gay men to political endeavours in Ireland. Of the USA, D'Emilio observes:

> The epidemic elucidated, in a manner that movement rhetoric could not, the continuing strength of gay oppression ... many had to admit how marginal and despised they were, despite the class or race or gender privileges they enjoyed. (pp. 262–3)

On this point, Altman (1986) also highlights that

> Whereas earlier rallying points required a certain perception that homosexuality was a political issue, a perception resisted by many gays, AIDS is literally a life or death issue that can affect every gay man, no matter how wealthy, powerful or closeted. (p. 103)

However, although there hasn't been widespread mobilization of gay men in Ireland in response to AIDS, the commitment of some gay men to AIDS organizations and AIDS political endeavours has had a number of positive effects for the Irish gay community.

D'Emilio (1992) has observed of the USA that through AIDS 'the 1980s have witnessed ... the spread of the [gay] movement to parts of the country that had barely been touched by it in the 1970s' (p. 266). In Ireland, similar developments have taken place. While AIDS organizations have grown up in areas such as Dublin or Cork where there had been some gay infrastructure previous to AIDS, they have also developed in cities like Limerick and Galway where, previous to AIDS, gay infrastructure was scant, if non-existent. While not attempting to label bodies such as AIDS Help West or Limerick AIDS Alliance as gay organizations, it is clear that they do provide a much-needed forum for gay men to meet and thus contribute to the development of a gay community in these areas. AIDS, then, has had the effect of broadening the development of gay community to parts of Ireland where, previous to the epidemic, gay communal endeavours had been relatively scarce.

While problems with political mobilization remain, there are some signs that the situation is improving. In Cork, where there has, in recent years, developed a division between the gay community and the AIDS Alliance, significant developments are under way for the creation of a more overtly gay AIDS organization. Dublin, which has had the benefit of the Lesbian and Gay Health Caucus since 1990, has been active in providing encouragement for the development of similar groups in other centres across the country. In addition, law reform may hold the key to more involvement of gay men in political endeavours, by bridging the gap which exists between the movement and the subculture. The large numbers present at the 1993 and 1994 Dublin Lesbian and Gay Pride marches would seem to support this theory. Nevertheless, I do fear that recruitment problems may prevail until the numbers of Irish gay men affected by AIDS necessitates the kind of mobilization visible in other countries.

Conclusion

In conclusion, then, it seems that AIDS has had differing effects on our political lives. It would appear that AIDS has not adversely affected our political legitimacy. However, in comparison with other Western countries, our community remains relatively politically unmotivated by the epidemic. But it is difficult to draw conclusions when forced to rely upon one's own impressions or loose comparisons with other Western countries. If writing and researching this article has made one thing plaintively clear, then it is how little we know about the epidemic's impact on gay men in Ireland. This article goes some way to rectifying this shortcoming, as will the forthcoming needs assessment which is being undertaken by GLEN and the Department of Health (GLEN, 1994). But together they expose only a fraction of the multitude of ways in which our lives and communities have been altered by AIDS. We need more information. We need to comprehend fully how AIDS has affected the development and maintenance of gay identity and community in Ireland. We need to understand how our lives have been altered: sexually, socially, culturally and politically. It is only when we know this that we can even begin to envision what the future of AIDS holds for Irish gay men. If I were to have a vision, then, I suppose it would be one of greater knowledge, the search for which is not dependent on the political attractiveness of funding either gay or AIDS research.

Notes

1. It would be incredibly facetious to claim that there weren't *any* out gay men prior to the 1980s, since the work of organizations like the IGRM was obviously done by out gay men. My point here is that the groundwork of groups like the IGRM in the 1970s, which endeavoured to provide a space in which it was possible to be gay, combined with the rapid change in attitudes on homosexuality during the 1980s, brought *far more* people out of the closet than would have been possible in previous eras. While not all of them could be classed as being 'out' in the fullest sense of the term, there was certainly more of a visible presence of gay men in Ireland during the 1980s, especially in urban areas.

2. I refer here to the Prohibition of Incitement to Hatred Act 1990, the 1993 amendment to the Unfair Dismissals Act 1977, as well as the promise of an amended Employment Equality Act and a new Equal Status Bill.

3. There is a marked absence of research into the effect AIDS has had on discrimination or overt violence against gay men in

Ireland. However, reports from other countries, especially the USA, show that gay men are often more at risk of discrimination or violence because of AIDS than other identifiable groups affected by the syndrome (Herek, 1989 and St Lawrence *et al.*, 1990).

4. Having said this, one of the major opposers of gay law reform, Family Solidarity, did attempt to use AIDS in their campaign to prevent decriminalization. In 1990, the group published '*The Homosexual Challenge: Analysis and Response*', wherein it actively cultivated a link between gay sex and AIDS. Dr Joseph McCarroll (1991), Secretary of the organization in 1991, summed up the attitude of the group by arguing that 'As the Government's own education teaches, sodomy and such acts pose a significant danger to health. They put those who practice them at high risk to the fatal AIDS disease. The need to protect health, then, provides a compelling and sufficient reason for maintaining the present laws against these acts. To remove the laws would send a social message legitimizing the very acts which the Government is trying to discourage.'

5. In addition, the removal of the laws criminalizing gay sex would also facilitate better funding of HIV prevention initiatives among gay men because, since the mid 1980s, the Department of Health has refused to fund HIV prevention material for gay men on the basis that 'information relating to gay sexual practices would be contrary to the criminal law' (Rose, 1994, p. 22).

6. While there have been certain reservations about the importance of AIDS for the lesbian community, many lesbians have contributed wholeheartedly to the fight against AIDS. An analysis of the impact of AIDS on the political legitimacy of the Irish lesbian community was beyond the scope of this article. However, reports from other countries show that although lesbians remain relatively physically unaffected by the epidemic, AIDS does have considerable implications for the political legitimacy of the lesbian community, due to its connection with the gay community in popular discourse (Faderman, 1992, p. 293–5; Schneider, 1992, p. 170–3).

7. There are a few notable exceptions. Out of the ashes of GHA rose the Dublin Lesbian and Gay Health Caucus, which continued the work of GHA by providing safer-sex information to lesbians and gay men both in Dublin and on a national level. Furthermore, in 1991, an *ad hoc* group of gay and bisexual men in Cork produced the *Man to Man Safe Sex Guide*, in conjunction with Cork AIDS Alliance.

References

Adam, B. (1987). *The Rise of a Gay and Lesbian Movement*. Boston: G.K. Hall.

Altman, D. (1986). *AIDS in the Mind of America*. New York: Doubleday.

Altman, D. (1988). 'Legitimation through disaster: AIDS and the gay movement', in E. Fee and D.M. Fox (eds.), *AIDS: The Burdens of History*. Berkeley: University of California Press, pp. 32–43.

Altman, D. (1992). 'AIDS and the reconceptualization of homosexuality', in A. Klusacek and K. Morrison (eds.), *A Leap in the Dark: AIDS, Art and Contemporary Cultures*. Quebec: Vehicule.

Barnes, M. (1989). 'Toward a ghastly death: the censorship of AIDS education'. *Columbia Law Review*, 89. p. 708.

D'Emilio, J. (1983). *Sexual Politics, Sexual Communities: The Making of a Homosexual Minority in the United States 1940–1976*. Chicago: University of Chicago Press.

D'Emilio, J. (1992). 'After Stonewall', in *Making Trouble: Essays on Gay History, Politics and the University*. London: Routledge.

Epstein, S. (1991). 'AIDS activism and the contested construction of knowledge'. *Socialist Review*, 21, p. 42.

Faderman, L. (1992) *Odd Girls and Twilight Lovers: A History of Lesbian Life in Twentieth Century America*. London: Penguin.

Family Solidarity (1990). *The Homosexual Challenge: Analysis and Response*. Dublin: Family Solidarity.

Gay and Lesbian Equality Network (1994). *Proposed Action-Research Project on HIV Prevention Strategies and the Gay Community: A Submission to the Department of Health*. Dublin: Mimeo.

Herek, G.M. (1989). 'Hate crimes against lesbians and gay men', *American Psychologist*, 44, June.

Kayal, P.M. (1993). *Bearing Witness: Gay Men's Health Crisis and the Politics of AIDS*. Oxford: Westview.

King, E. (1993). *Safety in Numbers: Safer Sex and Gay Men*. London: Cassell.

Kippax, S., Crawford, J., Connell, B., Dowsett, G., Watson, L., Rodden, P., Baxter, D., and Berg, R. (1992). 'The importance of gay community in the prevention of HIV transmission: a study of Australian men who have sex with men', in P. Aggleton, P. Davies and G. Hart (eds.), *AIDS: Rights, Risk and Reason*. London: Falmer Press.

McCarroll, J. (1991). 'Why homosexual acts should not be legalized'. *Irish Times*, 30 May.

Padgug, R.A. and Oppenheimer, G.M. (1992). 'Riding the tiger: AIDS and the gay community', in E. Fee and D.M. Fox (eds.), *AIDS:*

The Making of a Chronic Disease. Berkeley: University of California Press, pp. 245–278.

Philpott, G. (1994). 'Drama out of a crisis'. *Fortnight*, May.

Robson, C. (1991). 'Homosexual acts should not be crimes'. *Irish Times*, 19 July.

Rose, K. (1994). *Diverse Communities: The Evolution of Lesbian and Gay Politics in Ireland*. Cork: Cork University Press.

St Lawrence, J.S., Husfeldt, B.A., Kelly, J.A., Hood, H.V. and Smith, S. (1990). 'The stigma of AIDS: fear and prejudice toward gay men'. *Journal of Homosexuality*, 19, 30.

Schneider, B.E. (1992) 'Lesbian politics and AIDS work'. In K Plummer (ed.) *Modern Homosexualities: Fragments of a Lesbian and Gay Experience*. London: Routledge.

Wachter, R.M. (1992) 'AIDS, activism, and the politics of health'. *The New England Journal of Medicine*, 326, 2.

Weeks, J. (1977). *Coming Out: Homosexual Politics in Britain from the Nineteenth Century to the Present*. London: Quartet.

Weeks, J. (1988). 'Love in a cold climate', in P. Aggleton and H. Homans (eds.), *Social Aspects of AIDS*. London: Falmer Press.

Part V
Emigrants

The Accidental Immigrant

Anne Maguire

AMERICA was never even my dream holiday. Six months before I arrived in New York I would not have believed that I would be carrying my life in three bags through the arrivals gate in John F. Kennedy airport. At work, Betty had insisted that I submit an application for a Donnelly visa because everyone was doing it. I sent in two, and so joined the first wave of people to leave Ireland with a green card awaiting me on the other side of the Atlantic. The USA was, in fact, the only country I definitely knew I never wanted to visit: Ronald Reagan was President. Much of my political education included a knee-jerk reaction of fury and contempt for America because it was *the* imperialist power: warmongering, evil and shamelessly capitalistic. I did not choose the USA; it simply offered me a way out of Ireland when I needed it. London was not an option because of the rampant anti-Irish racism there. (I wouldn't be the type to behave and keep my mouth shut and so I had ruled England out.) But getting out of Ireland was always in the back of my mind. It was either going to be Dublin, where I was bored stupid with my job in the Civil Service, politically demoralized after losing every campaign I had worked on, and barely keeping my head above water in general, or getting the hell out before I went under completely.

I was a lesbian, but had never worked on any lesbian or gay-specific issues during my activist life in Dublin. My work was as a Republican and a feminist. My political awakening occurred during the Dirty protests (the Blanket protests) when Republican prisoners were demanding that their status as political prisoners be restored. The H-Block hunger strikes moved me further and solidified my Republican conviction. Through people I met during this time I was introduced to feminism and took to it as naturally as I had taken to getting the British out of Ireland. In hindsight, I realize that I was predisposed to both philosophies, or to being radical, and simply needed to learn and be able to articulate my beliefs.

When I was eighteen Joni Crone came out to the nation on the *Late Late Show*. In our living-room in Donnycarney, my parents and I silently witnessed this incredible act of bravery. I worked on Bernadette McAliskey's general election campaigns in my constituency, Dublin North Central, where she was a candidate. During these campaigns I met Anne Speed who was vigorous in her recruitment of both Noeleen McDonnell, my good friend, and me. Through Anne Speed my grounding in activism took root and blossomed. During the Anti-Amendment campaign I worked in my constituency again, and realized that I was beginning to formulate my own understanding and opinions about the Women's Movement and the forces fighting against women in Ireland. At a meeting in Anne Speed's house in Phibsboro, the idea of organizing a National Women's Conference took root and so I helped organize this conference in Rutland Street School in 1984. During that conference I was delighted by one particular British woman who, along with three other British lesbians, stayed with my family in Donnycarney. I followed her around to hear what she was saying, because every sentence out of her mouth seemed to begin with, 'As a lesbian ... ' This tireless activist, Sarah Roelofs, brought the lesbian out of me. Finally, when I was twenty-two, and had left home, I came out. At that time I was working in the Dublin-based *Women Against Strip-Searching in Armagh* group, where Siobhan Lennon, had a tremendous impact on me, she being the other anti-imperialist, Irish Republican feminist lesbian in the group. In October 1987, I left Ireland.

I arrived in New York decked out in my new coat and hat, terrified and full of grief about leaving my life in Ireland behind me. Marie Honan, who barely knew me, met me at the airport and didn't know what to do with this weepy woman and her matching luggage. My sister, Cathy, also lived in New York, where she worked as a live-in nanny in Brooklyn to put herself through art college. Paul O'Dwyer, whom I'd met a couple of times through a mutual friend, was in New York too. I had a telephone number for him safely packed away. My intention was to be strong and totally self-sufficient. I had to find a job.

Looking for work was excruciating. In the mornings I rose with Marie, put on a tweed skirt from Dunnes Stores, a jacket, nylon tights and a pair of court shoes and hit the streets. I never would have dressed in drag in Dublin so skirts, nylons and shoes that cut the feet off me were a new and uncomfortable experience. Through Paul I managed to get a part-time job in the Great American Health Food Bar near Wall Street, which paid four dollars an hour on the take-out counter. I had been in New York for three weeks and didn't realize that there were several ways coffee could be served: light, regular and dark. I didn't know what bagel-melts were. There were several concoctions of health shakes, salads and a whole variety of food and combinations that were completely alien to me.

It was hellish but at least one co-worker, a young African–American woman, thought it was hilariously funny and helped me out. She tried to get me to visit her church on Sundays and dealt with the fast pace at breakfast and lunch by repeating 'Praise the Lord'. One day when she was trying to recruit me for church I told her that I was a lesbian. She didn't care much, so we continued to make each other's day bearable.

The subways were another nightmare because of the system: how would I ever know when I was supposed to be going uptown or downtown? Marie's performance in the New York underground was impressive. She dragged me from one train to another without even having to refer to a map. She was amazing!

One day I was to meet Paul in the financial district for lunch and arrived three hours late: it was only when the train had emerged above ground into a landscape of abandoned and burned-out buildings that it had dawned on me I was going in the wrong direction.

The part-time work in the restaurant was not paying the bills. I needed a new job. Every agency in New York suggested that I take 'Girl Friday' jobs and, while I wasn't sure what skills I had after six and a half years working in the Department of Labour, I knew that I was not about to become a general dogsbody. I'd never sat in front of a typewriter in my life but the agencies insisted that I take a typing test when I couldn't type to save my life! Pure desperation drove me to perform my way to a job. Being white and English-speaking proved a definite advantage and it was automatically assumed that I was educated, that is, that I had a degree. So, depending on the position I was pursuing, my degree would change. I've had degrees in English, history and law. It worked. The reality is that my formal education ended at St Mary's Holyfaith secondary school. Nobody ever checked, though I've had a couple of close calls with the law degree.

I was extremely home sick, and torn about being in New York but determined to adjust and look after myself. I missed my home, family and friends, the life I knew. I also felt that I had no right to leave Ireland, because that was where I should be – fighting for what I believe in. My duty was in Ireland, whether it be to family, friends or the lofty notion of responsibility to one's country. However, I got over that by telling myself, and the people I had left behind, that I would be back within two years.

Initially I did try to fit in to the Irish and the gay communities in New York, but I couldn't hack either for various reasons. Marie took me to a lesbian bar my first week here, Kelly's on Bedford Street in the West Village. I had never seen lesbians in suits with briefcases before in my life. And I'd come across maybe three lesbians in Dublin with long hair! I was very nervous and didn't feel at all comfortable, but nonetheless I was curious and wanted to experience the scene. The first woman that I made eye contact with at the bar came over immediately and asked me for a light. I wanted to get out of there fast, away from these forward dykes. Overt sexuality and lesbians directly coming on to other lesbians, was not what I was used to. Later we went to the Duchess on Grove Street, which was much more like home, though the clientele would rarely be found in any pub in Ireland: the lesbians were almost exclusively African–American. The physical make-up and the feel of the bar reminded me of the pubs I was used to in Dublin. Nothing too fancy, a place where you could sit and not be bothered by anyone.

Later I went to many ACT UP meetings, and was left speechless. In my experience, hundreds of activists only got together for national conferences, not weekly meetings. I couldn't understand why people got a big cheer because it was their first meeting, or why anyone would bring attention to themselves in the first place by volunteering this information. Instead of being excited I was intimidated. The culture shock was profound. The meetings had a structure that was not familiar. The language was new to me, the medical terms and acronyms baffling. It took several meetings for me to figure out that PWA meant a 'person with AIDS'. Everybody seemed to be articulate, confident and in control of the situation. My knowledge of HIV and AIDS was minimal and I was completely ignorant of New York City and national politics and activism. I understood that people were dying and that the government and medical industry were not responding adequately because of homophobia, racism and sexism. But I could not relate to what I saw happening at ACT UP.

I quite often felt angry when I left the meetings, mostly because I didn't understand what was going on and also because I felt I didn't belong there. I had never seen lesbians and gay men like these lesbians and gay men before, and they scared me. It was like being on another planet. While I had certainly felt alienated in the gay community in Dublin, this was different. This was far more profound than merely not being excited or interested; this was about wanting, but not knowing how, to fit in. It reminded me somewhat of my first feelings of desperation around the Republican hunger strikes and not knowing what to do. Though both of these instances differ greatly, in many respects they were linked by a feeling of powerlessness. In hindsight, much of my experience during the first couple of years in New York was about the closet. I believe that had I been more secure as a lesbian the cultural obstacles could have been overcome.

Both Marie and I sought out the Irish Women's Study group and worked with them for over a year. They produced a video about women's contribution to the Nationalist struggle in Ireland and organized speaking tours with the Sinn Féin women's department. However, after a year I wanted something that was more action-orientated. I steered well clear of the Irish ghettos in the Bronx and Queens and wanted no involvement with the established Irish–American community. My circle of friends were mostly native-born Irish people and, to a certain point, these relationships sustained an emotional need and a contact with Ireland. Marie and I had become lovers. Upon leaving Dublin I had decided that there would be no room for romance; and for the first time in my life that was fine with me. My New York adventure would be enough excitement. However, Marie had her own plan and succeeded in seducing me, which was no mean feat given my resolve to remain single.

A substantial part of my first few years in New York was spent finding my way in a strange city. The need to make a place for myself, and not having any luck led to my involvement in the formation of the Irish Lesbian and Gay Organization (ILGO). We began meeting in April 1990. My journey was coming to an end. For most of us, this group provided a place to experience a 'coming home'. I had never consciously thought about being Irish until I left Ireland. And I had hardly explored or begun to find my place as a lesbian until I came to New York. When ILGO was formed I had been in New York for nearly two and a half years. Now I was ready and prepared to put the training I had received in Dublin, and the new lesbian sensibility I had developed in New York, into action.

At that first ILGO meeting (attended by nineteen gay men and two lesbians – Marie and I), we had our first political battle: What would we call the group? Some wanted to call it 'Cáirde' (friends) to make the connection with Ireland, while others of us felt such subtleties would be lost in New York. We also believed that it would be more positive to say exactly who we were and not to be closeted, no matter how well intentioned and symbolic 'cáirde' may have been. Step two was to decide whether 'lesbian' or 'gay' should go first in the title. Naturally, Marie and I insisted on 'lesbian' and we had support, but one man was afraid that everyone would think it was a lesbian-only group. I pointed out that all he needed to do was look around the room to allay his fears. At that meeting we also decided to march in the Gay Pride parade in New York in June, just two months away.

ILGO's primary function was (and the philosophy remains so today) to provide a safe place for Irish and Irish-American lesbians and gay men. Like many existing groups in Ireland, the group is social-, service- and support-orientated, qualities it shares with the ethnic and racially identified gay groups in New York. Our statement of purpose has always included the term 'political' too, though that has, on occasion, been contentious. Initially the term 'political' was interpreted as pertaining to 'The North'. This led to much anxiety at meetings when anyone with a Northern Irish accent spoke. Regardless of what the topic was it was understood that the person had a position and God forbid they air it. The assumption that all Northerners were Provos and all Southerners were either apolitical or anti-Republican was rampant. Most people in ILGO had never been involved in any type of group before, never mind a group that was, by it's very nature, political. My impression is that people felt that as long as the word 'political' remained unsaid we would be perceived as harmless and non-threatening. What is also interesting is that 'political' was not understood to bear any relation to homophobia or to the process of empowerment that was possible when a group of lesbian and gay immigrants get together and no longer feel isolated among people from their ethnic background.

This was only the beginning and people were very excited, though many were terrified of being 'found out'. There was an electricity in the air at the meetings. For most this was the first time they had been in contact with other Irish gay men and lesbians, and some people remarked later on that they were surprised that people at the meetings were normal! Within our first year the understanding of 'political' changed radically. It came to mean the St Patrick's Day parade and everything that went with it.

What is clear about ILGO and the St Patrick's Day parade is that most people, particularly those of us who are most actively involved, have no inclination to be associated with, never mind march in, the parade. This, very simply, is where our 'coming out' took place in Irish America and where we were told that we did not belong, nor were we welcome. Now we are saddled with 'The Parade' in perpetuity, much to my chagrin. During the course of this battle ILGO has lost members and gained members. Some people who turned up for meetings in our first year have returned years later to join in the work of the parade. Some left the group, scared off by the very public nature of the fight. ILGO had no idea that applying to march in the New York parade would cause such a stir. What we were faced with, ten days prior to the event on Fifth Avenue, in 1991, was whether or not to come right out of the closet or to back down from the virulent homophobia of the parade organizers, the

Ancient Order of Hibernians (AOH). At our monthly meeting in March, five people declared that they would march if the opportunity arose. The general feeling in the room was that we were not ready for this, and that we should wait until the following year. However, this was before the media ran with the story that put us in the spotlight. Once that happened, we decided to get together each evening to review all that was going on. We had meetings at City Hall with the AOH and city officials, and Paul O'Dwyer and I were elected as the ILGO representatives and as spokespeople to deal with the hundreds of calls we were getting from newspapers, TV and radio. Everyone was encouraged to wade in and Lucy Lynch, Tarlach MacNiallais, Marie and Kieran did media work when the load became totally overwhelming. It was an explosive period and towards the end we met several times each day and night.

What happened was incredible. Women and men who had joined the group, many of whom believed that they were the 'only ones' before ILGO was founded, were now rushing out of the closet. Some had only been to three or four meetings. ILGO had not yet celeberated its first anniversary. Phone calls were made to Ireland, as members came out to their parents; some reactions were positive and some were extremely painful. We were being swept along by a tremendous wave of excitement, pride and fighting spirit. We didn't have time to consider the broader consequences of our actions on a personal or a political level. The group was being pulled at from every direction: the Irish community was in turmoil; some in the gay community could not understand that our Irish identity was just as important as our gay identity; the media frenzy verged on the insane; and the pressure from City Hall and politicians to resolve the controversy was immense. We were on a roll that would not let up and we had to keep moving.

What was most important to us was to fight the homophobia of the American Irish community and in so doing, to experience the power and strength that came from working together as principled and courageous Irish women and men who happen to be lesbian and gay. That commitment, regardless of the bizarre setting, is what compels us to continue the struggle, wherever it takes us, to the bitter end.

In 1991 a compromise was reached and we marched with Division 7 of the AOH and with Mayor David Dinkins – the first Black mayor of New York. The vicious reaction to our presence that day made it clear that, in order to survive, we had to continue to fight against the hatred of lesbians and gay men in the Irish community and the homophobia of every institution which allows and promotes this bigotry. Rather than scaring us back into the closet, we were spurred on. We have never been allowed to march again. Parades in this country have not been the same since.

The St Patrick's Day parade symbolizes more than the coming of age of Irish-identified lesbians and gay men in the USA. It represents a constant reference point regarding issues of ethnic and racial identity, constitutional questions and the separation of church and state, lesbian and gay community politics, matters concerning Catholicism and other religious doctrines, homophobia, and other parades. The clearest message that the New York parade struggle has highlighted over the years is the extent of homophobia that runs through the powerful institutions of government, church and law.

As ILGO's work on the parade continues, a discernible radicalization has taken place among the activist membership. This positive movement, however, has a down side, as a huge amount of energy goes into the parade, sometimes to the detriment of other social activities. This has mostly come about because those of us who became active in the parade working group are the very people who, in the past, held the organization together. As is common in most organizations there is a core group of people who are willing to do the majority of work to ensure the survival of the organization. It was a natural step for those most actively involved in ILGO in 1991 to take on the parade. While I am wholeheartedly committed to providing a social and supportive environment within ILGO, it is certainly not the function I would choose for myself, particularly after expending a lot of energy over four and a half years holding the group together. And while the majority of people who come to ILGO are looking for contact with Irish lesbians and gay men, there is a conflict when others display an interest in pursuing a more active role in both the Irish and lesbian and gay community. Like most groups the trouble emerges because of the passivity and lack of commitment of the bulk of the membership. There is a reason for this apathy. Many people continue to feel disempowered in their lives and do not feel they have a right to be a part of anything (an attitude that is in large part due to the evil of the closet). Very few members move from the position of expecting to be cared for and catered to. This leaves everybody feeling frustrated: those who get upset about a lack of fun events and those who are angry about having to do everything. Naturally, there are people in between who are just happy to be among other Irish gays, but being mellow in the middle rarely achieves much.

Resolving this issue is not an easy process. It involves a conscious effort at recruitment and having a keen eye for those who may be able to shift towards organizing. Then begins the pursuit. Sometimes it's a simple matter of building up self-esteem and confidence, sharing skills and passing on organizational tools. Being gently solicitous is essential for maintaining, as well as building, the organization. Brow-beating never works. Prior to the 1994 parade we welcomed three new activist members – two lesbians and one gay man. Since the parade these three have taken on the responsibility of running the day-to-day business of ILGO with those of us who remain, and so the pattern continues.

A very interesting aspect of ILGO is the existence of a powerful lesbian leadership in what is a male-dominated organization. Since the beginning, the lesbian presence has been a formidable and radical force within the group. More recently, lesbians have consolidated this position through our total commitment to ILGO and an absolute belief in our own worth and power. In the early days women were overwhelmingly outnumbered by men in ILGO, and today our mailing list still reflects a predominantly male membership. In such an environment, it was necessary for lesbians to support each other. While there have been numerous ego and personality clashes throughout the years, the lesbians tended to talk things through, whereas the gay men were more likely to be involved in power struggles with each other. So while the gay men in ILGO battled it out, the lesbians resolved issues and got down to work. Ultimately, many of the male activists in the group isolated themselves from the other gay men. It is, I believe, the strength and commitment of the lesbians in ILGO which explains our predominance in the organization's leadership.

During the 1993 campaign the New York Lesbian Avengers voted to work on the St Patrick's Day parade with ILGO. Both Marie Honan and I are founding members of the Avengers. Sheila Quinn emerged as a prominent Avenger and added to the Irish presence along with Catch Keeley. Without these fearless and incredibly organized and smart lesbian activists the demonstration on Fifth Avenue that year could have been disastrous. Despite a court injunction thousands turned out, and among their numbers was a group of people, calling themselves the CD (Civil Disobedience) Rebels, who had decided that they were the real radicals, and that the parade issue would be better served by them rather than by ILGO and our supporters. They attempted to lead the demonstration, but the Avenger marshals went into action. They expertly guided ILGO and thousands of protesters out onto Fifth Avenue while also clearing the hundreds of media people out of the way and watching the police. The Rebels were ineffectual. In the daunting lead-up to the 1993 parade Marie and I would check in with longtime activists and founding Avengers, Maxine Wolfe and Sarah Schulman, when we needed sound advice, analysis and personal support.

Since then ILGO has worked with the Lesbian Avengers on the parade. Avenger Carrie Moyer designs our posters, and when it's time to go flyposting to publicize our plan the Avengers are the flyposting queens! Civil disobedience and marshal training is facilitated by Avengers and lesbians from ACT UP. Historically important activists like Sarah Schulman and Maxine Wolfe are now solidly involved in ILGO's struggle, which has been an incredible boost and a joyous learning experience full of sound politics and friendship. If the leadership in ILGO was not lesbian-identified we would never have had the benefit of the experience and expertise of the women in the Lesbian Avengers. Though we have made a concerted effort to work with other ethnic and racially identified gay groups in the city, the response has not had the same profound effect on our direction and success. This is certainly an area where ILGO could focus more of it's attention.

The presence in ILGO of strong lesbians has unfortunately resulted in much overt misogyny. Ultimately, most of the gay men who considered themselves to be the real leaders left the group (always with a bit of a bang). Their departures were invariably marked by an attack on the lesbians, or a specific lesbian, in the group. But while the men were jostling for position the leadership had been formed naturally and painlessly by the people who were doing the work. Today the remaining male activists are almost exclusively lesbian-loving men who appreciate strength and leadership regardless of gender. Recently, John-Francis Mulligan sat through a meeting to try to resolve the fact that a prominent man in ILGO wanted to set up a counter-organization under the pretext of fulfilling a cultural role for Irish gays. John-Francis could not believe the level of misogyny openly displayed at this meeting; we assured him that his inability to identify with these gay men was a compliment to his fine sensibility. Lesbians and gay men can, and have, worked effectively together. Sexism is inevitable but not insurmountable. The ILGO membership faces each battle as it arises and together as lesbians and gay men we resolve it ... for the most part!

On the first of October, 1995, I will have been in New York for eight years. I know that I have not assimilated and that I do not consider New York to be my home. Neither, in all honesty, can I say Ireland is my home, though often when we talk about 'home' here it means Ireland. Neither place is home. Because I could not survive where I felt I did not belong, I left. New York is a city of transients, full of people who don't belong anywhere else. The central conflict in my life is that while Ireland now seems somewhat alien, it's still where my life's interest and energy lie and where I want to be able to live. This conflict remains unresolved.

If I came back to Ireland, I wonder how long it would take not to be classed as a 'returned immigrant'. It took me long enough to adapt to the concept of being an immigrant, and so the idea of no longer being considered bona fide Irish is horrifying. One thing I am quite sure about is my Irishness. Are we the 'Yanks' of the Irish lesbian and gay diaspora? Does the term 'returned immigrant' simply reflect the truth of experience, or is there an inherent hostility to those who leave/flee, and later return, in their resultant categorization as 'other'? The contribution to, and influence of immigrants on their country of origin, is often minimalized and undermined, particularly by those it immediately affects in Ireland. The simple reason being that the work did not take place on the island itself. The construct of 'us' and 'them' leads to a less than even-handed equality when determining the elements that have contributed to progress and movement on our small island.

The greeting, 'Hello New York' jumped out at us from a photograph of the thirty lesbians and two gay men who marched in the St Patrick's Day parade in Cork in 1992. This brave act of solidarity and support caused much joy, pride, amusement and a little sadness in ILGO. On one level or another St Patrick's Day in Ireland, in America, and internationally, is now associated with 'out' Irish lesbians and gay men. While activism outside of the island has its limitations, historically it's had an impact on the country.

Mine is probably the classic immigrant situation: to be constantly haunted by home and the wish to return. Most often immigrants need the idea of 'home' in order to survive the reality of life as an exile. Many live with bitterness and vow never to return. As an immigrant, I fluctuate between feelings of relief, liberation, anger, grief and a sense of never being rooted to one spot. My fears about returning to live in Ireland are manifold. I am tired but resigned to living on the margins, but I do not want to settle in a country where, given the Irish woman I am, I will be placed on the fringes of the very outer margins. My worst fear is not finding a place to belong in the lesbian and gay community; that was one of my reasons for leaving, and so it preys on me. I need community to survive. If you don't belong in the ghetto where is there left to go?

A Land Beyond Tears

Fr Bernard J. Lynch

IN my life, and for as long as I can remember, both God and sex have vied with each other for my attention. But given the disincarnation of my religious indoctrination, the idea that any-body's sexuality could be perceived as a way into God was simply absurd. I grew up believing with Simon and Garfunkel that 'God laid His hands on us all' and 'Our backs were to the wall'. I swallowed whole the belief that if I were ever to get close to God, and by extension my own happiness, then this vital part of my humanity had to be oppressed, repressed and suppressed at any and every cost. In fact, underlying this was the Jensenistic belief that any kind of human pleasure was highly suspect. As I recalled elsewhere (*A Priest on Trial*, Bloomsbury, 1993), even a mundane penile erection was considered a venial sin. Consequently, I was over thirty years of age before I learned to fart without feeling guilt.

As I now understand and fully accept that 'God does not let sleeping dogs lie', and while for a time I was successful in ignoring my sexuality, in the innocent, if not naive assumption that if I did so then my sexuality would ignore me, I had to pay a very high price for my truncated development. I am the eldest of six children – three boys and three girls – and received my earliest education, both primary and secondary, at the Christian Brothers' Schools in Ennis, Co. Clare. I made up my mind to be a priest as a child, and have rarely vacillated from that conviction to this present time. Of course, like most young Irish boys growing up in the 1950s, my parents, church and school influenced me, but I must say that I had no consciousness at that time of entering a seminary in order to avoid facing my gayness. At seventeen years of age I still believed what the priest told me in confession: 'It is a phase you are going through . . . and you will grow out of it.' This same priest, of course, took voyeuristic delight in questioning young boys about every prurient detail of their sexual, pubescent adolescent activities: 'Did you come or not; against his belly or bottom; on top of him or he on top of you?' And all this addressed at boys of only eleven or twelve; at that particular time in my sexual development I was not capable of anything more than a dry orgasm.

Many years later while living in New York, where, psycho-sexually speaking, I grew up, I met a former school mate of mine from Ennis and after exchanging the usual pleasantries he said to me: 'Do you remember Fr. X?' and I blurted out: 'Not you too'. 'I come to you Father' – this was the introduction Fr. X asked each boy to make in the confession as a substitute for that usual greeting, 'Bless me Father'. In this way he said he would 'recognize immediately the nature of our problem' – *sex*. I am convinced that that same priest used his inquisitorial power in the confessional to satisfy his own masturbatory fantasies, while he condemned us for our sins against nature!

Catholic lesbian women and gay men are, through Baptism, robbed of their birthright. From their pre-conscious childhood they are taught that any and every form of affectional, physical same-sex feelings and desires are wrong. As His Holiness John Paul II most recently put it in his response to the European Court's 1994 legislation on the rights of lesbian/gay people to adopt children: 'They should be eradicated'. Is it any wonder then that love of self for God is a virtually impossible task for Catholic lesbian women and gay men? A quality that the Church should be enabling and enobling from birth with 'The new life of baptism' becomes instead a requiem, a death-knell. For those people who are lesbian, gay and transgendered sexually, their baptismal waters drown them in the 'labyrinth' of a merciless struggle to be fought over and against all of their mortal lives.

Today, with so many priests and bishops being publicly shamed because of their sexual improprieties, I ask how did we as a Church escape so much for so long? There is absolutely no allowance for any psychosexual development whatsoever. In the eyes of the institutional Church one moves from sexual kindergarten to post-doctoral sexual chastity – without grammar, high-school or undergraduate work of any kind. A lot of priests I know suffer from serious arrested sexual development. They are not child molesters, but their psychosexual emotional development stopped as soon as they entered the seminary. Some were as young as thirteen years of age. The fact that the celibate lie has been 'outed' is a *call* to all of us for personal integrity, not for shouts of hypocrisy. Although, given the present Roman sexual fascism towards sexual minorities, it is difficult, if not impossible, to imagine healthiness (holiness) and openness being welcomed by those who preside in authority over hypocrisy and lies. In Cardinal Ratzinger's letter on the 'Pastoral Care of Homosexual People' (1986), he advocates that gay people should remain closeted and engage in egodystonic (distanced) behaviour, with self-destructive consequences, over egosyntonic (integrated) behaviour that would lead to sexual and personal integrity.

He further states that anyone seeking human and civil rights for gay people ought not to be surprised if they have violence perpetrated against them. Most young priests and seminarians I know who are gay live the lie as best they can, but I have to ask: what does it profit to gain the whole world (let alone possible ordination) and suffer the loss of one's soul?

For me the question is and always will be: how to be human now? Not how to be gay or straight or, indeed, even Christian in a particular way. For surely, if being sexually orientated towards the same-sex gender does not make us more human, then it ought to be 'eradicated'. And the same can and ought to be said about our Christianity or our religion. Either they help us to become more fully alive, to ourselves and to others, or we are in really serious trouble.

To be born is to be human, it is also to *become* human. Becoming myself in all the fullness of my personhood (psychologically, emotionally, sexually, intellectually and spiritually) is the mark of personal existential existence. In the words of Alexander Pope: 'All knowledge is oneself to know'. St Iraneaus in the third century put it even more strongly: 'Gloria Dei, vivans homo' ('The glory of God is man/woman fully alive'). Consequently, the first paradigm of my thesis, as both a gay man and a Christian, is this:

Either my sexuality and that of all human beings is a way into God or it is not. Either it enables and enobles my humanity (which is another way of saying that it brings me closer to the God within and without) or it takes me further from my true self. For any self-alienation means alienation from God.

Anything or anyone that would hurt or destroy that self which we and others are created to be – the image of God – is not of God. I believe this 'image of God' is something we are born with, but it is also something we strive to become in all the fullness of our humanity. For the human authenticity and the religious authenticity are always one. It is not what we say about God that matters, but rather who we are as a result of our belief in Him. This is what I find so fascinating about Christianity: that our human historicity is in fact our divine historicity. In other words, every minute of our existential existence from birth to death is God's image in us trying to express itself in the image of Love. What can this say of our sexuality/relationality but that somehow God is continuously birthing forth in us, to use Dante's words, a 'love that holds the sun, the moon, and stars in place'.

Of course, this can and does go wrong. There is so much ego to be found and to be given up before we can as it were, surrender ourselves to the Lover God. On one level, life to me seems to be about finding our ego (who we are) and letting it go (who we can become). I have discovered this to be particularly true in the journeys I have made with those living with HIV/AIDS.

The mind wants a god that the heart understands, but if the heart understood God the mind would reject it. It would give the heart a heart attack. For God is for the heart, and if our heart is right our God is right. Most of us do not have our hearts to begin with. For those who are lesbian and gay the order of the heart is utterly and totally reversed. Everyone and everything, from conception and throughout the most formative years of life, tells us that either we should not exist or if we do then we are, at best, second rate. In fact we are the only minority born into families that hate us. Perhaps I should say that they do not know how to love us. Anyone who helps to enable us to be more human, more free, more joyful, more in love with life is indeed a reflection of the divine. As Spinoza would have it: 'He who loves God becomes God'. But what is it to be human, to become human? These are huge questions that minds greater than mine have struggled with across the ages and around the world.

First of all I would reiterate that becoming myself is *the* mark of personal existentialist meaning. Secondly, to be human is to be in relationship. This is my second paradigm. Tangential to this is the psychosexual fact that our sexuality is the seat of our relationality. Our sexuality is that apotheosis of power where we are instinctively attracted and attractive to life, to love and to God. To label this natural God-given instinct as 'disordered' for 10 per cent of the world's population is a most disordered statement. To say that when this instinct is acted upon in a responsible, humanizing way it is 'evil', is indeed a statement of evil that cries to the very heavens for correction. How can love be evil? How can something which makes our hearts beat with the very rhythm of the universe be anything but good and of God?

Commanding lesbian and gay people to refrain from all sexual relational activity makes as much sense as telling Beethoven not to compose music. It is part of our very souls to be in relationship. And when frustrated and mutilated by Church authorities, this God-given desire leads to serious psychosexual and spiritual sickness (as we now see in so many priests). If sexuality were simply about who people choose to sleep with, then it would at least be understandable why the Church takes such a narrow view of sex. But our sexuality has as much to do with how we relate to our grandparents, appreciate theatre, enjoy music and celebrate Mass, as it does with who we may find sexually attractive. A spirituality without sexuality is as truncated as a sexuality without spirituality.

The only sin is not to touch. The Commandment is: 'Go forth and touch'. AIDS is an illness that is very often contracted in people's attempts to be in touch, to experience some kind of affirmation and acceptance, to know even for a moment some kind of love. Institutional religion has failed in the face of this pandemic precisely because HIV is so indigenously associated with sex (Body of Christ) and blood (Blood of Christ), is so much part of the very essence of what constitutes us physiologically as human beings. Consequently, Church institutions have tried everything within their worldly power to pervert safer-sex education and responsible sexual information about the disease. It is, for example, so dishonest to talk about 'innocent victims'! Everyone with the virus is innocent or no one is innocent. I have not met anyone in their right mind who wanted to get the virus.

Over my years of ministry to people living with this disease, especially gay people who are HIV-positive or have AIDS, I have found that for many of them the words 'God', 'Jesus' and 'Church' have become more vulgar and obscene than the word 'fuck'. It is not simply a question of throwing the baby out with the bath-water. No, the bath-water, in the case of lesbian/gay people, has been so polluted by the statements issuing from Church representatives such as Mgr. Foley, the Vatican spokesperson on AIDS ('AIDS is the natural result of unnatural acts', 1986). And worse, that the baby (God/Christ/Spirituality, if you will) has also been contaminated by association, and is understandably seen as a part of the oppression the Church visits on the oppressed. As a group of Irish gay people said to me many years ago: 'Our only problem with you is that you make the Catholic Church look credible.'

Most of the Irish lesbian/gay cultural Catholics I have worked with have a virulent hatred of the institution that oppresses them. To compound their sense of injustice they are often painfully aware of the many gay priests and religious in the Church, some of whom are sexually active and others with life-partners, who front an organization that continuously and consistently denies every human and civil right to sexual minorities. (At the same time, some of those same priests will themselves take advantage of every gain (and having been there I know), frequenting clubs, dancing at gay discos and picking up young men for sexual liaisons.) Yet they fail to lift a finger against the terror of oppression that gnaws at the very souls of the people who we, as priests, are ordained to serve. Both Cardinal Spellman and J. Edgar Hoover are, I suppose, the two most notorious examples of such hypocrisy in recent history.

While I am well aware that the shadow side exists in all of us, what angers me is that in the era of AIDS this kind of behaviour robs the very people who most need a God – Christ, spirituality – in order to make some meaning of a meaningless and ignominious disease, that all too often attacks when one is not even mature enough to imagine one's life never mind one's death. What is there to be done,

one may ask, when Church dogma and doctrine becomes one more opportunistic infection in people's struggle to be free. For me, the only credible option in this pandemic is to speak out against such institutional destruction of people's lives. This can be a statement of protest against inhuman and unchristian behaviour, as well as a prophetic stance for social justice for all oppressed people. While I don't and cannot judge those who choose otherwise, I believe that to identify with the present Roman hegemony of sexual oppression is like trying to be Christian in the Third Reich. For some I am sure this was possible, and is possible. For me, whether through weakness or strength, it is not possible to give allegiance to an institution that destroys people through the dialectical abuse of its power. Sexual minorities, and especially those living with the HIV virus, have had every bone in the souls of their bodies broken and their relationship to God practically destroyed by the institutional Church.

Paradoxically, I love the Church for so much that it does represent, and for the many good people in it. After all, I sincerely acknowledge that through it I too received 'the deposit of faith', for which I am eternally grateful. I love the Mass, the Sacraments, the sacred music, art and culture. These I shall always take with me for as long as I am in this time called life, and beyond. In that deepest 'ontological' sense I am always Catholic and always a priest. But I choose to be an outcast with the outcasts, wandering neither aimlessly nor in a desert but with a hope that is beyond optimism, for indeed there is not a lot to be optimistic about. The word courage has lost meaning, so much has already been taken away. Yes, hope beyond optimism, which ultimately is the abandon to love.

What is there to hope for in our future in Ireland? In this abandon of love what exactly do I believe we are going to gain? Coming out of the closet can and often does mean loss of job and position of respectability within society. It can also mean estrangement and even permanent separation from one's family of origin. (You are welcome home, but don't bring the subject up again and don't even think of bringing one of your so-called faggot friends or lovers ... what would the neighbours think?) The average lesbian/gay person has not only to work against his or her own internalized homophobia and years of self-negating socio-cultural exposure, but is often faced with a much harder task when it comes to their own parents and families in Ireland if they are to experience a glimpse of the joy and acceptance their heterosexual siblings take so much for granted. All too often after years of agonizing denial and pretence when eventually, and painstakingly, they can admit who they are and why they have for so long been so unhappy, they are met by either outright rejection or a refusal to acknowledge what they have shared with their blood and tears. Of the two it is preferable to be rejected rather than ignored. At the very least it means that on some level one has been heard, even if the response is negative.

Again, as in the case of the Church, many lesbian/gay people leave their families and go abroad eschewing all contact, save for the basic obligations of christenings, weddings and funerals. Indeed the funeral, for so many Irish people dying of AIDS, is often the occasion when all comes into the light. It is then that all the forces of patriarchal heterosexist homophobic culture are brought to bear on the dying young man, who is urged not to bring further discredit on the family by revealing the cause of his illness. I have often heard the imploration: 'Don't come home . . . we'll come and see you'. I recall how a certain Irish Mgr. told me on behalf of his nephew's family from Co. Kildare: 'Father, find a corner and bury him, we cannot have that sort of thing back here.'

Again and again life-partners are denied access to their loved ones, as in a recent case of two people I know. Stephen and Michael had been loving partners since Michael first arrived in London from Ireland in the mid-1980s. Michael came from Co. Laois and Stephen from Yorkshire. When Michael first became ill he, like so many others, told his parents he had cancer. Michael grew more and more ill, until eventually Stephen persuaded him to go to Ireland and see his family before he became too weak to travel. Stephen offered to go with him. What ensued is related here in Stephen's own words:

> From my arrival, the family made it clear to me that I was not welcome. They sent no fewer than three priest friends to impress upon me the necessity of my immediate return. Meanwhile, Michael was getting sicker, and the pressure of those around him had a debilitating effect on his already compromised immune system. He wanted me to stay but I couldn't. I left, both hurt and enraged.

Michael died three days later. 'Of course, I never got to say goodbye and was told that if I showed up at the funeral his brothers would personally eject me. I am still very angry about the whole thing.'

I would like to think that this kind of drama around AIDS is uncommon. But I have to say, unfortunately, that in my experience the opposite is true. How, I ask, can it be otherwise when people's minds are so indoctrinated with homophobic dogma from the very highest authorities in our Church? I have said elsewhere, and shall continue to say: 'The Catholic Church is a conduit to AIDS.' It spreads the virus by giving gay people no option but to be sexually active in an unsafe way with a multiplicity of partners. This is forgiven. Responsible, loving sexual relationships are, however, anathema and unforgivable. According to Church teaching, to be in a faithful, monogamous, safe same-sex relationship is 'To live in Sin'. Incredible! Church teaching also forbids heterosexuals with the virus to use condoms to save their partners' lives. Given the barrage of unchristian teaching issuing from the Vatican over the past ten years regarding the lives and loves of gay people, I am, in fact, heartened that so many Catholics see through the sham and give us, in this our darkest hour, something to live for – great enough to die for.

Therein lies my hope for the future amid all the losses of family, friends, church, job, health insurance and old age pension. Yes there are people, ordinary, good religious people, both clerical and lay, who know in their heart of hearts that we are essentially no different to themselves in who we are or what we strive to become. And that some of us would choose to be hated for who we are rather than be loved for who we are not. Yes, hated for who we are, so that those lesbian, gay and transgender children who come after us in Ireland, and elsewhere, will more easily tread the path not taken. I pray for the day when never again will a lesbian daughter or a gay son hear the words from their parents: 'I am only sorry that I did not have you aborted.' Yes, I not only pray but work for that Kingdom, when parents shall rejoice in the unusual, but natural, experience of procreating a lesbian daughter or gay son in the divine image of eternal love.

Keeping it Close: Experiencing Emigration in England

Cherry Smyth

The shape of the island is the shape of all the journeys around it that a history of emigration has set in motion.

Fintan O'Toole

IN the 1840s, before the Famine, there were 8 million people in Ireland. Almost a quarter of the population died of starvation, and another quarter emigrated. The population did not recover its 1890 level until 1990, and actually fell by 0.4 per cent in 1991. It is estimated that one out of every twelve people living in the Republic in 1982 had emigrated by 1989.[1] It is thought that between 80 and 85 per cent of those who leave to study elsewhere never return.

Leaving

It is against this tragic, perpetual sense of disappearance that I want to talk about leaving Ireland, about a search for home, a struggle against displacement. Despite the prediction of Mr Foley, a palmist, when I was seventeen, that I too would 'cross the water', I initially refused to follow the inevitable path pointing towards England.

Having grown up in the Protestant tradition, yet seeing myself as Irish, I already experienced a sense of unbelonging, an internal emigration, because I was not Catholic and therefore could not really be Irish. Learning Irish was not an option in school, and tuning into Gaelic programmes on RTE made me feel like a tourist in my own land. Catholicism, Gaelic, Irish music and dancing were all part of a club to which I had been implicitly denied membership. Hoping to find an Irish identity I could claim, I moved from Portstewart, a small seaside town in Co. Derry, to Dublin to go to college. I ditched my British passport, took an Irish one, but was perceived as a 'Northerner' and therefore 'less' Irish. It was not until I moved to London four years later that I became 'Irish'. Eight years later when I visited New York I experienced myself as 'European' as well.

Somewhere in those crossings I became a lesbian feminist, a queer dyke, a femme top. I refused the fixity of the identity I had been expected to conform to with a vengeance. My affinities with people of colour and other minority groups come from a sense of shared oppression, of being named and ridiculed in order to be contained, an experience that José Arroyo confirms.

> I grew up in Canada. I was astonished that as soon as I went into the US I was Hispanic. I was certainly not Hispanic to myself, I was not Hispanic in Montreal, but to the immigration people at the border, I was Hispanic.[2]

In London I can pretend that I haven't really left. I only came to college here. I only came to work here. I've no intention of settling here. 'Sure, Belfast is only an hour from Heathrow.' Yet in England I may as well be a million miles away. I discover that I am more at home in Manhattan.

> Ireland is a diaspora, and as such is both a real place and a remembered place, both the far west of Europe and the home back east of the Irish-American. Ireland is something that often happens elsewhere. (O'Toole, 1994)

I never left. I don't believe I ever left. I decided I was going to work in London for a while. I had benchmarks of six months and then I'd move jobs and do it for another year. I don't think I ever made a decision that I'd left home and certainly not one that says I'm never going back.
(Dee, thirty-one, from Downpatrick)

There are three key issues for lesbians and gays leaving Ireland – work, education and sexuality. Sometimes it involves a combination of all three, sometimes a realization in hindsight that same-sex desire was a motivating factor. For me, the passage for leaving was facilitated by education as, at that time, I could get a grant to attend college in England.

I first left when I was nineteen. Work, sexuality and confusion about who and what I was encouraged me. I found Dublin very repressive and negative towards women's sexuality. All my brothers went to university, so there was no money left over. (Elizabeth, twenty-nine, from Dublin)

My teenage ambition was to get out of the North and never come back, to enter a Dublin shop without being frisked, to not have to nervously watch every 'unattended vehicle', to not have the sense that each time I went out for a drink I could be blown to bits. Growing up in a overtly militarized country developed a keen anti-British attitude, as well as a level of fearfulness from which it took many years to recover. My adolescent fear of sexuality was fused with a terror of being shot or maimed in a public place. On a very simple level, my mistrust of men was compounded by the corruption and inequality of politics in the North (an almost totally male preserve) and an association of men with violence. Although moving to Dublin lessened my fear of death, I continued to feel oppressed as a woman until I moved to London and joined the women's peace movement. The sense of the hopelessness of politics was alleviated by moving to England, where I found a structure in which my voice could be heard, whether I was Catholic or Protestant, from the North or not.

I left to study straight after my A levels. I didn't really think about it. It was an accident more than a decision to come to England. The Troubles weren't part of my reason for leaving, but since then both that and my sexuality are part of why I don't come back. (Heather, thirty-one, from Ballymena)

Coming out

I want to examine the movement between the need for a collective identity as Irish and for a collective identity as a lesbian. To me, the two seemed irreconcilable for a long time. Although my sexuality was not the primary motivation for my leaving – further education and a chance to belong to a vibrant, unapologetic women's movement in England came first on the list – my lesbianism has since framed my decisions to return or not, to develop links with Irish dykes and fags and to question narrow monopolies on identity, whether national or sexual. My coming out as a lesbian paralleled and informed my emergence as a post-Prod Nationalist. Common sexuality allowed me to identify with Republican lesbians and gay men in a new way, just as feminism had given me the opportunity to forge new links with women across different backgrounds of class, nationality and race.

When I came out I felt that I had to choose between my sexual and my national identity. What if my parents declared that I would never be allowed home again? Would I be prepared to be out, exiled in England at that price? I held off the announcement for four years, for fear of rejection, not just by my parents, but by Ireland as a whole, where at the time, homosexuality was illegal in the South and reluctantly legal in the North. The duplicity of my double life – homo in England, hetero in Northern Ireland – was exaggerated by living in a culture which I did not see as my own. Living in London certainly gave me the courage to come out to myself, but it didn't give me a language to talk to my sexphobic parents about what they perceived as purely genital and strictly repulsive.

Oddly enough, British policy on Northern Ireland worked as a catalyst for my confession, when in October 1988, the broadcasting ban silenced certain political groups, from Sinn Féin to the

Ulster Defence Association. If I too was silenced, I was somehow colluding with the British oppression of the Irish. It was suddenly important that I not become yet another 'invisibilized' Irish lesbian, and that I begin a campaign against the homophobic institutions of the state and family that were somehow symbolized by the ban. Freud works in mysterious ways! The reception was mixed. I was not banished, but polite silence was requested. 'It's all very well', I remember my mother saying, 'doing those things in England, so long as you don't do them here. The ill-feeling runs too deep.' Most lesbians and gays I've met in London have made the choice to come out to family at home. Perhaps it is another signal of our separateness. We can more easily afford to come out and then leave again, than live down the road as 'out' members of the family.

> There's a fear that they'll say I never want to see you again, and you'll lose that big chunk of your life. But I'd left it so long and I was really angry and fed up pretending. (Elizabeth)

> Being out is no problem in my immediate family. My mum's dead and my dad's gay. (Heather)

Living the life

Many of us who left had not lived in a big city before, had not yet experienced the responsibilities and freedoms of adulthood, and England seemed to represent opportunities to express ourselves in ways we'd only dreamed of. Missing the humour, the connectedness is compensated for by escape from the hypocrisy and provincialism of the small towns many of us came from. I love the anonymity, the lack of predetermination, the fact that no one knows what my father does, and that no one ever suggests that I ought to be married 'at my age'. I thrive on the multiculturalism, the range of arts, food, music, colours that I can witness just walking to the shop. In Ireland I had an extended family whom I begrudgingly had to visit and with whom I took endless cups of over-brewed tea. In London I have what has been dubbed a 'pretended'[3] family of lovers, ex-lovers and friends, which gives me the support and validation necessary to live.

In Pratibha Parmar's view, it is precisely the anonymity and space of the city that allows us such freedom:

> Questions of place and location are crucial. It is in the urban space that we can escape from the claustrophobia of our tight-knit cultural and familial obligations and pressures. It is also in the urban metropolis that we can find anonymity and escape the bounty hunters that hunt us down as transgressors, in order to reclaim us with their patriarchal notions of woman as daughter, as wife, as sister but never as individual in her own right.[4]

> I've so much more freedom here. I do and say things I want to say and do. I can be a lawyer if I want. There's no judgement. (Elizabeth)

> I don't miss the small scene. I like clubbing and the rave scene here, and just seeing other dykes around is very affirming. I think I fancy only four dykes in the whole of Cork. (Niambh, thirty-one, from Cork)

However, there is a tendency for some of my assumptions about Irish culture and society to become fossilized circa 1982, the year I left, and to neglect to remember how many more freedoms I would have there now as a feminist, as a lesbian. Some of us seem to conflate the oppressive attitudes of our families with Ireland as a whole, and feel relieved to have 'escaped' rather than obliged to stay and fight to change it. In that choice, there lingers betrayal and regret.

> I won't go back to it –
> My nation displaced
> into old dactyls ...
> where time is time past.
> A palsy of regrets.
> No. I won't go back.
> My roots are brutal:

> From 'Mise Eire' by Eavan Boland

Sticking it out

The cost of freedoms of lifestyle, identity and politics are enormous, insidious and wearying. Everyone I spoke to missed the rural environment and experienced a sense of being cut off:

> I miss my friends and family. I find that about London, just the size and sheer geography of it very inhibitive to seeing people regularly and forming deeper relationships. The size of Cork and the way the society runs, you pop in for tea and bump into people more. So I've made better friends in Ireland. (Niambh)

Obviously the immediate loss of family, friends, culture and reference points marks the lives of any emigrant, but living in London has very specific disadvantages:

> If I collapsed in a heap
> here, right here where I'm standing
> would some big-hearted stranger
> step forward benignly
> from these sullen Londoners,
> these hurrying, self-conceited Londoners
> who slip me by, curtly
> as if I were a cess-pit
> befouling their way?

> From 'Piccadilly: Nightfall'
> by Cathal Ó'Searcaigh

Almost every day the media, workers in the office, comedians, manage to perpetuate the notion that the Irish are dangerous, violent, stupid, inferior. There is immense pressure to assimilate, to sound English, to lie low. Two incidents come to mind. I am driving at 33 miles an hour in a 30-mile-an-hour zone. A policeman pulls me over and asks me if I am aware that I was speeding. 'No,' I say. 'Where are you going?' he asks. I tell him. 'Is that an Irish accent?' he asks. 'Yes,' I reply. 'Have you been drinking?' he asks. I am in a gay bar and a woman asks me to dance. 'Where are you from?' she asks.

'Ireland,' I reply. 'So you're a Paddy then?' I turn swiftly and walk away as though she has slapped my mouth.

Some of the people I interviewed admitted that when they first came to England they wanted to disassociate from being Irish, and made clear attempts to assimilate to prevent this kind of abuse:

> As I pass for straight and for English I often find myself challenging attitudes that people let slip about Irish people. When people discover that I'm Irish, I've had it inferred that I'm not so smart, not so sophisticated, not so cultured. (Julie, twenty-four, from Portrush, Northern Ireland)

> A lot of my work around equal opportunities has concentrated around racism, but only in relation to black people. Every time I try to mention anti-Irish racism, it's not seen as valid. (Heather)

Keeping it close

> No matter that
> my name is Greek
> my surname is Portuguese
> my language alien.
> There are ways
> of belonging.

> From 'De Souza Prabhu'
> by Eunice de Souza

One of the ways of resisting anti-Irish prejudice is to hold on to and promote an idealized picture of Ireland which feeds into the romanticized postcard version that we all know is deeply false. It becomes more difficult to retain an 'authentic' identity the longer we stay away and the more idiomatic language and cultural gestures we shed. Many of us perceive Ireland as home when we're in England and yet when we return, England becomes the place we want to be:

I don't think I'm that far off being assimilated now. What gives me the right to call myself Irish anymore? I know nothing about gay life there and less about the rest of it. Maybe I'm not English, but I'm not Irish any more. Maybe I am kind of stuck halfway over the Isle of Man. (Julie)

Some Irish lesbians resist assimilation by relationships with each other, reinforcing cultural and linguistic ties:

The familiarity with an Irish lover is very different, the number of things that don't need explaining. And there is a broader acceptance in my family than when I brought an English woman home. (Dee)

I like the easy knowledge of each other. You can refer back to cultural things, and my lover can come into my family and we slip back into the Cork scene very easily because she's from there as well. (Niambh)

For others, intimacy with other Irish lesbians is too cloyingly familiar. Perhaps it's also a symptom of our internalized homophobia and anti-Irish racism which associates other Irish women with the institutions and attitudes that have been oppressive. With issues of merging already a danger in lesbian relationships, I've found that I like the taste of difference. None of the women I spoke to, however, had ongoing or frequent relationships with white English women. Although most denied that it was a conscious thing, they were often surprised to examine their track records to find that even lovers who they perceived initially as English were in fact Welsh, Scots, or had one or two parents of Irish descent.

My social circle has very few Irish lesbians in it. I'm a little scared to develop that because it feels too close to home. It feels like being exposed. (Julie)

Then there is what gay men have dubbed the 'Spud Queen' fetish, the desire non-Irish gay men have to seek out Irish lovers. As yet it has no name in the lesbian community in London, but there's no denying the prevalence of it, which most of us view with ambivalence. Often for me, issues of trust have been more difficult with

English women, where I have felt that fucking me is their way of understanding their role in 'the Irish question'. If the power imbalance is not addressed in conversations in or out of bed, I remain cautious and distant. On the other hand, the majority of English lesbians and gays care little what happens, or has happened, in Ireland and make no effort to inform themselves politically. Even in saying this, I feel the scruff of my neck tingle as though I will be punished for such 'ingratitude'. The colonized imagination is wilful and persistent.

One of my English lovers had a Celtic thing, and all her lovers had been Irish or Scottish, so I felt that I was the next in a long line. Another one was trying to get back to her Irish roots because her grandmother was Irish, and when the grandmother died she broke up with me a week later. (Julie)

Coming home

There are two postcards on my mirror – a red heart with the word 'QUEER' scratched into it in silver (a reproduction of a painting by the late Derek Jarman) and a postcard of a boarded-up cottage beside a line of wind-bent trees in Glencolombkille. There rests my contradictory sense of belonging, my split allegiance to place: one indefatigably urban, defiant, incorrigible; the other undeniably rural and possessing a different quality of resilience. My absence from Ireland is the absence in the ruins of a thousand cottages in Donegal and also from the political movements and victories that have been won over the past decade. My presence in London is a presence at marches, meetings, clubs, talks, exhibitions, readings – one of self-definition and endless intellectual and sexual exploration. For years they seemed irreconcilable. For years I felt guilty that I had left, had chosen to live in the country of the occupying army and could travel away from the constant fear of violent injury and death.

Not many emigrants have the chance to come back as themselves. This is more true for lesbians and gays. It was not until I visited Derry for the first ever Lesbian and Gay Pride event in 1992 to give a poetry reading, that I felt that I had come home and left nothing of myself behind. 'Home' shifts locations back and forth, back and forth.

I'm afraid of getting into a situation whereby I'm here twelve years down the road going, 'Oh I only came for a week and here I am still.' I've heard of so many cases of that. Even though I like London, I find it large and so polluted I don't want to stay here any length of time. I'd go back if I was going to have a child, for the family support and the rural environment. (Niambh)

Long-term, Ireland is home. I don't think I've ever thought of England as being home. The closest to it was when I was involved with a woman with a couple of kids and I got into a role with them. That felt like a home environment. But it wasn't complete home because it wasn't home. (Heather)

I do want to go back. I'd like to go back if I could open a gay bar, but sexuality would be a problem for me, being a teacher. Ironically, because of the new legislation around sexuality, I'd have more safeguards against discrimination in my work there than I do here. But I think it will take longer for attitudes to change. (Niambh)

Everyone I spoke to found it immensely ironic that they had moved to England for more sexual freedom only to witness Ireland gain more progressive legislative changes. It challenges further collusion with the reactionary image of an Ireland which froze at the point when we left. Most women were hesitant to be convinced that attitudes would change immediately. The women from the North also expressed concern that it was still extremely homophobic and, because of the entrenched communities and the war, that there had been little chance for dissenting minorities to have a voice.

Perhaps the legislation will not encourage lesbians and gays in exile to return at once, but it may stem the flow of sexual emigration from Ireland. The fact that sexuality is at the cutting edge of the struggle to challenge the monopoly of what it is to be Irish in the 1990s makes each one of us who have left salute the guts and endurance of those who stayed to fight.

My vision of the future once contained simply the word 'peace'. Now my human rights as a dyke are just as important to my vision of a new Ireland. I hope that the three main areas that motivate emigration – work, education and sexuality – can be developed to provide better opportunities for lesbians and gays to fulfil their potential without leaving.

Emigration teaches you of reinvention and loss as you move between nostalgia and disdain. It is essential for lesbian and gays crossing the Irish Sea, the Atlantic, the world, to maintain links with the growing queer movement in Ireland and with other Irish queers in the diaspora. We must find access to new technologies, so that the cost of frequent ferry or plane journeys does not prohibit the knowledge of how communities here and there have developed our/ their own ways of being Irish queers. At times, when I've gone back to Ireland, I've felt an uncomfortable embarrassment when people think I'm English, which undermines my right to speak as an Irish lesbian. While in the USA it seems as though Irish identity is bolstered, in England, it is diminished. In an ideal future, anti-Irish racism will be more fully acknowledged as the insidious and overt discrimination it presents; Irish lesbians and gays in England will have as powerful and subversive a presence as those in the USA and will be consulted and included in political and cultural movements in Ireland.

As Ireland is reinvented shakily towards peace, there must be space for a secular, socialist, non-sectarian voice and practice, and a letting go of old traditions of bigotry and revenge. I cannot envisage returning for good, nor can I build a future based on a life in England. I vacillate. I journey back and forth. I take home with me in a suitcase. I imagine becoming global and that being enough.

Incessant boat people are we,
Forced from Larne to Stranraer,
Dun Loaghaire–Fishguard,
Limerick–Quebec.
Pale with separation
We drag slowly with suitcases and memories
To other lands.

From 'Coming Home' by Cherry Smyth (Boyes, 1993)

I would like to thank all the Irish lesbians living in London who contributed time and thoughtfulness to this piece.

Notes

1. *Irish Times*, 30 May 1994.
2. Comments made during a presentation to the Troublesome Visibilities Conference, St. Martin's College, April 1994.
3. In Section 28 of the Local Government Act 1988, a local authority is forbidden to 'promote the teaching in any maintained school of the acceptability of homosexuality as a pretended family relationship'.
4. See Note 2.

References

Boland, Eavan (1989). *Selected Poems*. London: Carcanet.
Boyes, Sara (ed.) (1993). *Frankenstein's Daughter*. Exeter: Stride.
De Souza, Eunice (1990). *Ways of Belonging*. Edinburgh: Polygon.
Ó'Searcaigh, Cathal (1993). *An Bealach 'na Bhaile'*. Dreubhàn, Connemara: Clo Iar-Chonnachta.
O'Toole, Fintan (1994). *Black Hole, Green Card*. Dublin: New Island Books.

Geasa
Cathal Ó'Searcaigh

Tráthnóna teann teasbhaigh
a bhí ann i ndeireadh an earraigh
agus bruth na hóige i mo chuislí;
An sú ag éirí i ngach beo
agus bachlóga ag broidearnaigh
ar ghéaga na gcrann fearnóige
taobh liom. Mé ag amharc ina treo,
ag cúlchoimeád uirthi go fáilí
fríd scoilt i gclaí an gharraí;
Í tarnocht agus ar a sleasl"i,
caite síos ar sheanchuilt bhuí;
faobhar na hóige ar a cuid cuair
agus í ag diúl na gréine le cíocras;
a cneas comh glé ...
                          le béal scine.
Mé easnamhach
ar an uaigneas
measc cloch

                    gan seasamh
                    san uaigneas
                    measc cloch

235: *Geasa*/The Bond

M'easnamh mar mhiodóg
ag gabháil ionam go putóg
nó tuigeadh domh go hóg
agus go grod ... gan ionam
ach buachaill ar a chéad bhod
nach ndéanfadh meallacht mná
fíoch agus flosc na féithe
a ghríosadh ionam go bráth;
is nach síolrófaí de chlann
do mo leithéidíse a choíche
ach cibé clann bheag bhearsaí
a shaolofaí domh san oíche
as broinn mhéith na Béithe;
is ba mhór an crá croí domh
na geasa dubha draíochta
a leagadh orm go síoraí
as féith seo na filíochta.

Ach tráthnóna teann teasbhaigh
a bhí ann agus bruth na hóige i mo chuislí;
Ag breathnú uirthi, ag baint lán
mo dhá shúl, as a corp álainn, éadrocht,
chan ise a bhí romham sínte,
chan ise a bhí mo ghriogadh
ach bogstócach mo shamhlaíochta
agus é 'mo bheophianadh ...
Ach b'fhada go gcasfaí orm é ina bheatha,
b'fhada go bhfaighinn sásamh
óna chneas álainn fionnbhán,
óna chumthacht tharnocht
ach amháin ...
                    i mo dhán ...

The Bond

Frankie Sewell (a translation of 'Geasa')

It was a hard hot afternoon
as spring came unsprung
and youth bubbled in my veins;
juices coursed through every living thing
and buds pulsed on Alder branches
next to me. Secretly, I watched her
through a handy wee slit in the garden wall
as she lay back naked
on an old yellow quilt,
the youth-sharpened curves of her body
greedily sucking in sun, her skin as bright ...
                                                    as the edge
                                                    of a knife.

And I was left wanting,
out on my own
among stones

                    left cold,
                    alone
                    among stones

237: *Geasa/The Bond*

Absence stung me with daggers to the bones
as I learnt young and sudden
(a pubescent teen) that no bewitching woman
could scorch my veins with flux and fury;
and the only children to spring from my loins
would be a family of verse born
from the juicy womb of my Muse;
O, and it hurt so deep,
this dark magic bond
placed on me forever
by Poetry.

On a hard hot afternoon,
youth bubbling in my veins,
my eyes full drunk
with her bright beautiful body –
only it wasn't her stretched before me,
not her turning me on,
but a slender youth I imagined,
burning me alive ...
It would take years to meet him in the flesh,
years to satisfy my wish
for his pale, wonderful skin,
his clear, naked form –
but sometimes ...

                    in poems ...